Zora Neale Hurston's *Their Eyes Were Watching God*

A CASEBOOK

ZORA NEALE HURSTON'S

Their Eyes Were Watching God

◆   ◆   ◆

A   CASEBOOK

Edited by
Cheryl A. Wall

OXFORD
UNIVERSITY PRESS

2000

OXFORD

UNIVERSITY PRESS

Oxford   New York
Athens   Auckland   Bangkok   Bogotá   Buenos Aires   Calcutta
Cape Town   Chennai   Dar es Salaam   Delhi   Florence   Hong Kong   Istanbul
Karachi   Kuala Lumpur   Madrid   Melbourne   Mexico City   Mumbai
Nairobi   Paris   São Paulo   Shanghai   Singapore   Taipei   Tokyo   Toronto   Warsaw

And associated companies in
Berlin   Ibadan

Copyright © 2000 by Oxford University Press, Inc.

Published by Oxford University Press, Inc.
198 Madison Avenue, New York, New York 10016

Oxford is a registered trademark of Oxford University Press.

Library of Congress Cataloging-in-Publication Data
Zora Neale Hurston's Their eyes were watching God: a casebook
edited by Cheryl A. Wall.
p. cm. — (Casebooks in contemporary fiction)
Includes bibliographical references.
ISBN 0-19-512173-2 ISBN 0-19-512174-0 (pbk.)
1. Hurston, Zora Neale. Their eyes were watching God.   2. Afro-American
women in literature.   3. Afro-Americans in literature.   I. Wall, Cheryl A.   II. Series.
PS3515.U789 T639   2000
813'.52—dc21   00-024714

3 5 7 9 8 6 4 2

Printed in the United States of America
On acid-free paper

Acknowledgments

I WISH TO THANK my research assistants, Stephanie Harzewski and Rick Lee, for their expertise and enthusiasm. I am indebted to William Andrews, the editor of this series, for the example of his scholarship as well as for his collegiality and his patience. My daughter, Camara, remains my sweet inspiration; it is a joy to watch her as she finds "the jewel down inside herself." Most of all, I thank my sister Gatsie on whom I can always depend for a good thought.

Credits

Hazel V. Carby, "The Politics of Fiction, Anthropology and the Folk: Zora Neale Hurston" in *New Essays on "Their Eyes Were Watching God,"* edited by Michael Awkward (Cambridge University Press, 1990).

Henry Louis Gates, Jr., "Zora Neale Hurston and the Speakerly Text," in *The Signifying Monkey: A Theory of African-American Literary Criticism* (Oxford University Press, 1988).

Zora Neale Hurston, excerpt from *Twentieth Century Authors* (H.W. Wilson Company, 1942).

Barbara Johnson, "Metaphor, Metonymy, and Voice in *Their Eyes Were Watching God*" in *Black Literature and Literary Theory*, edited by Henry Louis Gates, Jr. (Routledge, 1984).

Carla Kaplan, "Erotics of Talk: 'That Oldest Human Longing' in *Their Eyes Were Watching God,"* *American Literature,* 67:1 (March 1995) 115–142 (Duke University Press, 1995).

Daphne Lamothe, "Vodou Imagery, African American Tradition and Cultural Transformation in Zora Neale Hurston's *Their Eyes Were Watching God,"* *Callaloo* 22.1 (1999): 157–175 (Johns Hopkins University Press, 1999).

Mary Helen Washington, "'I Love the Way Janie Crawford Left Her Husbands,'" in *Invented Lives: Narratives of Black Women 1860–1960* (Doubleday, 1987).

Sherley Anne Williams, Foreword, in *Their Eyes Were Watching God* (Board of Trustees of the University of Illinois, University of Illinois Press, 1978).

Contents

Zora Neale Hurston's *Their Eyes Were Watching God*

A C A S E B O O K

Introduction

CHERYL A. WALL

◆ ◆ ◆

A PUBLISHER'S ADVERTISEMENT IN the *New York Times Book Review* inviting readers to "spend the summer with a classic" offers these titles: *The Unbearable Lightness of Being* by Milan Kundera, *A Tree Grows in Brooklyn* by Betty Smith, *Brave New World* by Aldous Huxley, *The Crying of Lot 49* by Thomas Pynchon, *One Hundred Years of Solitude* by Gabriel García Márquez, and *Their Eyes Were Watching God* by Zora Neale Hurston.[1] Mixing novels from diverse national and stylistic traditions and disregarding once-fixed categories of "literary" and "popular," the list makes "classic" the common denominator. Since all of these novels are frequently taught and most have been the object of sustained critical attention, "classic" is an apt adjective, as well as an effective advertising ploy. Yet unremarkable as the list may seem in 1999, it would have been inconceivable even a decade earlier. The struggle to reclaim the legacy of Zora Neale Hurston has not only gained "classic" status for the novel most believe to be her greatest work, but it has in the process helped to redefine what "classic" means.

The blurb for *Their Eyes* quotes Alice Walker's ringing endorsement, "there is no book more important to me than this one." The statement is taken from Walker's preface to Robert Hemenway's 1977 biography, a key document in the reconstruction of Hurston's life and the reclamation of her art. In "Zora Neale Hurston: A Cautionary Tale and a Partisan View,"

3

and in a series of celebrated essays including "In Search of Our Mothers' Gardens" and "Looking for Zora," Walker embraced Hurston as a literary foremother and introduced her folklore and fiction to tens of thousands of readers. Imagining herself in the preface "condemned to a desert island for life, with an allotment of ten books to see [her] through," Walker chooses Hurston's *Mules and Men* and *Their Eyes*, the latter for the pleasure it provides. She takes joy in "identifying with the black heroine, Janie Crawford, as she acted out many roles in a variety of settings, and functioned (with spectacular results) in romantic and sensual love."[2]

Readers followed Walker's lead, responding in kind to the lyricism, the laugh-out-loud humor, the spirituality, and the pleasure of Hurston's texts. The University of Illinois Press published an edition of *Their Eyes* in 1978 that sold more than 300,000 copies. The first edition, published in 1937, had sold a fraction of that number. HarperCollins, the publisher that now holds the rights to all of Hurston's writing, issued a new edition of the novel in 1991. HarperCollins does not release sales figures, but one can safely assume that given the conglomerate's publicity departments and distribution networks—one can now buy the novel in airports—the sales of its edition of *Their Eyes* have far outstripped those of the academic press.[3]

Impressive as its commercial success has been, its critical success earns *Their Eyes* the "classic" appellation. Hurston's rediscovery is one of the most dramatic chapters in African American literary history. As Henry Louis Gates, Jr. observes, "Hurston is the first writer that [his] generation of black and feminist critics has brought into the canon. . . . [She] is now a cardinal figure in the Afro-American canon, the feminist canon, and the canon of American fiction."[4] Scholars and critics investigating the impact of oral forms on African American literature find a theoretical foundation as well as a wealth of material in Hurston's writings. Her novels, particularly *Their Eyes Were Watching God,* provide grist for the mills of critics of every persuasion. Feminist critics explore the revision of the romance script in *Their Eyes*—rather than living happily ever after with her lover, Janie lives on without him—as well as its representation of "a maiden language." Andrew Delbanco, a scholar of American literature, argues that "Hurston belongs among the American classics." Not only is she "a brilliant transcriber of dialect," but a writer who, in her own voice, "renders the world in phrases that are palpable and wonderfully immediate." Poststructuralists locate moments in *Their Eyes* that challenge the existence of a binary and hierarchical model of language and of the reality it represents. Scholars of the African diaspora identify cultural practices and beliefs that are common to societies in the Caribbean and Africa as well as the United States.[5]

More evidence for Hurston's significance comes from the frequency with which present-day authors allude to her work. Black American writers like Ishmael Reed and white American writers like Susan Straight have extended Hurston's legacy by repeating and revising her signature tropes. So too have such premier theater artists as Ossie Davis, Ruby Dee, and George Wolfe. Hurston's texts inspire artists in various media, including the choreographer Diane McIntyre and the filmmaker Julie Dash. Yet nowhere do those texts resonate more strongly than in the pages of scores of books by African American women published in the last quarter of the twentieth century. Walker's "search" suggests one reason that Hurston's rediscovery coincides with a renaissance of writing by black women. Allusions to Hurston's art and life recur in texts by writers as varied as Maya Angelou, Toni Cade Bambara, bell hooks, Paule Marshall, Terry McMillan, Toni Morrison, Gloria Naylor, and Ntozake Shange. Walker is only Hurston's most noted legatee. At the beginning of her career, Walker eloquently described her quest for models. Her essays constructed an artistic tradition in which she could locate her own writing. She found in Hurston a writer who challenged "conventional standards" and who believed that beauty was a cardinal principle in African American culture. That belief resonated for Walker, who, because of her mother's love of beauty and creativity with flowers, asserted that "even [her] memories of poverty are seen through a screen of blooms."[6] Inspired by Hurston's example, Walker proposed her own alternative definitions of beauty and art. These expanding definitions by Walker and her peers have done much to create the critical space in which Hurston's art has achieved "classic" status.

The book to which writers, scholars, and readers return most often is *Their Eyes Were Watching God*. Hurston explains in her autobiography, *Dust Tracks on a Road*, that she wrote the novel "under internal pressure in seven weeks" while she was conducting ethnographic fieldwork in Haiti, on a fellowship from the Guggenheim Foundation, and recovering from a failed romance (p. 155). Her lover was a much younger man. Hurston later reflected that "I tried to embalm all the tenderness of my passion for him" in her book. The circumstances were hardly promising, but the novel, published in September 1937, almost exactly a year after she arrived in Port-au-Prince, is her masterpiece. The protagonist, Janie Crawford, begins a quest for romance, which she belatedly finds, and ultimately achieves spiritual fulfillment. Through a deepening engagement with African American culture, Janie gains the wisdom and strength to claim her voice and her self. Many vibrant voices speak through the novel; some seek to silence Janie, while others inspire her. Hurston renders the speech of her characters with perfect pitch. She writes the oral culture brilliantly. The folktales and personal narratives that her characters relate, the courtship rituals, speeches, sermons, and diverse oral performances that they enact become for readers of the novel what they are for its characters: "crayon enlargements of life." As the novel progresses, its narrative voice, no less than the voices of its characters, is inflected by the tonalities and rhythms of black vernacular English. "Words walking without masters" is an apt metaphor for both the novel's folk speech and its singular prose.

While it is not unusual for literary reputations to fluctuate, Hurston's stock has risen precipitately. When she died in the Saint Lucie County Welfare Home in Fort Pierce, Florida, on 28 January 1960, none of her seven books was in print. She had not published a novel in twelve years. Her life and career had long been spiraling downward. In the early years of the preceding decade, for example, Hurston had published a smattering of articles in national magazines. When the woman who employed her as a maid in Miami noticed Hurston's byline in the *Saturday Evening Post*, she called a reporter. The resulting publicity was hugely discomfiting to Hurston, who soon moved on. For the rest of the decade, she lived a hand-to-mouth existence in a series of Florida hamlets. In 1952, she was in Live Oak, working as a stringer for the *Pittsburgh Courier*, an African American newspaper that was distributed nationally. She was living in Eau Gallie when, in a letter to the editor of the *Orlando Sentinel* in 1955, Hurston wrote that the United States Supreme Court's Brown vs. Topeka decision was an attack on blacks' self respect; she could "see no tragedy in being too dark to be invited to a white school social affair." The letter, which was immediately distributed to newspapers throughout the South as proof that blacks did not want integration, cost her what little regard national black leaders and media still had for her opinion. By 1957 her byline could be read only in the *Fort Pierce Chronicle*, the local black weekly. Her funeral was front-page news in the *Chronicle*, which highlighted the generosity of neighbors who collected money for Hurston's funeral. She had died penniless.[7]

Her body was buried in an unmarked grave in a segregated cemetery, but that was not Hurston's final resting place. A decade after her death, Hurston's work began to be rediscovered by a new generation of readers. The children of the Civil Rights movement appreciated the pride Hurston took in the language and folkways of southern blacks. Unlike some of Hurston's contemporaries, these readers were not embarrassed by the representations of black life in her books. Rather, in an era of cultural assimilation, Hurston's writing gave these readers an inheritance that they were eager to claim. In the wake of the Civil Rights movement, the

Women's movement gained force in communities and on campuses across the United States; it produced new audiences for narratives about women. Feminists admired the strength and audacity of Hurston's female characters. All of Hurston's books are now in print, including four novels: *Jonah's Gourd Vine* (1934), *Their Eyes Were Watching God, Moses, Man of the Mountain* (1939), and *Seraph on the Suwanee* (1948); two volumes of folklore and ethnography; *Mules and Men* (1935) and *Tell My Horse* (1938); and a memoir, *Dust Tracks on a Road* (1942). Hurston also published more than fifty short stories, essays, and plays during her lifetime. Since her death several volumes collecting these along with never published pieces have come to print.[8] The longer it endures, the more "classic" Hurston's work becomes.

Not only are her books widely taught but Hurston is today among the best known twentieth-century African American writers. Her name and image circulate throughout the popular culture—from the stage to film and television. The story of her life has assumed legendary status. Growing up in Eatonville, Florida, the first all-black town incorporated in the United States, Zora learned early to love the tales she heard told on the porch of Joe Clarke's store, "the heart and spring of the town," as well as the books she read in school. She never acknowledged that she was in fact born on 7 January 1891 in Notasulga, Alabama, a hamlet near Tuskegee; her parents, John and Lucy Potts Hurston, moved to Eatonville shortly after Zora's birth. John, a preacher/poet who earned his living as a carpenter, was thrice elected mayor; her mother, who had been a country schoolteacher, urged her precocious daughter to "jump at de sun." Zora's idyllic childhood ended when her mother died. At fourteen, Zora was on her own. For two decades, she scrambled to support herself and to gain an education. Her life became what she described as a series of "wanderings": living with relatives and working as a domestic in Memphis, traveling with a Gilbert & Sullivan troupe as lady's maid to its star, leaving the troupe in Baltimore and enrolling in night school at Morgan Academy in Baltimore, working as a manicurist and attending Howard University in Washington off and on for six years, and arriving in New York City during the first week of January 1925, with "$1.50, no job, no friends, and a lot of hope." Her great ambition was to be a writer. Stories that she had written at Howard had caught the eye of Charles S. Johnson, the editor of *Opportunity* who, in Hurston's view, was the prime mover of "the so-called Negro Renaissance."[9] He continued to publish her stories. "Spunk" took a second-place prize at the *Opportunity* awards dinner that May and later appeared in *The New Negro*.

Hurston turned thirty-four the week she reached New York, but she persuaded those she met there that she was ten years younger. (Her age was only one aspect of her life she kept private; scholars have found records of two marriages she never disclosed.) In New York she found a benefactor who proffered a scholarship to Barnard College, where she began studying anthropology with Franz Boas, who pioneered the discipline in the United States.[10] Although she continued to write stories and plays, and joined Gwendolyn Bennett, Countee Cullen, Langston Hughes, and Wallace Thurman to plan the first and only issue of *Fire!!*, the legendary literary magazine, Hurston determined to pursue a career as a social scientist. Two years after arriving in New York and armed with a new understanding of her childhood world, she boarded a southbound train. Her first stop was Eatonville, where she began collecting folklore—the folktales, spirituals, sermons, work songs, blues, and children's games—that many New Negroes disparaged but which to Hurston constituted the "arts of the people before they find out there is any such thing as art."[11] At a time when the Great Migration, the movement that brought blacks by the hundreds of thousands from the rural South to the urban North, seemed a sign of progress, as did the poetry and fiction of the emergent Harlem Renaissance, Hurston moved against the tide.[12] As many black intellectuals adopted a rhetoric of racial uplift, Hurston celebrated the art of "the Negro farthest down." She spent the next six years crisscrossing Florida, Alabama, and Louisiana, signing on at lumber camps and apprenticing herself to hoodoo doctors, in order to document the art created by "the unlettered Negro" who had "given the Negro's best contribution to American culture."[13]

While conducting her research, Hurston reminisced in *Dust Tracks*, "I picked up glints and gleams out of what I had and stored it away to turn to my own use." Hurston's writing is suffused with the similes, the metaphors, and the rhythms that are the poetry of black vernacular expression. Her desire, in scholar Karla Holloway's phrase, "to render the oral culture literate" led to the technical innovations of her prose. Few of her nineteenth-century predecessors wrote in black idiom—a term Hurston preferred to dialect—in part because their project was to emphasize the common culture they shared with their mainly white readers. Hurston's project was in part to demonstrate that black Americans had created a culture of their own, one that might not be appreciated if judged by the standards of the dominant society. Indeed, Hurston argued, "we each have our own standards of art, and thus we are all interested parties and so unfit to pass judgment upon the art concepts of others."[14] Hurston's view of the relative standard of art derived from her work as an anthropologist. She soon found that her view could be applied to her own art as well as that of the folk. The analytical tools she honed have served her critics well.

Drawing on her field notes, Hurston began to define this alternative aesthetic in the essay "Characteristics of Negro Expression" that she contributed to Nancy Cunard's massive anthology, *Negro*, in 1934.

> Every phase of Negro life is highly dramatized. No matter how joyful or how sad the case there is sufficient poise for drama. Everything is acted out. Unconsciously for the most part of course. There is an impromptu ceremony already ready for every hour of life.
>
> No little moment passes unadorned.[15]

Moments of ritualized improvision—courtship rituals, a lamplighting ceremony, a solo played on an imaginary guitar—became hallmarks of her fiction. So too did the "will to adorn," reflected in the profusion of metaphors and similes that recur in folktales and in Hurston's fiction. Nanny implores her granddaughter: "Put me down easy, Janie. Ah'm a cracked plate." One of his Eatonville neighbors complains about Joe: "he talks tuh unlettered folks wid books in his jaws." After Joe's death, Janie "sent her face to Joe's funeral, and herself went rollicking with the springtime across the world." Here, as throughout her oeuvre, Hurston created fiction to accord with the aesthetic principles she identified in African American culture.

Hurston's effort was not merely to interpolate folk sayings in her fiction; it was to create a literary language informed by the perspective as well as the poetry of rural black southerners. While most critics have agreed that her ear was attuned to the poetry, they have debated whether Hurston represented the perspective accurately. Her black male contemporaries thought not. They faulted her books for an alleged lack of racial militancy. Alain Locke, for example, wrote that *Their Eyes* was an "oversimplification" of southern black life and wondered when Hurston would "come to grips with motive fiction and social document fiction." Richard Wright offered a more hostile response. He wrote in *New Masses* that the novel lacked a theme "that lends itself to serious interpretation." He located it instead in the tradition of minstrelsy, a tradition that "Miss Hurston *voluntarily* continues. . . . Her characters eat and laugh and cry and work and kill; they swing like a pendulum eternally in that safe and narrow orbit in which America likes to see the Negro live: between laughter and tears." [16]

Defining the novel in essence as one of feeling rather than of ideas was, from Wright's masculinist perspective, another way of saying that *Their Eyes* is a woman's story. The feminists who initially reclaimed Hurston's novel clearly responded to its politics, a politics of gender to which Wright was oblivious. Subsequent critics have found in the novel a wealth of commentary on the politics of race, ethnicity, and culture. But while *Their Eyes* cannot be read as though it has no politics, it should not be read as though it is only political.[17] Hurston was determined not to create characters according to type—minstrel or otherwise. Her decision to concentrate on intraracial community rather than interracial conflict was similarly deliberate. She was more interested in probing "that which the soul lives by" than in documenting the oppression and exploitation that defined the material existence of most African Americans in the 1930s. Even her most ardent admirers have sometimes wished that she had acknowledged more explicitly the then unyielding power of the forces of oppression. And yet, Hurston represented the reality that the most insidious aspect of racism is the extent to which its victims internalize the attitudes of their oppressors. Nanny, Joe Starks, Mrs. Turner, and eventually even Tea Cake begin to take their measure from the society that holds them in contempt. The deepest wounds of oppression, whether of racism, sexism, or class, are those that scar the soul.

Choosing selections for this casebook was difficult, because after almost four decades of neglect, *Their Eyes Were Watching God* has become one of the most widely discussed novels in the African American tradition. All of the selections in this volume have been previously published. Several are among the most frequently cited pieces of Hurston criticism. Others suggest new directions for Hurston studies. All confirm the richness of Hurston's novel, as one that lends itself to reading after reading, both as an object of critical inquiry and a source of ongoing pleasure.

In the first piece, a brief article written for a reference book, Hurston describes her childhood, her education, her favorite authors, and her work. One might say that she interviews herself. While she plays fast and loose with the facts of her life, she conveys a good bit of the spirit with which she lived it. Certainly, she gives readers a flavor of her personal exuberance ("I love sunshine the way it is done in Florida") and political iconoclasm (among the public figures she admires is Robert E. Lee who "fought for an unfortunate cause, but . . . was a worthy foe"). She recounts her dissatisfaction with the portrayal of blacks in fiction when she began her career and her subsequent determination "to write about my people as they are, and not to use the traditional lay figures."

Poet, novelist, and scholar Sherley Anne Williams wrote the foreword to the 1978 University of Illinois Press edition of *Their Eyes Were Watching God* that found its way onto college syllabi across America. The essay's reading of the novel's central metaphors was one of the first to demonstrate the self-conscious design of Hurston's art. Most memorably, Williams offers an evocative account of the shock of recognition and affirmation she experienced upon reading *Their Eyes*. It was a pleasure long deferred. She writes, "it did, however, finally become my turn to read *Their Eyes Were Watching God*, and I became Zora Neale's for life. In the speech of her characters, I heard my own country voice and saw in the heroine something of my own country self. And this last was most wonderful because it was most rare." Williams speaks for a generation of black women readers, who had not often encountered representations of their lives in books.[18] But she reminds us as well that "Janie's quest for fulfillment becomes any woman's tale."

Mary Helen Washington, one of the first scholars to map the literary history of African American women, described the mission she was undertaking in the introduction to her pioneering anthology *Black-Eyed Susans: Classic Stories by and about Black Women*: "we are, in fact, in for quite a revelation in the country of the black woman writer, for the territory is still wilderness. Consider Zora Neale Hurston."[19] Washington identified Hurston then as the author of "what is probably the most beautiful love story of a black man and woman in literature." In the essay reprinted here, "I Love the Way Janie Crawford Left Her Husbands," Washington takes a second look. Homing in on the problematic development of the female hero in Hurston's writing, Washington contrasts John Pearson, the male protagonist of *Jonah's Gourd Vine*, and Janie Crawford, the female protagonist of *Their Eyes Were Watching God*. Even in the representation of Janie, Washington finds, the female hero is not entirely free to speak.

While the earliest feminist interpretations held that Janie achieves selfhood by claiming her voice, Barbara Johnson asserts that it is by accepting the inevitability of self-division that Janie gains the power of speech. She shows how Janie's revelation that "she had an inside and an outside now and suddenly she knew how not to mix them" has profound implications both for Janie's quest for a unified identity and for her ability to speak. In figurative language, Johnson observes, "inside and outside are never the same." Although the essay graphs the literary contexts of the novel's production, "Metaphor, Metonymy, and Voice" may seem to some to be less about *Their Eyes* than about an ongoing debate among poststructuralist theorists. But for that very reason the article demonstrates how the rhetorical richness of Hurston's novel serves the purposes of various critical constituencies, thereby assuring its canonical status.

Excerpted from Gates's groundbreaking study, *The Signifying Monkey: A Theory of Afro-American Literary Criticism*, "Zora Neale Hurston and the Speakerly Text" surveys the social and literary history that for generations mitigated against the use of black vernacular English by African American writers. It then carefully explicates the rhetorical strategies Hurston deployed to recuperate the vernacular for literature. Through her use of "free indirect discourse," according to Gates, Hurston was able not only to represent the speech and thought of her protagonist but of the collective black community. Gates marshals persuasive evidence for his assertion that the narrative voice Hurston created in *Their Eyes Were Watching God* is "her legacy to Afro-American fiction."

Gates inserts Hurston and her text into the African American literary tradition as it developed from the slave narrative to Paul Laurence Dunbar, Jean Toomer, James Weldon Johnson, Sterling Brown, Richard Wright, and Ralph Ellison. Hurston's relation to that all-male canon is akin to Janie's relation to the mule-talkers on the porch of Joe Starks's store. Hurston writes herself free by signifying on the tradition, just as Janie "speaks herself free" by signifying on Joe. [20] In addition to the influential theory Gates elaborates here, he offers one of the finest close readings of Hurston's novel that we have.

In "The Politics of Fiction, Anthropology, and the Folk: Zora Neale Hurston," Hazel Carby is more interested in Hurston's ideological positions than in the novel's thematics of voice. Carby casts a skeptical eye on the recuperation of Hurston as a cultural icon, as she critiques the representation of black "folk" culture in *Their Eyes Were Watching God* and interrogates the reception of the novel in the 1980s and 1990s. While Hurston was disdainful of the elitist manner in which black folk culture was reproduced on stage and in fiction, Carby reminds us that Hurston's own representations were necessarily mediated. Hurston no more than choirmaster Hall Johnson (an African American) or novelist DuBose Heyward (a white American) had access to *the* "authentic" folk culture. No such entity existed. More controversial is Carby's argument that Hurston's representation of "the folk" as a *rural* people and African American culture as primarily oral is ahistorical. She quotes with approval Wright's critique of *Their Eyes* and restages the debate between the two authors.[21] Carby asserts that *Their Eyes Were Watching God* is set in the Eatonville of Hurston's childhood rather than in the period of its creation; as a consequence the novel displaces the key social movement of its time—the urban migration of

African Americans. By embracing the novel now, Carby contends, readers evade the urgent social crises of *our* time.

Carla Kaplan reasserts the importance of orality in the novel, in terms of both speech and sexuality. Rather than focussing on Janie's acquisition of a voice (it claims that Janie has had one all along), "The Erotics of Talk" argues that the novel's concern is with the lack of listeners. Questions of audience are central to this reading which situates the text in the context of the cultural politics of the Harlem Renaissance. Indeed, Kaplan locates the action of the text as coterminous to the New Negro movement. In this context, the novel's representation of its black female protagonist as a sexual subject is highly controversial. By affirming "the value and status of self-revelation as a means of social transformation," Kaplan argues, Hurston challenged a cardinal tenet of the movement.

Daphne Lamothe begins her essay, "Vodou Imagery, African American Tradition and Cultural Transformation in *Their Eyes Were Watching God*" by reminding us that Zora Neale Hurston wrote the novel in 1937 while in Haiti collecting folklore on Vodou. *Tell My Horse*, which documents the findings of that expedition, was published the next year. But, Lamothe contends, the findings are foreshadowed in the novel. Hurston discovered a dynamic system of belief that in no way resembled the stereotypes of popular culture. Neither was Vodou a site of nostalgia; instead it became Hurston's "means of comprehending transformation." She linked her protagonist Janie with aspects of Vodou goddess, Ezili Freda, the mulatta goddess of love, and Ezili Dantò, the black goddess who is associated with maternal rage. Images from Vodou are threaded throughout the novel. Through these images, Lamothe argues, *Their Eyes* "links the southern folk with a Black Atlantic experience rooted in slavery, armed revolution and African spirituality."

Lamothe's essay reads Hurston's novel through critical paradigms that did not exist when it was initially rediscovered. Yet here, too, Hurston's scholarly investigations and her poetic imagination made her prescient. Her understanding of cultural connections within and across geographic and imaginary space anticipated the concept of the Black Atlantic. She had in fact represented the cultural kinship among people of African descent as early as 1932, when she chose a Bahamian fire dance as the finale to a concert of African American folklore she produced. Lamothe's exploration of Vodou allusions in *Their Eyes* evokes the definition of "classic" that Houston Baker advances in *Workings of the Spirit*: "A *classic* in any culture, one might say, is a space in which the spirit works."[22]

In the frame tale of the novel Janie begins to tell her story to Pheoby, her "kissin'-friend" of twenty years and her ideal listener: "Ah depend on you for a good thought," Janie explains to Pheoby. "And Ah'm talking to you from dat standpoint." Pheoby's "hungry listening" propels Janie onward. We as readers overhear Janie's story, as it were, and we listen from many different standpoints. The essays assembled here confirm that whatever perspective we bring to the novel, it will reward the most careful reading we can give it.

Notes

1. The *New York Times Book Review*, 11 July 1999, p.16.

2. Robert Hemenway, *Zora Neale Hurston: A Literary Biography* (Urbana: University of Illinois Press, 1977). Walker's preface and the other essays cited here were collected in *In Search of Our Mothers' Gardens* (New York: Harcourt Brace Jovanovich, 1983), 86. Walker also edited the first Hurston reader, *I Love Myself When I Am Laughing . . .* (New York: The Feminist Press, 1979).

3. See Michael Awkward, introduction to *New Essays on "Their Eyes Were Watching God"* (New York: Cambridge University Press, 1990), 4–6, 22. Fawcett Books had published a mass-market paperback before the Illinois edition appeared. In 1991 Illinois published a hardcover edition, illustrated by Jerry Pinkney with a foreword by Ruby Dee. In her essay in this volume, Hazel Carby offers one interpretation of the novel's commercial success.

4. *The Signifying Monkey: A Theory of Afro-American Literary Criticism* (New York: Oxford University Press, 1988), 180.

5. See, for example, John Callahan, *In the African American Grain: The Pursuit of Voice in Twentieth-Century Black Fiction* (Urbana: University of Illinois Press, 1988). Representative feminist readings include Ann DuCille, *The Coupling Convention: Sex, Text, and Tradition in Black Women's Fiction* (New York: Oxford University Press, 1993); Rachel DuPlessis, *Writing Beyond the Ending: Narrative Strategies of Twentieth Century Women Writers* (Bloomington: Indiana University Press, 1985); and Sandra Gilbert and Susan Gubar, *No Man's Land: The Place of the Woman Writer in the Twentieth Century* (New Haven: Yale University Press, 1988). Andrew Delbanco, *Required Reading: Why Our American Classics Matter Now* (New York: Farrar, Straus and Giroux, 1997), 203–204. For a poststructuralist analysis, see Sharon Davie, "Free Mules, Talking Buzzards, and Cracked Plates: The Politics of Dislocation in *Their Eyes Were Watching God*," *PMLA* 108 (1993): 446–459.

6. *In Search of Our Mothers' Gardens*, 241. For a comparative analysis of the literary and ideological perspectives of Hurston, Walker, and Richard Wright, see Cheryl A. Wall, "On Freedom and the Will to Adorn: Debating Aesthetics and/as Ideology," in George Levine, ed., *Aesthetics and Ideology* (New Brunswick, NJ: Rutgers University Press, 1994), 283–303.

7. For information about Hurston's later life, see Hemenway, *Zora Neale Hurston,* and Cheryl A. Wall, *Women of the Harlem Renaissance* (Bloomington: Indiana University Press, 1995).

8. These collections include *The Collected Essays of Zora Neale Hurston, vols. 1 and 2* (New York: HarperCollins, 1997, 1998); *The Complete Short Stories of Zora Neale Hurston* (New York: HarperCollins, 1996); *I Love Myself . . . A Zora Neale Hurston Reader,* edited by Alice Walker; *The Sanctified Church,* with a foreword by Toni Cade Bambara (Berkeley, CA: Turtle Island, 1985); *Spunk: The Collected Stories of Zora Neale Hurston* (Berkeley, CA: Turtle Island, 1985); *Zora Neale Hurston: Folklore, Memoirs and Other Writings;* and *Zora Neale Hurston: Novels and Short Stories,* edited by Cheryl A. Wall (New York: The Library of America, 1995).

9. *Dust Tracks on a Road* (1942. New York: HarperCollins, 1991), 121–122. Additional information is taken from Hemenway, *Zora Neale Hurston,* and Wall, *Women of the Harlem Renaissance.*

10. The benefactor was Annie Nathan Meyer. Hurston met her more famous patron, Charlotte Osgood Mason, in the fall of 1927, shortly before she embarked on her first collecting expedition; Mrs. Mason supported much of Hurston's field work for the next five years.

11. Hurston, "Folklore and Music," in *Zora Neale Hurston: Folklore, Memoirs and Other Writings,* 876.

12. Consider, for example, Alain Locke who wrote about the Great Migration in the title essay of *The New Negro:* "With each successive wave of it, the movement of the Negro becomes more and more a mass movement toward the larger and the more democratic chance—in the Negro's case a deliberate flight not only from countryside to city, but from medieval to modern." (1925. New York: Atheneum, 1992), 6.

13. Hurston made the statement to Frank Hayes, a reporter for the *Chicago Daily News,* in November 1934. Quoted in Hemenway, 205.

14. "Characteristics of Negro Expression," in *Hurston: Folklore, Memoirs and Other Writings,* 834.

15. "Characteristics of Negro Expression," 830.

16. Locke, "Literature by and about the Negro," *Opportunity,* 1 June 1938; Richard Wright, "Between Laughter and Tears," *New Masses,* 5 October 1937, 22, 25.

17. For an examination of Hurston's politics and philosophy, see Deborah Plant, *Every Tub Must Sit on Its Own Bottom* (Urbana: University of Illinois Press, 1995).

18. As a writer Williams would fashion lyrical black voices of her own in the novel *Dessa Rose* (New York: Wm. Morrow, 1986) and in two volumes of poetry, *The Peacock Poems* (Middletown, CT: Wesleyan University Press, 1975) and *Some One Sweet Angel Chile* (New York: William Morrow, 1982).

19. Introduction, *Black-Eyed Susans: Classic Stories by and about Black Women* (New York: Anchor Books, 1975), xi.

20. Many scholars construct an African American literary tradition that is less androcentric than the one Gates theorizes upon here. See for example Hazel Carby, *Reconstructing Womanhood: The Emergence of the Afro-American Woman Novelist* (New York: Oxford University Press, 1987); Deborah McDowell, *"The Changing Same": Black Women's Literature, Criticism, and Theory* (Bloomington: Indiana University Press, 1995); and Claudia Tate, *Domestic Allegories of Political Desire: The Black Heroine's Text at the Turn of the Century* (New York: Oxford University Press, 1992). Gates is himself the editor of the Schomburg Library of Nineteenth-Century Black Women Writers.

21. Perhaps to heighten the drama of the debate, Carby misinterprets Hurston's assertion that she did not belong to "the sobbing school of Negrohood" as Hurston's way of distinguishing her work from Wright's. In 1928 when Hurston published "How It Feels to Be Colored Me," the article in which she proclaims her position, Wright had not established his. He moved to Chicago in December 1927, took the examination for the postal service in the spring, and began work as a temporary employee that summer. The ideological conflict between Wright and Hurston arose later.

22. Houston Baker, *Workings of the Spirit: The Poetics of Afro-American Women's Writing* (Chicago: University of Chicago Press, 1990), 74.

Zora Neale Hurston
on Zora Neale Hurston

❖   ❖   ❖

I WAS BORN AT Eatonville, Florida (the first *incorporated* Negro town in America). My father, the Rev. John Hurston, was a Baptist preacher and carpenter. My mother, Lucy Hurston, sewed for the community. They both came from Alabama and had been in Eatonville three years when I was born.

I went to grammar school in the village and was generally considered a bright pupil, but impudent and a bit stubborn. There were many beatings, both at home and at school, and a great deal of talk at both places about "breaking my spirit." One mile away was a white village, mostly inhabited by white people from Wisconsin, Michigan, and upper New York State. They often visited our village school, and they found me and I found them. They gave me books to read and sent me more when they went North in the summer. I played with their children on their estates. I felt no fear of white faces. The Southern whites in the neighborhood were very friendly and kind, and so I failed to realize that I was any different from them, in spite of the fact that my own village had done its best to impress upon me that white faces were something to fear and be awed by. So I have never been able to achieve race prejudice. I just see people. I see the *man* first, and his race as just another detail of his description.

I went to high school at Morgan Academy of Morgan College, Baltimore. Started in college at Howard University at Washington, D.C., but transferred to Barnard College in my sophomore year and took my B.A. there in 1928. Dr. Franz Boas got me a fellowship in anthropology to do research in folklore, and I returned to the South immediately upon my graduation. This work went on for four years. By reason of my work, I was invited to join the American Folklore Society, American Ethnological Society, and American Anthropological Society.

While I was working I began to think of writing. I had done a few things for school publications as an undergraduate. I saw that what was being written by Negro authors was all on the same theme—the race problem, and saturated with our sorrows. By the time I graduated from college, I had sensed the falsity of the picture, because I did not find that sorrow. We talk about the race problem a great deal, but go on living and laughing and striving like everybody else. So I saw that what was being written and declaimed was a pose. A Negro writer or speaker was supposed to say those things. It has such a definite pattern as to become approximately folklore. So I made up my mind to write about my people as they are, and not to use the traditional lay figures.

I love sunshine the way it is done in Florida. Rain the same way—in great slews or not at all. I am very fond of growing things; I shall end my days as a farmer if I have my way. I like strong displays of nature like thunderstorms, with Old Maker playing the zigzag lightning through his fingers. I feel a kinship with animals and things. I am sorry that snakes are so misunderstood and hated by their kinfolk on two legs. I dislike cold weather and all of its kinfolk: that takes in bare trees and a birdless morning.

I love courage in every form. I worship strength. I dislike insincerity, and most particularly when it vaunts itself to cover up cowardice. Pessimists and grouches and sycophants I do despise. I like all kinds of pretty-looking tasteless salads.

In authors I like Anatole France, Maxim Gorky, George Bernard Shaw, Victor Hugo, Mark Twain, Dickens, Robert Nathan, Willa Cather, Irvin S. Cobb, Anne Lindbergh, the Chinese philosophers, and Sinclair Lewis. I read every bit of Irish folk material that I can get hold of. Among public figures I like Lindbergh, Thomas E. Dewey, A. L. Lewis, George W. Carver, the Duke of Windsor; among deceased Americans, Lincoln, Edison, Franklin, Washington, Alexander Hamilton, Robert E. Lee (he fought for an unfortunate cause, but he was a worthy foe), Robert G. Ingersoll, Thomas Paine.

I want my resident to be Orange County, Fla., but my career keeps me living in my Chevrolet. At present I am drama coach at North Carolina College for Negroes, at Durham, N.C. My work in progress is a novel of upper-class Negro life, two full length plays, and several short stories.

Encountering Zora Neale Hurston

SHERLEY ANNE WILLIAMS

◆   ◆   ◆

I FIRST ENCOUNTERED Zora Neale Hurston in an Afro-American literature course I took in graduate school. She was one of numerous authors surveyed in the two-semester course, which began with Lucy Terry in 1746 and ended with the Black Arts writers of the sixties. Hurston's works were studied as a sort of holdover from the Harlem Renaissance, that period that coincided, at least in part, with the Jazz Age and witnessed the first concerted outpourings of formal artistic expression among Afro-Americans. The most important stylistic developments of the period were the attempt to use Afro-American folk culture as a basis for creating distinctive black contributions to serious or "high" culture, and the attempt to repudiate the false and degrading stereotypes promulgated in Anglo-American popular (and high) culture by exploring the individual consciousness hidden behind the enveloping Sambo mask. *Their Eyes Were Watching God* was published in 1937, almost ten years after the stock market crash of 1929, the date most often given as the end of the Harlem Renaissance.[1] The book's rural southern settings, the use of dialect and folkloric materials, even its romantic theme represent much that was distinctive and significant about this period.

It would have been difficult for most of the students in that class to prove these statements. We "read at" Zora Neale in the same way we had read at most of the writers studied to that point (and quite a few that came after): in snatches. And although I'd never seen—much less read—an embarrassing number of the works discussed in the course, I felt lucky to be there. Afro-American literature was still an exotic subject then, rarely taught on any regular basis. Most of the works of the writers we studied had been out of print for a long time, and students relied on lectures, anthology selections (when available), what samplings could be garnered in a Saturday spent in a rare-book collection or an evening in the reserve book reading room, and Robert Bone's *The Negro Novel in America* for our impressions of William Wells Brown, Frances Harper, William Attaway, Jessie Fauset, and Zora Neale Hurston. We were fortunate to be in Washington, D.C., with its several large university and public libraries and the Library of Congress. But library holdings really couldn't make up for those out-of-print books. The few personal or library copies of this or that were shared around, but there were about forty students in the class. By the time a person got the book, it had usually been discussed at least four weeks prior, and the owner needed it back to write a paper. So, like many students in the class, out of sheer frustration I ended by concentrating on contemporary authors (i.e., Wright, Ellison, Baldwin), whose works were more readily available.

It did, however, finally become my turn to read *Their Eyes Were Watching God,* and I became Zora Neale's for life. In the speech of her characters I heard my own country voice and saw in the heroine something of my own country self. And this last was most wonderful because it was most rare. Black women had been portrayed as characters in numerous novels by blacks and nonblacks. But these portraits were limited by the stereotypical images of, on the one hand, the ham-fisted matriarch, strong and loyal in the defense of the white family she serves (but unable to control or protect her own family without the guidance of some white person), and, on the other, the amoral, instinctual slut. Between these two stereotypes stood the tragic mulatto: too refined and sensitive to live under the repressive conditions endured by ordinary blacks and too colored to enter the white world.

Even the few idealized portraits of black women evoked these negative stereotypes. The idealizations were morally uplifting and politically laudable, but their literary importance rests upon just that: the correctness of their moral and political stance. Their value lies in their illuminations of the society's workings and their insights into the ways oppression is institutionalized. They provide, however, few insights into character or consciousness. And when we (to use Alice Walker's lovely phrase) go in search of our mother's gardens, it's not really to learn who trampled on them or how or even why—we usually know that already. Rather, it's to learn what our mothers planted there, what they thought as they sowed, and how they survived the blighting of so many fruits. Zora Hurston's life and work present us with insights into just these concerns.

The date of her birth, like many of the facts of her life, is a matter of uncertainty. Robert E. Hemenway, in a first and much-needed biography, *Zora Neale Hurston* (Urbana: University of Illinois Press, 1977), cites January 7, 1901, as the date that makes the most sense.[2] Eatonville, Florida, the small, all-black town where Zora was born, is the setting for two of her four published novels, *Jonah's Gourd Vine* (1934) and *Their Eyes Were Watching God.* The gatherings on the front porch of the town's general store came to symbolize for Hurston the richness of Afro-American oral culture, and she struggled for much of her career to give literary renderings of that oral richness and to portray the complex individuality of its unlettered, "uncultured" *folk* creators. Hurston studied cultural anthropology under Franz Boas, first as a student at Barnard College and later at Columbia University. In 1927 she returned to the South, where she lived off and on for the rest of her life, collecting examples of and participating in the dynamic culture created in the saw mills, turpentine camps, and small-town jook joints and cafés. She had at her command a large store of stories, songs, incidents, idiomatic phrases, and metaphors; her ear for speech rhythms must have been remarkable. Most importantly, she had the literary intelligence and developed the literary skill to convey the power and beauty of this heard speech and lived experience on the printed page.

Hurston's evocations of the lifestyles of rural blacks have not been equaled; but to stress the ruralness of Hurston's settings or to characterize her diction solely in terms of exotic "dialect" spellings is to miss her deftness with language. In the speech of her characters, black voices—whether rural or urban, northern or southern—come alive. Her fidelity to diction, metaphor, and syntax—whether in direct quotations or in paraphrases of characters' thoughts—rings, even across forty years, with an aching familiarity that is a testament to Hurston's skill and to the durability of black speech. Yet Zora's personality and actions were so controversial that for a long time she was remembered more as a *character* of the Renaissance than as one of the most serious and gifted artists to emerge during this period. She was a notable tale-teller, mimic, and wit, confident to the point of brashness (some might even say beyond), who refused to conform to conventional notions of ladylike behavior and middle-class decorum. To one of her contemporaries, she was the first black nationalist; to another, a handkerchief-head Uncle Tom. Larry Neal, in his recent introduction to her autobiography, *Dust Tracks on a Road* (1942; reprinted, New York: J. B. Lippincott, 1971), calls her a "kind of Pearl Bailey of the literary world . . . a conservative in her political outlook with a remarkable understanding of a blues aesthetic and its accompanying sensibility." To Alice Walker and others of our generation, Zora was a woman bent on discovering and defining herself, a woman who spoke and wrote her own mind.

Something of the questing quality that characterized Zora's own life informs the character of Janie—without, of course, the forcefulness of Hurston's own personality. In this and other instances, the character is more conventional than the author, for despite obvious idealizations, Janie operates in a "real" world. Her actions, responses, and motivations are consistent with that reality and the growing assertiveness of her own self-definitions. Where Janie yearns, Zora was probably driven; where Janie submits, Zora would undoubtedly have rebelled. Author and character objectify their definitions of self in totally different ways. Zora was evidently unable to satisfactorily define herself in a continuing relationship with a man, whereas such definition is the essence of Janie's romantic vision and its ultimate fulfillment provides the plot of the novel. But in their desire and eventual insistence that their men accord them treatment due equals, they are one.

Janie is raised by her grandmother, Nanny, an ex-slave who has suffered most of the abuses heaped upon black women in slavery: hard physical labor, poor rations, whippings, the threat of being separated from children and mate, coerced sexual relations with the master, and vindictive treatment at the hands of the mistress. Nanny doesn't fare much better in freedom; her daughter, whom she'd hoped to make into a schoolteacher as the fulfillment of her own frustrated dreams, is raped by a local schoolteacher. Janie is the result of this brutal coupling. After Janie's birth, the mother runs away, leaving Janie in Nanny's care. Nanny sees in the baby girl another chance to fulfill her own dreams "of whut a woman oughta be and to do." Nanny works for a white family, and Janie is raised (as the saying goes) in the white folks' yard, elevated above the common run of black people and separated from the sustenance that the community provides. She is six before she even realizes that she is black. The revelation doesn't devastate Janie. Rather, it stands as both a symbol of Nanny's unrealistic attempts to shield the girl from life and a metaphor for Janie's lack of self-knowledge.

Janie is just entering young womanhood when Nanny, frightened by the advent of that maturity, tries to school Janie about the lot of black women: "Honey, de white man is de ruler of everything as fur as Ah been able tuh find out. . . . de white man throw down de load and tell de nigger man tuh pick it up. He pick it up because he have to, but he don't tote it. He hand it to his women-folks. De nigger woman is de mule uh de world so fur as Ah can see." The image of the black woman as the mule of the world becomes a metaphor for the roles that Janie repudiates in her quest for self-fulfillment and the belief against which the book implicitly argues. Love, for the old ex-slave, is "de very prong all us black women gits hung on": that is, as Nanny goes on to explain, wanting a dressed-up dude who can't keep himself in shoe leather, much less provide for someone else; his women tote that burden for him. Love doesn't kill; it just makes a black woman sweat. Nanny dies believing that the only armor against this fate is money or the protection of good white people.

Janie holds onto her vision of a fulfilled and fulfilling love through two loveless marriages. Nanny arranges Janie's first marriage, to Logan Killicks, an older farmer whose sixty acres ought to provide Janie with the security Nanny has been able to achieve only through working for white families. Killicks, however, can't see any further than his plow, and Janie is stifled by his plodding nature. Realizing that Janie doesn't return his love, he tries to destroy her spirit by threatening to make her help with the back-breaking labor of the farm. Nanny's metaphor is almost actualized, but Janie rebels. She runs away with Joe Starks, an ambitious go-getter who pauses on his way to becoming "a big voice" in the world (mayor and postmaster, principal landowner and businessman in Eatonville) to marry Janie. Joe stops making "speeches with rhymes" to Janie almost as soon as the wedding ceremony is over. Instead of love talk, he buys her the best of everything.

Joe provides Janie with the "front porch" existence of Nanny's dreams, but in doing so, he isolates her from direct participation in any life except his own. His stranglehold on her life and definition of self is symbolized in his prohibition against her participation in the tale-tellings, mock flirtations, and other comic activities that center around or emanate from the porch of his general store. Despite his own pleasure in these sessions, he charges that the people who gather at them are "trashy," and Janie is Mrs. Mayor Starks. They don't even own their own houses, and a woman of Janie's respectability shouldn't want to pass the time of day with them. Thus, "when Lige or Sam or Walter or some of the other big picture talkers were using a side of the world for a canvas, Joe would hustle her off inside the store to sell something." The link between selling and Joe's attempt to isolate Janie from authentic membership in the community is striking and deliberate: Janie is Joe's personal possession, "de mayor's wife." It is an image that, as Hurston says of their marriage, is soon deserted by the spirit. But it is not only class that Joe uses as a means of browbeating Janie into submission. She is a woman; her place is in the home (or wherever he tells her to be, like the store, where he forces her to clerk because her many mistakes give him another opportunity to belittle her intelligence). Someone has to think for women, children, chickens, and cows. The instances of Joe's chauvinism are obvious and many. The metaphor of the mule is further reified in Joe's insistence that Janie tote his narrow, stultifying notions of what behavior is appropriate to her class and sex. Rooted at first only in the specificity of the Afro-American female experience, the metaphor has been transformed into one for the female condition; Janie's individual quest for fulfillment becomes any woman's tale.

Joe dies of a kidney ailment after some years of marriage. Janie, now a widow with property and still a very attractive woman, meets and marries Vergible "Tea Cake" Woods, an itinerant laborer and gambler much younger than herself. Tea Cake is love and laughter and talking in rhymes. However, he fulfills Janie's dreams because he requires only that she be herself. At home with himself, he has no need to dominate Janie or curb her self-expression in order to prove his masculinity. In contrast to the social status that her previous marriages gave her (and the book is filled with contrasts), Janie's place in her relationship with Tea Cake is on the muck, a booming farming area, picking beans at his side. Janie has come *down*, that paradoxical place in Afro-American literature that is both a physical bottom and the setting for the character's attainment of a penultimate self-knowledge (think of Ellison's Invisible Man in his basement room or the hero of Baraka's *The System of Dante's Hell* in the Bottoms). Down on the muck, Janie's horizons are expanded by the love and respect she shares with Tea Cake. She becomes a participant in the life that Nanny, Logan, Joe, and other friends and advisors would have her believe is beneath her. "The men held big arguments here like they used to do on the store porch. Only here, she could listen and laugh and even talk some herself if she wanted to. She got so she could tell big stories herself from listening to the rest." Janie comes at last into her own, at home with herself, her man, and her world. This unity is symbolized in a final play on the black-woman-as mule image. Tea Cake asks and Janie consents to work in the fields with him, because neither wants to be parted from the other even during the working day. Their love for each other makes the stoop labor of bean picking seem almost play. The differences between the image and the reversal of that image are obvious: Tea Cake has asked, not commanded; his request stems from a desire to be with Janie, to share every aspect of his life with her, rather than from a desire to coerce her into some mindless submission. It isn't the white man's burden that Janie carries; it is the gift of her own love.

Notes

1. Contemporary critics are less dogmatic about the dates; some consider the entire period between the world wars, 1919–39, as the Renaissance. See, for example, Eugene B. Redmond, *Drum-Voices* (New York: Doubleday, 1976).

2. The point is not so much Zora's actual age, but rather, that the contradictory dates indicate how closely the gregarious Zora guarded her private life. Hemenway's book is a gold mine on Zora, her work, and the Renaissance.

"I Love the Way Janie Crawford Left Her Husbands"

Zora Neale Hurston's Emergent Female Hero

MARY HELEN WASHINGTON

◆ ◆ ◆

IN THE PAST FEW years of teaching Zora Neale Hurston's *Their Eyes Were Watching God*,[1] I have become increasingly disturbed by this text, particularly by two problematic relationships I see in the novel: women's relationship to the community and women's relationship to language. *Their Eyes* has often been described as a novel about a woman in a folk community, but it might be more accurately described as a novel about a woman outside of the folk community. And while feminists have been eager to seize upon this text as an expression of female power, I think it is a novel that represents women's exclusion from power, particularly from the power of oral speech. Most contemporary critics contend that Janie is the articulate voice in the tradition, that the novel celebrates a woman coming to self-discovery and that this self-discovery leads her ultimately to a meaningful participation in black folk traditions.[2] Perhaps. But before bestowing the title of "articulate hero" on Janie, we should look to Hurston's first novel, *Jonah's Gourd Vine*, to its main character, Reverend John Pearson, and to the power that Hurston is able to confer on a male folk hero.[3]

From the beginning of his life, John Pearson's relationship to the community is as assured as Janie's is problematic. Living in a small Alabama town and then in Eatonville, where Janie also migrates, he discovers his preaching voice early and is encouraged to use it. His ability to control and manipulate the folk language is a source of power within the community. Even his relationships with women help him to connect to his community, leading him to literacy and to speech, while Janie's relationship with men deprive her of community and of her voice. John's friendship with Hambo, his closest friend, is much more dynamic than Janie and Pheoby's because Hurston makes the male friendship a deeper and more complex one, and because the community acknowledges and comments on the men's friendship. In his introduction to *Jonah's Gourd Vine*, Larry Neal describes John Pearson's exalted function in the folk community:

> John Pearson, as Zora notes in her letter to [James Weldon] Johnson is a poet. That is to say, one who manipulates words in order to convey to others the mystery of that Unknowable force which we call God. And he is more; he is the intelligence of the community, the bearer of its traditions and highest possibilities.[4]

One could hardly make such an unequivocal claim for Janie's heroic posture in *Their Eyes.* Singled out for her extraordinary, angelicized beauty, Janie cannot "get but so close to them [the people in Eatonville] in spirit." Her friendship with Pheoby, occurring apart from the community, encapsulates Janie and Pheoby in a private dyad that insulates Janie from the jealousy of other women. Like the other women in the town, she is barred from participation in the culture's oral tradition. When the voice of the black oral tradition is summoned in *Their Eyes,* it is not used to represent the collective black community but to invoke and valorize the voice of the black *male* community.[5]

As critic Margaret Homans points out, our attentiveness to the possibility that women are excluded categorically from the language of the dominant discourse should help us to be aware of the inadequacy of language, its inability to represent female experience, its tendency not only to silence women but to make women complicitous in that silence.[6] Part of Janie's dilemma in *Their Eyes* is that she is both subject and object—both hero and heroine—and Hurston, apparently could not retrieve her from that paradoxical position except in the frame story, where she is talking to her friend and equal, Pheoby Watson. As object in that text, Janie is often passive when she should be active, deprived of speech when she should be in command of language, made powerless by her three husbands and by Hurston's narrative strategies. I would like to focus on several passages in *Jonah's Gourd Vine* and in *Their Eyes* to show how Janie is trapped in her status as object, as passive female, and to contrast the freedom John Pearson has as subject to aspire to a heroic posture in his community.

In both *Their Eyes* and *Jonah's Gourd Vine* sexuality is established in the early lives of Janie and John as a symbol of their growing maturity. The symbol of Janie's emerging sexuality is the blossoming pear tree being pollinated by the dust-bearing bee. Early in the text, when Janie is about fifteen, Hurston presents her stretched out on her back beneath a pear tree, observing the activity of the bees:

> She saw a dust-bearing bee sink into the sanctum of a bloom; the thousand sister-calyxes arch to meet the love embrace and the ecstatic shiver of the tree from root to tiniest branch creaming in every blossom and frothing with delight. So this was marriage! She had been summoned to behold a revelation. Then Janie felt a pain remorseless sweet that left her limp and languid.

She leaves this scene of the pear tree looking for "an answer seeking her" and finds that answer in the person of Johnny Taylor who, in her rapturous state, looks like a golden glorious being. Janie's first sexual encounter is observed by her grandmother and she is summarily punished.[7] To introduce such a sexual scene at the age when Janie is about to enter adulthood, to turn it into romantic fantasy, and to make it end in punishment certainly limits the possibility of any growth resulting from that experience.

John's sexual encounters are never observed by any adult and thus he is spared the humiliation and the punishment Janie endures for her adolescent experimentation. In an early scene when he is playing a game called "Hide the Switch" with the girl in the quarters where he works, he is the active pursuer, and, in contrast to Janie's romantic fantasies, John's experience of sexuality is earthy and energetic and confirms his sense of power:

> . . . when he was "it" he managed to catch every girl in the quarters. The other boys were less successful but girls were screaming under John's lash behind the cowpen and under sweet-gum trees around the spring until the moon rose. John never forgot that night. Even the strong odor of their sweaty bodies was lovely to remember. He went in to bed when all of the girls had been called in by their folks. He could have romped till morning.

A recurring symbol Hurston uses to represent John's sexuality is the train, which he sees for the first time after he meets Lucy, the woman destined to become his first wife. A country boy, John is at first terrified by the "panting monster," but he is also mesmerized by this threatening machine whose sides "seemed to expand and contract like a fiery-lunged monster." It looks frightening, but it is also "uh pretty thing" and it has as many destinations as John in his philandering will have. As a symbol of male sexuality, the train suggests power, dynamism, and mobility.[8]

Janie's image of herself as a blossom waiting to be pollinated by a bee transforms her figuratively and literally into the space in which men's action may occur.[9] She waits for an answer and the answer appears in the form of two men, both of whom direct Janie's life and the action of the plot. Janie at least resists her first husband, Logan, but once Jody takes her to Eatonville, he controls her life as well as the narrative. He buys the land, builds the town, makes Janie tie up her hair, and prescribes her relationship with the rest of the town. We know that Hurston means for Janie to free herself from male domination, but Hurston's language, as much as Jody's behavior, signifies Janie's status as an object. Janie's arrival in Eatonville is described through the eyes and speech of the men on the front porch. Jody joins the men, but Janie is seen "through the bedroom window getting settled." Not only are Janie and the other women barred from participation in the ceremonies and rituals of the community, but they become the objects of the sessions on the porch, included in the men's tale-telling as the butt of their jokes, or their flattery, or their scorn. The experience of having one's body become an object to be looked at is considered so demeaning that when it happens to a man, it figuratively transforms him into a woman. When Janie launches her most devastating attack on Jody in front of all the men in the store, she tells him not to talk about her looking old because "When you pull down yo' britches you look lak de change uh life." Since the "change of life" ordinarily refers to a woman's menopause, Janie is signifying that Jody, like a woman, is subject to the humiliation of exposure. Now that he is the object of the gaze, Jody realizes that other men will "look" on him with pity: "Janie had robbed him of his illusion of irresistible maleness that all men cherish."

Eventually Janie does speak, and, interestingly, her first speech, on behalf of women, is a commentary on the limitations of a male-dominated society.

> Sometimes God gits familiar wid us womenfolks too and talks His inside business. He told me how surprised He was 'bout y'all turning out so smart after Him makin' yuh different; and how surprised y'all is goin' tuh be if you ever find out you don't know half as much 'bout us as you think you do.

Speech does not lead Janie to power, however, but to self-division and to further acquiescence in her status as object. As her marriage to Jody deteriorates she begins to observe herself: "one day she sat and watched the shadows of herself going about tending store and prostrating itself before Jody, while all the time she herself sat under a shady tree with the wind blowing through her hair and her clothes."

In contrast to Janie's psychic split in which her imagination asserts itself while her body makes a show of obedience, John Pearson, trapped in a similarly constricting marriage with his second wife, Hattie, experiences not self-division but a kind of self-unification in which the past memories he has repressed seep into his consciousness and drive him to confront his life with Hattie: "Then too his daily self seemed to be wearing thin, and the past seeped thru and mastered him for increasingly longer periods. He whose present had always been so bubbling that it crowded out past and future now found himself with a memory." In this new state John begins to remember and visit old friends. His memories prompt him to confront Hattie and even to deny that he ever married her. Of course his memory is selective and self-serving, and quite devastating to Hattie, but it does drive him to action.

Even after Janie acquires the power of speech that allows her to stand up to Jody, Hurtston continues to objectify her so that she does not take action. Immediately after Jody's death she goes to the looking glass where, she tells us, she has told her girl self to wait for her, and there she discovers that a handsome woman has taken her place. She tears off the kerchief Jody has forced her to wear and lets down her plentiful hair: "The weight, the length, the glory was there. She took careful stock of herself, then combed her hair and tied it back up again." In her first moment of independence Janie is not seen as autonomous subject but again as visual object, "seeing herself seeing herself," draping before herself that "hidden mystery" that attracts men and makes her superior to women. Note that when she turns to the mirror, it is not to experience her own sensual pleasure in her hair. She does not tell us how her hair felt to her—did it tingle at the roots? Did she shiver with delight?—no, she takes stock of herself, makes an assessment of herself. What's in the mirror that she cannot experience without it: that imaginary other whom the mirror represents, looking on in judgment, recording, not her own sensations but the way others see her.

Barbara Johnson's reading of *Their Eyes* suggests that once Janie is able to identify the split between her inside and outside selves, incorporating and articulating her own sense of self-division, she develops an increasing ability to speak.[10] I have come to different conclusions: that Hurston continues to subvert Janie's voice, that in crucial places where we need to hear her speak she is curiously silent, that even when Hurston sets out to explore Janie's internal consciousness, her internal speech, what we actually hear are the voices of men. Once Tea Cake enters the narrative his name and his voice are heard nearly twice as often as Janie's. He walks into Janie's life with a guitar and a grin and tells her, "Honey since you loose me and gimme privilege tuh tell yuh all about mahself. Ah'll tell yuh." And from then on it is Tea Cake's tale, the only reason for Janie's account of her life to Pheoby being to vindicate Tea Cake's name. Insisting on Tea Cake's innocence as well as his central place in her story, Janie tells Pheoby, "Teacake ain't wasted no money of mine, and he ain't left me for no young gal, neither. He give me every consolation in the world. He'd tell 'em so too, if he was here. If he wasn't gone."

As many feminist critics have pointed out, women do get silenced, even in texts by women, and there are critical places in *Their Eyes* where Janie's voice needs to be heard and is not, places where we would expect her as the subject of the story to speak. Perhaps the most stunning silence in the text occurs after Tea Cake beats Janie. The beating is seen entirely through the eyes of the male community, while Janie's reaction is never given. Tea Cake becomes the envy of the other men for having a woman whose flesh is so tender that one can see every place she's been hit. Sop-de-Bottom declares in awe, "wouldn't Ah love tuh whip uh tender woman lak Janie!" Janie is silent, so thoroughly repressed in this section that all that remains of her is what Tea Cake and the other men desire.

Passages that are supposed to represent Janie's interior consciousness begin by marking some internal change in Janie, then gradually or abruptly shift so that a male character takes Janie's place as the subject of the discourse; at the conclusion of these passages, ostensibly devoted to the revelation of Janie's interior life, the male voice predominates. Janie's life just before and after Jody's death is a fertile period for such self-reflection, but Hurston does not focus the attention of the text on Janie even in these significant turning points in Janie's life. In the long paragraph that tells us how she has changed in the six months after Jody's death, we are told that Janie talked and laughed in the store at times and was happy except for the store. To solve the problem of the store she hires Hezikiah "who was the best imitation of Joe that his seventeen years could make." At this point, the paragraph shifts its focus from Janie and her growing sense of independence to Hezikiah and his imitation of Jody, describing Hezikiah in a way that evokes Jody's presence and obliterates Janie. We are told at the end of the paragraph, in tongue-in-cheek humor, that because "managing stores and women storeowners was trying on a man's nerves," Hezikiah "needed to take a drink of liquor now and then to keep up." Thus Janie is not only removed as the subject of this passage but is subsumed under the male-defined category of worrisome women. Even the much-celebrated description of Janie's discovery of her split selves: "She had an inside and an outside now and suddenly she knew how not to mix them" represents her internal life as divided between two men: her outside self exists for Joe and her inside self she is "saving up" for "some man she had never seen."[11]

Critic Robert Stepto was the first to raise the question about Janie's lack of voice in *Their Eyes*. In his critique of Afro-American narrative he claims that Hurston creates only the illusion that Janie has achieved her voice, that Hurston's strategy of having much of Janie's tale told by an omniscient third person rather than by a first person narrator undercuts the development of Janie's "voice."[12] While I was initially resistant to this criticism of *Their Eyes*, my reading of *Jonah's Gourd Vine* suggests that Hurston was indeed ambivalent about giving a powerful voice to a woman like Janie who is already in rebellion against male authority and against the roles prescribed for women in a male-dominated society. As Stepto notes, Janie's lack of voice is particularly disturbing in the courtroom scene, which comes at the end of her tale and, presumably, at a point where she has developed her capacity to speak. Hurston tells us that down in the Everglades "She got so she could tell big stories herself," but in the courtroom scene the story of Janie and Tea Cake is told entirely in third person: "She had to go way back to let them know how she and Tea Cake had been with one another." We do not hear Janie speaking in her own voice until we return to the frame where she is speaking to her friend, Pheoby.[13]

There is a similar courtroom scene in *Jonah's Gourd Vine*, and there is also a silence, not an enforced silence but the silence of a man who deliberately chooses not to speak. John is hauled into court by his second wife, Hattie, on the grounds of adultery. Like the court system in *Their Eyes*, this too is one where "de laws and de cote houses and de jail houses all b'longed tuh white folks" and, as in Janie's situation, the black community is united against John. His former friends take the stand against him, testifying on Hattie's behalf in order to spite John, but John refuses to call any witnesses for his defense. After he has lost the trial, his friend Hambo angrily asks him why he didn't allow him to testify. John's eloquent answer explains his silence in the courtroom, but more than that, it shows that he has such power over his own voice that he can choose when and where to use it, in this case to defy a hypocritical, racist system and to protect the black community:

Ah didn't want de white folks tuh hear 'bout nothin' lak dat. Dey knows too much 'bout us as it is, but dey some things dey ain't tuh know. Dey's some strings on our harp fuh us tuh play on an sing all tuh ourselves. Dey thinks wese all ignorant as it is, and dey thinks wese all alike, and dat dey knows us inside and out, but you know better. Dey wouldn't make no great 'miration if you had uh tole 'em Hattie had all dem mens. Dey wouldn't zarn 'tween uh woman lak Hattie and one lak Lucy, uh yo' wife befo' she died. Dey thinks all colored folks is de same dat way.

John's deliberate silence is motivated by his political consciousness. In spite of the community's rejection of him, he is still their defender, especially in the face of a common adversary. Hurston does not allow Janie the insight John has, nor the voice, nor the loyalty to her people. To Mrs. Turner's racial insults, Janie is nearly silent, offering only a cold shoulder to show her resistance to the woman's bigotry. In the courtroom scene Janie is divorced from the other blacks and surrounded by a "protecting wall of white women." She is vindicated, and the black community humbled. Janie is the outsider; John is the culture hero, their "inspired artist," the traditional male hero in possession of traditional male power.

But John's power in the community and his gift for words do not always serve him well. As Robert Hemenway asserts in his critical biography of Hurston, John is "a captive of the community's need for a public giver of words."

> His language does not serve to articulate his personal problems because it is directed away from the self toward the communal celebration. John, the man of words, becomes the victim of his bardic function. He is the epic poet of the community who sacrifices himself for the group vision.[14]

For John, words mean power and status rather than the expression of feeling. When he first discovers the power of his voice, he thinks immediately of how good he sounds and how his voice can be exploited for his benefits:

> Dat sho sound good . . . If mah voice sound *dat* good de first time Ah ever prayed in, de church house, it sho won't be de las'.

John never feels the call to preach until the day on Joe Clarke's porch when the men tease John about being a "wife-made man." One of his buddies tells him that with a wife like Lucy any man could get ahead in life: "Anybody could put hisself on de ladder wid her in de house." The following Sunday in his continuing quest for manhood and power, John turns to preaching. The dramatic quality of his preaching and his showmanship easily make him the most famous preacher and the most powerful man in the area. John's inability to achieve maturity and his sudden death at the moment of his greatest insight suggest a great deal about Hurston's discomfort with the traditional male hero, with the values of the community he represents, with the culture's privileging of orality over inward development. Janie Starks is almost the complete antithesis of John Pearson: "She assumes heroic stature not by externals, but by her own struggle for self-definition, for autonomy, for liberation from the illusions that others have tried to make her live by or that she has submitted to herself."[15]

While Janie's culture honors the oral art, "this picture making with words," Janie's final speech in *Their Eyes* actually casts doubt on the relevance of oral speech:

> Talkin' don't amunt tuh uh hill uh beans when you can't do nothing else
> . . . Pheoby you got tuh *go* there tuh *know* there. Yo papa and yo' mamma
> and nobody else can't tell yuh and show yuh. Two things everybody's got
> tuh do fuh theyselves. They got tuh go tuh God, and they got tuh find out
> about livin' fuh theyselves.

Janie's final comment that experience is more important than words is an implicit criticism of the culture that celebrates orality to the exclusion of inner growth. The language of men in *Their Eyes* and in *Jonah's Gourd Vine* is almost always divorced from any kind of interiority. The men are rarely shown in the process of growth. Their talking is a game. Janie's life is about the experience of relationships. Logan, Jody, and Tea Cake and John Pearson are essentially static characters, whereas Pheoby and Janie allow experience to change them. John, who seems almost constitutionally unfitted for self-examination, is killed at the end of the novel by a train, that very symbol of male power he has been seduced by all of his life.[16]

Vladimir Propp, in his study of folklore and narrative, cautions us not to think that plots directly reflect a given social order but "rather emerge out of the conflict, the contradictions of different social orders as they succeed or replace one another." What is manifested in the tensions of plots is "the difficult coexistence of different orders of historical reality in the long period of transition from one to the other . . ."[17]

Hurston's plots may very well reflect such a tension in the social order, a period of transition in which the conflictual coexistence of a predominantly male and a more egalitarian culture is inscribed in these two forms of culture heroes. Both novels end in an ambiguous stance: John dies alone, so dominated by the ideals of his community that he is completely unable to understand his spiritual dilemma. And Janie, having returned to the community she once rejected, is left in a position of interiority so total it seems to represent another structure of confinement. Alone in her bedroom she watches pictures of "love and light against the walls," almost as though she is a spectator at a film. She pulls in the horizon and drapes it over her shoulder and calls in her soul to come and see. The language of this section gives us the illusion of growth and development, but the language is deceptive. The horizon represents the outside world—the world of adventure where Janie journeyed in search of people and a value system that would allow her real self to shine. If the horizon is the world of possibility, of journeys, of meeting new people and eschewing materialistic values, then Janie seems to be canceling out any further exploration of that world. In Eatonville she is a landlady with a fat bank account and a scorn for the people that ensures her alienation. Like the heroine of romantic fiction, left without a man she exists in a position of stasis with no suggestion of how she will employ her considerable energies in her now—perhaps temporarily—manless life.

Hurston was obviously comfortable with the role of the traditional male hero in *Jonah's Gourd Vine*, but *Their Eyes* presented Hurston with a problem she could not solve—the questing hero as woman. That Hurston intended Janie to be such a hero—at least on some level—is undeniable. She puts Janie on the track of autonomy, self-realization, and independence. She allows her to put on the outward trappings of male power. Janie dresses in overalls, goes on the muck, learns to shoot—even better than Tea Cake—and her rebellion changes her and potentially her friend Pheoby. If the rightful end of the romantic heroine is marriage, then Hurston has certainly resisted the script of romance by having Janie kill Tea Cake (though he exists in death in a far more mythical and exalted way than in life). As Rachel Blau Du Plessis argues, when the narrative resolves itself in the repression of romance and the reassertion of quest, the result is a narrative that is critical of those patriarchal rules that govern women and deny them a role outside of the boundaries of patriarchy.[18]

While such a critique of patriarchal norms is obvious in *Their Eyes*, we still see Hurston's ambivalence about Janie's role as "hero" as opposed to "heroine."[19] Like all romantic *heroines*, Janie follows the dreams of men. She takes off after Jody because "he spoke for far horizon," and she takes off after Tea Cake's dream of going "on de muck." By the rules of romantic fiction, the *heroine* is extremely feminine in looks. Janie's long, heavy, Caucasianlike hair is mentioned so many times in *Their Eyes* that, as one of my students said, it becomes another character in the novel. A "hidden mystery," Janie's hair is one of the most powerful forces in her life, mesmerizing men and alienating the women. As a trope straight out of the turn-of-the-century "mulatto" novel *(Clotel, Iola Leroy, The House Behind the Cedars)*, the hair connects Janie inexorably to the conventional romantic heroine. Employing other standard devices of romantic fiction, Hurston creates the excitement and tension of romantic seduction. Tea Cake—a tall, dark, mysterious stranger—strides into the novel and wrenches Janie away from her prim and proper life. The age and class differences between Janie and Tea Cake, the secrecy of their affair, the town's disapproval, the sense of risk and helplessness as Janie discovers passionate love and the fear, desire, even the potential violence of becoming the possessed are all standard features of romance fiction. Janie is not the subject of these romantic episodes; she is the object of Tea Cake's quest, subsumed under his desires, and, at times, so subordinate to Tea Cake that even her interior consciousness reveals more about him than it does about her.

In spite of his infidelities, his arrogance, and his incapacity for self-reflection, John Pearson is unambiguously the heroic center of *Jonah's Gourd Vine.* He inhabits the entire text, his voice is heard on nearly every page, he follows his own dreams, he is selected by the community to be its leader, and he is recognized by the community for his powers and chastised for his shortcomings. The preacher's sermon as he eulogized John at his funeral is not so much a tribute to the man as it is a recognition that the narrative exists to assert the power of the male story and its claim to our attention. Janie has, of course, reformed her community simply by her resistance to its values. The very fact of her status as outsider makes her seem heroic by contemporary standards. Unable to achieve the easy integration into the society that John Pearson assumes, she stands on the outside and calls into question her culture's dependence on externals, its lack of self-reflection, and its treatment of women. Her rebellion changes her and her friend Pheoby, and, in the words of Lee Edwards, her life becomes "a compelling model of possibility for anyone who hears her tale."[20]

Notes

1. Zora Neale Hurston, *Their Eyes Were Watching God* (Urbana: University of Illinois Press, 1978).

2 Robert Hemenway, *Zora Neale Hurston: A Literary Biography* (Urbana: University of Illinois Press, 1977), 239. Hemenway says that Janie's "blossoming" refers personally to "her discovery of self and ultimately to her meaningful participation in black tradition." But at the end of *Their Eyes,* Janie does not return to an accepting community. She returns to Eatonville as an outsider, and even in the Everglades she does not have an insider's role in the community as Tea Cake does.

3. Zora Neale Hurston, *Jonah's Gourd Vine* (Philadelphia: J. B. Lippincott, 1971).

4. Ibid., 7.

5. Henry Louis Gates, Jr., "Zora Neale Hurston and the Speakerly Text," in *The*

Signifying Monkey (New York: Oxford University Press, 1987). Gates argues that *Their Eyes* resolves the implicit tension between standard English and black dialect, that Hurston's rhetorical strategies create a kind of new language in which Janie's thoughts are cast—not in black dialect per se but a colloquial form of standard English that is informed by the black idiom. By the end of the novel this language (or free indirect discourse) makes Janie's voice almost inseparable from the narrator's—a synthesis that becomes a trope for the self-knowledge Janie has achieved. While Gates sees the language of *Their Eyes* representing the collective black community's speech and thoughts in this "dialect-informed" colloquial idiom that Hurston has invented, I read the text in a much more literal way and continue to maintain that however inventive this new language might be it is still often used to invoke the thoughts, ideas, and presence of men.

6. Margaret Homans, "Her Very Own Howl," *SIGNS* 9 (Winter 1983): 186–205.

7. One of the ways women's sexuality is made to seem less dignified than men's is to have a woman's sexual experience seen or described by an unsympathetic observer. A good example of the double standard in reporting sexual behavior occurs in Ann Petry's "In Darkness and Confusion," in *Black Voices: An Anthology of Afro-American Literature*, ed. Abraham Chapman (New York: New American Library 1968), 161–191. The young Annie Mae is observed by her uncle-in-law who reports that her sexual behavior is indecent. In contrast, his son's sexual adventures are alluded to respectfully as activities a father may not pry into.

8. The image of the train as fearsome and threatening occurs in Hurston's autobiography, *Dust Tracks on a Road: An Autobiography*, ed. Robert Hemenway (Urbana: University of Illinois Press, 1984). When she is a young girl on her way to Jacksonville, Zora, like John Pearson, is at first terrified of its "big, mean-looking eye" and has to be dragged on board "kicking and screaming to the huge amusement of everybody but me." Later when she is inside the coach and sees the "glamor of the plush and metal," she calms down and begins to enjoy the ride, which, she says "didn't hurt a bit." In both *Dust Tracks* and *Jonah's Gourd Vine* the imagery of the train is clearly sexual, but, while Zora sees the train as something external to herself, something that is powerful but will not hurt her, John imagines the train as an extension of his own power.

9. Teresa De Lauretis, *Alice Doesn't: Feminism, Semiotics, Cinema* (Bloomington: Indiana University Press, 1984), 143. De Lauretis notes that the movement of narrative discourse specifies and produces the masculine position as that of mythical subject and the feminine position as mythical obstacle, or, simply "the space in which that movement occurs."

10. I am indebted to Barbara Johnson for this insight which she suggested when I presented an early version of this paper to her class of Afro-American women writers at Harvard in the fall of 1985. I was struck by her comment that Jody's

vulnerability makes him like a woman and therefore subject to this kind of attack.

11. Barbara Johnson, "Metaphor, Metonymy, and Voice in *Their Eyes Were Watching God,"* in *Black Literature and Literary Theory,* ed. Henry-Louis Gates, Jr. (New York: Methuen, 1984), 204–219. Johnson's essay probes very carefully the relation between Janie's ability to speak and her ability to recognize her own self-division. Once Janie is able "to assume and articulate the incompatible forces involved in her own division," she begins to achieve an authentic voice. Arguing for a more literal reading of *Their Eyes,* I maintain that we hear precious little of Janie's voice even after she makes this pronouncement of knowing that she has "an inside and an outside self." A great deal of the "voice" of the text is devoted to the men in the story even after Janie's discovery of self-division.

12. Robert Stepto, *From Behind the Veil: A Study of Afro-American Narrative* (Urbana: University of Illinois Press, 1979), 164–167.

When Robert Stepto raised this issue at the 1979 Modern Language Association Meeting, he set off an intense debate. While I do not totally agree with his reading of *Their Eyes* and I think he short-changes Hurston by alloting so little space to her in *From Behind the Veil,* I do think he is right about Janie's lack of voice in the courtroom scene.

13. More accurately the style of this section should be called *free indirect discourse* because both Janie's voice and the narrator's voice are evoked here. In his *Introduction to Poetics: Theory and History of Literature,* vol. 1 (Minneapolis: University of Minnesota Press, 1982), Tzvetan Todorov explains Gerard Genette's definition of free indirect discourse as a grammatical form that adopts the indirect style but retains the "semantic nuances of the 'original' discourse."

14. Hemenway, *Zora Neale Hurston,* 198.

15. Mary Helen Washington, "Zora Neale Hurston: A Woman Half in Shadow," in *I Love Myself When I Am Laughing . . . And Then Again When I Am Looking Mean and Impressive: A Zora Neale Hurston Reader,* ed. Alice Walker (Old Westbury, N.Y.: Feminist Press, 1979), 16. In the original version of this essay, I showed how Joseph Campbell's model of the hero, though it had been applied to Ralph Ellison's invisible man, could more appropriately be applied to Janie, who defies her status as the mule of the world, and, unlike Ellison's antihero, does not end up in an underground hideout.

Following the pattern of the classic mythological hero, defined by Campbell in *The Hero with a Thousand Faces* (Princeton, NJ: Princeton University Press, 1968), Janie leaves her everyday world to proceed to the threshold of adventure (leaves Nanny and Logan to run off with Jody to Eatonville); she is confronted by a power that threatens her spiritual life (Jody Starks and his efforts to make her submissive to him); she goes beyond that threat to a world of unfamiliar forces some of which threaten her and some of which give aid (Tea Cake, his wild adventures, and his ability to see her as an equal); she descends into an underworld where she must undergo the supreme ordeal (the journey to the Everglades; the killing of Tea Cake and the trial); and the final work is that of the return when the hero reemerges from the kingdom of dread and brings a gift that restores the world (Janie returns to Eatonville and tells her story to her friend Pheoby who recognizes immediately her communion with Janie's experience: "Ah done growed ten feet higher from jus' listenin' tuh you, Janie").

16. Anne Jones, "Pheoby's Hungry Listening: Zora Neale Hurston's *Their Eyes Were Watching God*" (paper presented at the National Women's Studies Association, Humboldt State University, Arcata, California, June 1982).

17. De Lauretis, *Alice Doesn't*, 113. In the chapter "Desire in Narrative," De Lauretis refers to Vladimir Propp's essay "Oedipus in the Light of Folklore," which studies plot types and their diachronic or historical transformations.

18. Rachel Blau Du Plessis, *Writing Beyond the Ending: Narrative Strategies of Twentieth-Century Women Writers* (Bloomington: Indiana University Press, 1985). Du Plessis asserts that "it is the project of twentieth-century women writers to solve the contradiction between love and quest and to replace the alternate endings in marriage and death that are their cultural legacy from nineteenth-century life and letters by offering a different set of choices."

19. Du Plessis distinguishes between *hero* and *heroine* in this way: "the female hero is a central character whose activities, growth, and insight are given much narrative attention and authorial interest." By *heroine* she means "the object of male attention or rescue" *(Writing Beyond the Ending*, n. 22), 200, Hurston oscillates between these two positions, making Janie at one time a conventional romantic heroine, at other times a woman whose quest for independence drives the narrative.

20. Lee R. Edwards, *Psyche as Hero: Female Heroism and Fictional Form* (Middletown, CT: Wesleyan University Press, 1984), 212.

Metaphor, Metonymy, and Voice in *Their Eyes Were Watching God*

BARBARA JOHNSON

◆　◆　◆

N OT SO VERY long ago, metaphor and metonymy burst into
prominence as the salt and pepper, the Laurel and Hardy, the Yin and
Yang, and often the Scylla and Charybdis of literary theory. Then, just as
quickly, this cosmic couple passed out of fashion again. How did it happen
that such an arcane rhetorical opposition was able to acquire the brief but
powerful privilege of dividing and naming the whole of human reality,
from Mommy and Daddy or Symptom and Desire all the way to God and
Country or Beautiful Lie and Sober Lucidity?[1]

The contemporary sense of the opposition between metaphor and
metonymy was first formulated by Roman Jakobson in an article entitled
"Two Aspects of Language and Two Types of Aphasic Disturbances."[2] That
article, first published in English in 1956, derives much of its celebrity from
the central place accorded by the French structuralists to the 1963 transla-
tion of a selection of Jakobson's work, entitled *Essais linguistiques,* which included the aphasia study. The words metaphor and metonymy are not, of
course, of twentieth-century coinage: they are classical tropes traditionally
defined as the substitution of a figurative expression for a literal or proper
one. In metaphor, the substitution is based on resemblance or analogy; in
metonymy, it is based on a relation or association other than that of similarity (cause and effect, container and contained, proper name and quali-

41

ties or works associated with it, place and event or institution, instrument and user, etc.). The use of the name Camelot to refer to John Kennedy's Washington is thus an example of metaphor, since it implies an analogy between Kennedy's world and King Arthur's, while the use of the word Watergate to refer to the scandal that ended Richard Nixon's presidency is a metonymy, since it transfers the name of an arbitrary place of origin onto a whole sequence of subsequent events.

Jakobson's use of the two terms is an extension and polarization of their classical definitions. In studying patterns of aphasia (speech dysfunction), Jakobson found that they fell into two main categories: similarity disorders and contiguity disorders. In the former, grammatical contexture and lateral associations remain while synonymity drops out; in the latter, heaps of word substitutes are kept while grammar and connectedness vanish. Jakobson concludes:

> The development of a discourse may take place along two different semantic lines: one topic may lead to another either through their similarity or through their contiguity. The metaphoric way would be the most appropriate term for the first case and the metonymic way for the second, since they find their most condensed expression in metaphor and metonymy respectively. In aphasia one or the other of these two processes is restricted or totally blocked—an effect which makes the study of aphasia particularly illuminating for the linguist. In normal verbal behavior both processes are continually operative, but careful observation will reveal that under the influence of a cultural pattern, personality, and verbal style, preference is given to one of the two processes over the other.
>
> In a well-known psychological test, children are confronted with some noun and told to utter the first verbal response that comes into their heads. In this experiment two opposite linguistic predilections are invariably exhibited: the response is intended either as a substitute for, or as a complement to the stimulus. In the latter case the stimulus and the response together form a proper syntactic construction, most usually a sentence. These two types of reaction have been labeled substitutive and predicative.
>
> To the stimulus *hut* one response was *burnt out;* another, *is a poor little house.* Both reactions are predicative; but the first creates a purely narrative context, while in the second there is a double connection with the subject *hut:* on the one hand, a positional (namely, syntactic) contiguity, and on the other a semantic similarity.
>
> The same stimulus produced the following substitutive reactions: the tautology *hut;* the synonyms *cabin* and *hovel;* the antonym *palace,* and the

metaphors *den* and *burrow*. The capacity of two words to replace one another
is an instance of positional similarity, and, in addition, all these responses are
linked to the stimulus by semantic similarity (or contrast). Metonymical responses to the same stimulus, such as *thatch, litter,* or *poverty,* combine and
contrast the positional similarity with semantic contiguity.

In manipulating these two kinds of connection (similarity and contiguity) in both their aspects (positional and semantic)—selecting, combin-
ing, and ranking them—an individual exhibits his personal style, his verbal
predilections and preferences.[3]

Two problems immediately arise that render the opposition between
metaphor and metonymy at once more interesting and more problematic
than at first appears. The first is that there are not two poles here but four:
similarity, contiguity, semantic connection, and syntactic connection. A
more adequate representation of these oppositions can be schematized as
in Figure 1. Jakobson's contention that poetry is a syntactic extension of
metaphor ("The poetic function projects the principle of equivalence from
the axis of selection into the axis of combination"[4]), while realist narrative
is an extension of metonymy, can be added to the graph as in Figure 2.

The second problem that arises in any attempt to apply the meta-
phor/metonymy distinction is that it is often very hard to tell the two
apart. In Ronsard's poem "Mignonne, allons voir si la rose . . ." the
speaker invites the lady to go for a walk with him (the walk being an example of contiguity) to see a rose which, once beautiful (like the lady), is now
withered (as the lady will eventually be): the day must therefore be seized.

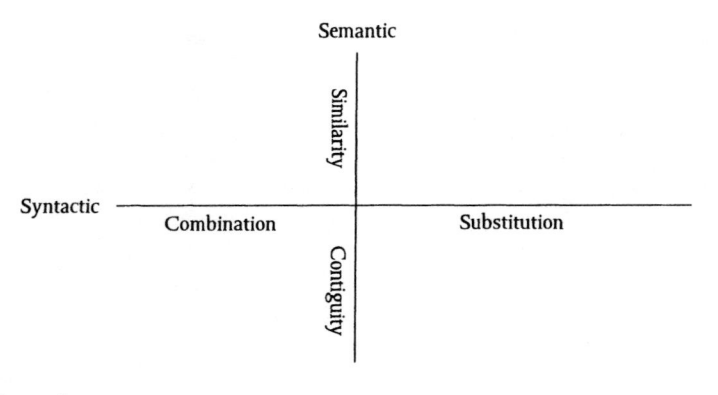

Figure 1

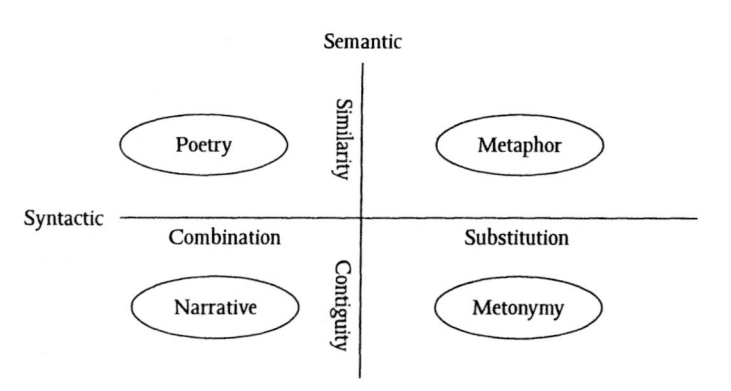

Figure 2

The metonymic proximity to the flower is designed solely to reveal the metaphoric point of the poem: enjoy life while you still bloom. The tendency of contiguity to become overlaid by similarity and vice versa may be summed up in the proverb "Birds of a feather flock together"—"Qui se ressemble s'assemble." One has only to think of the applicability of this proverb to the composition of neighborhoods in America to realize that the question of the separability of similarity from contiguity may have considerable political implications. The controversy surrounding the expression "legionnaires' disease" provides a more comical example: while the name of the disease derives solely from the contingent fact that its first victims were at an American Legion Convention, and is thus a metonymy, the fear that it will take on a metaphoric color—that a belief in some natural connection or similarity may thereby be propagated between legionnaires and the disease—has led spokesmen for the legionnaires to attempt to have the malady renamed. And finally, in the sentence "The White House denied the charges," one might ask whether the place name is a purely contiguous metonymy for the presidency, or whether the whiteness of the house isn't somehow metaphorically connected to the whiteness of its inhabitant.

One final prefatory remark about the metaphor/metonymy distinction: far from being a neutral opposition between equals, these two tropes have always stood in hierarchical relation to each other. From Aristotle to George Lakoff,[5] metaphor has always, in the Western tradition, had the privilege of revealing unexpected truth. As Aristotle puts it: "Midway between the unintelligible and the commonplace, it is a metaphor which most produces knowledge."[6] Paul de Man summarizes the preference for metaphor over metonymy by aligning analogy with necessity and conti- guity with chance: "The inference of identity and totality that is constitutive of metaphor is lacking in the purely relational metonymic contact: an ele- ment of truth is involved in taking Achilles for a lion but none in taking Mr. Ford for a motor car."[7] De Man then goes on to reveal this "element of truth" as the product of a purely rhetorical—and ultimately metonymi- cal—sleight of hand, thus overturning the traditional hierarchy and decon- structing the very basis for the seductiveness and privilege of metaphor.

I should like now to turn to the work of an author acutely conscious of, and superbly skilled in, the seductiveness and complexity of metaphor as privileged trope and trope of privilege. Zora Neale Hurston, novelist, folk- lorist, essayist, anthropologist and Harlem Renaissance personality, cut her teeth on figurative language during the tale-telling or "lying" sessions that took place on a store porch in the all-black town of Eatonville, Florida, where she was born around 1901. She devoted her life to the task of recording, pre- serving, novelizing and analyzing the patterns of speech and thought of the rural black south and related cultures. At the same time, she deplored the appropriation, dilution, and commodification of black culture (through spirituals, jazz, etc.) by the pre-Depression white world, and she constantly tried to explain the difference between a reified "art" and a living culture in which the distinctions between spectator and spectacle, rehearsal and perfor- mance, experience and representation are not fixed. "Folklore," she wrote, "is the arts of the people before they find out that there is such a thing as art."

> Folklore does not belong to any special area, time, nor people. It is a world and an ageless thing, so let us look at it from that viewpoint. It is the boiled down juice of human living and when one phase of it passes another begins which shall in turn give way before a successor.
>
> Culture is a forced march on the near and the obvious. . . . The intel- ligent mind uses up a great part of its lifespan trying to awaken its con- sciousness sufficiently to comprehend that which is plainly there before it. Every generation or so some individual with extra keen perception grasps something of the obvious about us and hitches the human race forward slightly by a new "law." Millions of things had been falling on men for thou- sands of years before the falling apple hit Newton on the head and he saw the law of gravity.[8]

Through this strategic description of the folkloric heart of scientific law, Hurston dramatizes the predicament not only of the anthropologist but also of the novelist: both are caught between the (metaphorical) urge to universalize or totalize and the knowledge that it is precisely "the near and the obvious" that will never be grasped once and for all but will only be (metonymically) named and renamed, as different things successively strike different heads. I shall return to this problem of universality at the end of this essay, but first I should like to take a close look at some of the figurative operations at work in Hurston's best-known novel, *Their Eyes Were Watching God.*[9]

The novel presents, in a combination of first- and third-person narration, the story of Janie Crawford and her three successive husbands. The first, Logan Killicks, is chosen by Janie's grandmother for his sixty acres and as a socially secure harbor for Janie's awakening sexuality. When Janie realizes that love does not automatically follow upon marriage and that Killicks completely lacks imagination, she decides to run off with ambitious, smart-talking, stylishly dressed Joe Starks, who is headed for a new all-black town where he hopes to become what he calls a "big voice." Later, as mayor and store owner of the town, he proudly raises Janie to a pedestal of property and propriety. Because this involves her submission to his idea of what a mayor's wife should be, Janie soon finds her pedestal to be a straitjacket, particularly when it involves her exclusion—both as speaker and as listener—from the tale-telling sessions on the store porch and at the mock funeral of a mule. Little by little, Janie begins to talk back to Joe, finally insulting him so profoundly that, in a sense, he dies of it. Some time later, into Janie's life walks Tea Cake Woods, whose first act is to teach Janie how to play checkers. "Somebody wanted her to play," says the text in free indirect discourse; "Somebody thought it natural for her to play" (p. 146). Thus begins a joyous liberation from the rigidities of status, image and property—one of the most beautiful and convincing love stories in any literature. In a series of courtship dances, appearances, and disappearances, Tea Cake succeeds in fulfilling Janie's dream of "a bee for her blossom" (p. 161). Tea Cake, unlike Joe and Logan, regards money and work as worth only the amount of play and enjoyment they make possible. He gains and loses money unpredictably until he and Janie begin working side by side picking beans on "the muck" in the Florida everglades. This idyll of pleasure, work, and equality ends dramatically with a hurricane during which Tea Cake, while saving Janie's life, is bitten by a rabid dog. When Tea Cake's subsequent hydrophobia transforms him into a wild and violent animal, Janie is forced to shoot him in self-defense. Acquitted of murder by an all-white jury, Janie returns to Eatonville, where she tells her story to her friend Phoeby Watson.

The passage on which I should like to concentrate both describes and dramatizes, in its figurative structure, a crucial turning point in Janie's relation to Joe and to herself. The passage follows an argument over what Janie has done with a bill of lading, during which Janie shouts, "You sho loves to tell me what to do, but Ah can't tell you nothin' Ah see!"

"Dat's 'cause you need tellin'," he rejoined hotly. "It would be pitiful if Ah didn't. Somebody got to think for women and chillun and chickens and cows. I god, they sho don't think none themselves."

"Ah knows uh few things, and womenfolks thinks sometimes too!"

"Aw naw they don't. They just think they's thinkin'. When Ah see one thing Ah understands ten. You see ten things and don't understand one."

Times and scenes like that put Janie to thinking about the inside state of her marriage. Time came when she fought back with her tongue as best she could, but it didn't do her any good. It just made Joe do more. He wanted her submission and he'd keep on fighting until he felt he had it.

So gradually, she pressed her teeth together and learned how to hush. The spirit of the marriage left the bedroom and took to living in the parlor. It was there to shake hands whenever company came to visit, but it never went back inside the bedroom again. So she put something in there to represent the spirit like a Virgin Mary image in a church. The bed was no longer a daisy-field for her and Joe to play in. It was a place where she went and laid down when she was sleepy and tired.

She wasn't petal-open anymore with him. She was twenty-four and seven years married when she knew. She found that out one day when he slapped her face in the kitchen. It happened over one of those dinners that chasten all women sometimes. They plan and they fix and they do, and then some kitchen-dwelling fiend slips a scorchy, soggy, tasteless mess into their pots and pans. Janie was a good cook, and Joe had looked forward to his dinner as a refuge from other things. So when the bread didn't rise and the fish wasn't quite done at the bone, and the rice was scorched, he slapped Janie until she had a ringing sound in her ears and told her about her brains before he stalked on back to the store.

Janie stood where he left her for unmeasured time and thought. She stood there until something feel off the shelf inside her. Then she went inside there to see what it was. It was her image of Jody tumbled down and shattered. But looking at it she saw that it never was the flesh and blood figure of her dreams. Just something she had grabbed up to drape her dreams over. In a way she turned her back upon the image where it lay and looked further. She had no more blossomy openings dusting pollen over her man,

neither any glistening young fruit where the petals used to be. She found
that she had a host of thoughts she had never expressed to him, and numerous emotions she had never let Jody know about. Things packed up and
put away in parts of her heart where he could never find them. She was saving up feelings for some man she had never seen. She had an inside and an
outside now and suddenly she knew how not to mix them. (pp. 110–113)

This opposition between an inside and an outside is a standard way of
describing the nature of a rhetorical figure. The vehicle, or surface meaning, is seen as enclosing an inner tenor, or figurative meaning. This relation
can be pictured somewhat facetiously as a gilded carriage—the vehicle—
containing Luciano Pavarotti, the tenor. Within the passage cited from
Their Eyes Were Watching God, I should like to concentrate on the two paragraphs that begin respectively "So gradually . . ." and "Janie stood where he
left her. . . ." In these two paragraphs Hurston plays a number of interesting variations on the inside/outside opposition.

In both paragraphs, a relation is set up between an inner image and
outward, domestic space. The parlor, bedroom and store full of shelves
already exist in the narrative space of the novel: they are figures drawn
metonymically from the familiar contiguous surroundings. Each of these
paragraphs recounts a little narrative of, and within, its own figurative
terms. In the first, the inner spirit of the marriage moves outward from the
bedroom to the parlor, cutting itself off from its proper place, and replacing itself with an image of virginity, the antithesis of marriage. Although
Joe is constantly exclaiming, "I god, Janie," he will not be as successful as
his namesake in uniting with the Virgin Mary. Indeed, it is his godlike self-
image that forces Janie to retreat to virginity. The entire paragraph is an externalization of Janie's feelings onto the outer surroundings in the form of
a narrative of movement from private to public space. While the whole of
the figure relates metaphorically, analogically, to the marital situation it is
designed to express, it reveals the marriage space to be metonymical, a
movement through a series of contiguous rooms. It is a narrative not of
union but of separation centered on an image not of conjugality but of
virginity.

In the second passage, just after the slap, Janie is standing, thinking,
until something "fell off the shelf inside her." Janie's inside is here represented as a store that she then goes in to inspect. While the former paragraph was an externalization of the inner, here we find an internalization
of the outer: Janie's inner self resembles a store. The material for this
metaphor is drawn from the narrative world of contiguity: the store is the

place where Joe has set himself up as lord, master, and proprietor. But here Jody's image is broken, and reveals itself never to have been a metaphor but only a metonymy of Janie's dream: "looking at it she saw that it never was the flesh and blood figure of her dreams. Just something she had grabbed up to drape her dreams over."

What we find in juxtaposing these two figural mininarratives is a kind of chiasmus, or crossover, in which the first paragraph presents an externalization of the inner, a metaphorically grounded metonymy, while the second paragraph presents an internalization of the outer, or a metonymically grounded metaphor. In both cases, the quotient of the operation is the revelation of a false or discordant "image." Janie's image, as Virgin Mary, acquires a new intactness, while Joe's lies shattered on the floor. The reversals operated by the chiasmus map out a reversal of the power relations between Janie and Joe. Henceforth, Janie will grow in power and resistance, while Joe deteriorates both in his body and in his public image.

The moral of these two figural tales is rich with implications: "She had an inside and an outside now and suddenly she knew how not to mix them." On the one hand, this means that she knew how to keep the inside and the outside separate without trying to blend or merge them into one unified identity. On the other hand it means that she has stepped irrevocably into the necessity of figurative language, where inside and outside are never the same. It is from this point on in the novel that Janie, paradoxically, begins to speak. And it is by means of a devastating figure—"You look like the change of life"—that she wounds Jody to the quick. Janie's acquisition of the power of voice thus grows not out of her identity but out of her division into inside and outside. Knowing how not to mix them is knowing that articulate language requires the copresence of two distinct poles, not their collapse into oneness.

This, of course, is what Jakobson concludes in his discussion of metaphor and metonymy. For it must be remembered that what is at stake in the maintenance of both sides—metaphor and metonymy, inside and outside—is the very possibility of speaking at all. The reduction of a discourse to oneness, identity—in Janie's case, the reduction of woman to mayor's wife—has as its necessary consequence aphasia, silence, the loss of the ability to speak: "she pressed her teeth together and learned how to hush."

What has gone unnoticed in the theoretical discussions of Jakobson's article is that behind the metaphor/metonymy distinction lies the much more serious distinction between speech and aphasia, between silence and the capacity to articulate one's own voice. To privilege *either* metaphor *or* metonymy is thus to run the risk of producing an increasingly aphasic *critical* discourse. If both, or all four, poles must be operative in order for speech to function fully, then the very notion of an "authentic voice" must be redefined. Far from being an expression of Janie's new wholeness or identity as a character, Janie's increasing ability to speak grows out of her ability not to mix inside with outside, not to pretend that there is no difference, but to assume and articulate the incompatible forces involved in her own division. The sign of an authentic voice is thus not self-identity but self-difference.

The search for wholeness, oneness, universality and totalization can nevertheless never be put to rest. However rich, healthy, or lucid fragmentation and division may be, narrative seems to have trouble resting content with it, as though a story could not recognize its own end as anything other than a moment of totalization—even when what is totalized is loss. The ending of *Their Eyes Were Watching God* is no exception:

> Of course [Tea Cake] wasn't dead. He could never be dead until she herself had finished feeling and thinking. The kiss of his memory made pictures of love and light against the wall. Here was peace. She pulled in her horizon like a great fish-net. Pulled it from around the waist of the world and draped it over her shoulder. So much of life in its meshes! She called in her soul to come and see.

The horizon, with all of life caught in its meshes, is here pulled into the self as a gesture of total recuperation and peace. It is as though self-division could be healed over at last, but only at the cost of a radical loss of the other.

This hope for some ultimate unity and peace seems to structure the very sense of an ending as such, whether that of a novel or that of a work of literary criticism. At the opposite end of the "canonical" scale, one finds it, for example, in the last chapter of Erich Auerbach's *Mimesis,* perhaps the greatest of modern monuments to the European literary canon. That final chapter, entitled "The Brown Stocking" after the stocking that Virginia Woolf's Mrs. Ramsay is knitting in *To the Lighthouse,* is a description of certain narrative tendencies in the modern novel: "multipersonal representation of consciousness, time strata, disintegration of the continuity of exterior events, shifting of narrative viewpoint," etc:

> Let us begin with a tendency which is particularly striking in our text from Virginia Woolf. She holds to minor, unimpressive, random events: measuring the stocking, a fragment of a conversation with the maid, a telephone

call. Great changes, exterior turning points, let alone catastrophes, do not occur.

Auerbach concludes his discussion of the modernists' preoccupation with the minor, the trivial, and the marginal by saying:

> It is precisely the random moment which is comparatively independent of the controversial and unstable orders over which men fight and despair. . . . The more numerous, varied, and simple the people are who appear as subjects of such random moments, the more effectively must what they have in common shine forth. . . . So the complicated process of dissolution which led to fragmentation of the exterior action, to reflection of consciousness, and to stratification of time seems to be tending toward a very simple solution. Perhaps it will be too simple to please those who, despise all its dangers and catastrophes, admire and love our epoch for the sake of its abundance of life and the incomparable historical vantage point which it affords. But they are few in number, and probably they will not live to see much more than the first forewarnings of the approaching unification and simplifcation.[10]

Never has the desire to transform fragmentation into unity been expressed so succinctly and authoritatively—indeed, almost prophetically. One cannot help but wonder, though, whether the force of this desire has not been provoked by the fact that the primary text it wishes to unify and simplify was written by a woman. What Auerbach calls "minor, unimpressive, random events"—measuring a stocking, conversing with the maid, answering the phone—can all be identified as conventional *women*'s activities. "Great changes," "exterior turning points" and "catastrophes" have been the stuff of heroic *male* literature. Even plot itself—up until *Madame Bovary,* at least—has been conceived as the doings of those who do not stay at home, i.e., men. Auerbach's urge to unify and simplify is an urge to re-subsume female difference under the category of the universal, which has always been unavowedly male. The random, the trivial, and the marginal will simply be added to the list of things all *men* have in common.

If "unification and simplification" is the privilege and province of the male, it is also, in America, the privilege and province of the white. If the woman's voice, to be authentic, must incorporate and articulate division and self-difference, so, too, has Afro-American literature always had to assume its double-voicedness. As Henry Louis Gates, Jr., puts it in "Criticism in the Jungle":

In the instance of the writer of African descent, her or his texts occupy
spaces in at least two traditions—the individual's European or American literary tradition, and one of the three related but distinct black traditions.
The "heritage" of each black text written in a Western language, then, is
a double heritage, two-toned, as it were. . . . Each utterance, then, is
double-voiced.[11]

This is a reformulation of W. E. B. Du Bois's famous image of the "veil" that
divides the black American in two:

The Negro is a sort of seventh son, born with a veil, and gifted with second
sight in this American world—a world which yields him no true self-
consciousness, but only lets him see himself through the revelation of the
other world. It is a peculiar sensation, this double-consciousness, this sense
of always looking at one's self through the eyes of others, of measuring
one's soul by the tape of a world that looks on in amused contempt and pity.
One ever feels his twoness—an American, a Negro; two souls, two
thoughts, two unreconciled strivings; two warring ideals in one dark body,
whose dogged strength alone keeps it from being torn asunder.

   The history of the American Negro is the history of this strife—this
longing to attain self-conscious manhood, to merge his double self into a
better and truer self.[12]

James Weldon Johnson, in his *Autobiography of an Ex-Colored Man,* puts it this
way:

This is the dwarfing, warping, distorting influence which operates upon
each and every colored man in the United States. He is forced to take his
outlook on all things, not from the view-point of a citizen, or a man, or
even a human being, but from the view-point of a *colored* man. . . . This
gives to every colored man, in proportion to his intellectuality, a sort of
dual personality.[13]

What is striking about the above two quotations is that they both assume
without question that the black subject is male. The black woman is totally
invisible in these descriptions of the black dilemma. Richard Wright, in his
review of *Their Eyes Were Watching God,* makes it plain that for him, too, the
black female experience is nonexistent. The novel, says Wright, lacks

a basic idea or theme that lends itself to significant interpretation. . . .
[Hurston's] dialogue manages to catch the psychological movements of the
Negro folk-mind in their pure simplicity, but that's as far as it goes. . . .
The sensory sweep of her novel carries no theme, no message, no thought.[14]

No message, no theme, no thought: the full range of questions and experiences of Janie's life are as invisible to a mind steeped in maleness as Ellison's Invisible Man is to minds steeped in whiteness. If the black *man's* soul is divided in two, what can be said of the black woman's? Here again, what is constantly seen exclusively in terms of a binary opposition—black versus white, man versus woman—must be redrawn at least as a tetrapolar structure (see Figure 3). What happens in the case of a black woman is that the four quadrants are constantly being collapsed into two. Hurston's work is often called nonpolitical simply because readers of Afro-American literature tend to look for confrontational *racial* politics, not sexual politics. If the black woman voices opposition to male domination, she is often seen as a traitor to the cause of racial justice. But, if she sides with black men against white oppression, she often winds up having to accept her position within the Black Power movement as, in Stokely Carmichael's words, "prone." This impossible position between two oppositions is what I think Hurston intends when, at the end of the novel, she represents Janie as acquitted of the murder of Tea Cake by an all-white jury but condemned by her fellow blacks. This is not out of a "lack of bitterness toward whites," as one reader[15] would have it, but rather out of a knowledge of the standards of male dominance that pervade both the black and the white worlds. The black crowd at the trial murmurs, "Tea Cake was a good boy. He had been good to that woman. No nigger woman ain't never been treated no better" (p. 276). As Janie's grandmother puts it early in the novel:

Honey, de white man is de ruler of everything as fur as Ah been able tuh find out. Maybe it's some place way off in de ocean where de black man is in

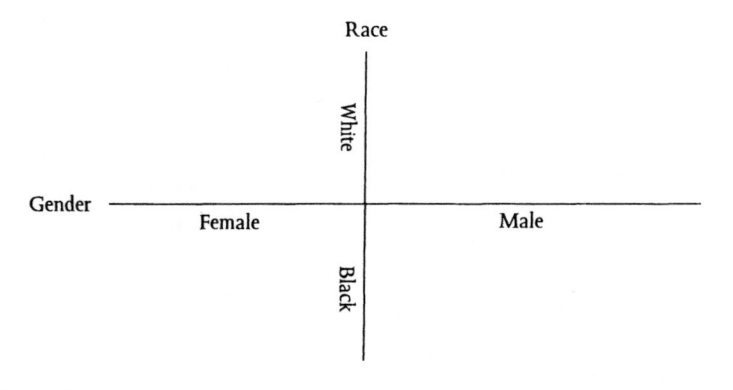

Figure 3

power, but we don't know nothin' but what we see. So de white man throw down de load and tell de nigger man tuh pick it up. He pick it up because he have to, but he don't tote it. He hand it to his womenfolks. De nigger woman is de mule uh de world so fur as Ah can see. (p. 29)

In a very persuasive book on black women and feminism entitled *Ain't I a Woman,* Bell Hooks (Gloria Watkins) discusses the ways in which black women suffer from both sexism and racism within the very movements whose ostensible purpose is to set them free. Watkins argues that "black woman" has never been considered a separate, distinct category with a history and complexity of its own. When a president appoints a black woman to a cabinet post, for example, he does not feel he is appointing a person belonging to the category "black woman"; he is appointing a person who belongs *both* to the category "black" *and* to the category "woman," and is thus killing two birds with one stone. Watkins says of the analogy often drawn—particularly by white feminists—between blacks and women:

> Since analogies derive their power, their appeal, and their very reason for being from the sense of two disparate phenomena having been brought closer together, for white women to acknowledge the overlap between the terms "blacks" and "women" (that is, the existence of black women) would render this analogy unnecessary. By continuously making this analogy, they unwittingly suggest that to them the term "women" is synonymous with "white women" and the term "blacks" synonymous with "black men."[16]

The very existence of black women thus disappears from an analogical discourse designed to express the types of oppression from which black women have the most to suffer.

In the current hierarchical view of things, this tetrapolar graph can be filled in as in Figure 4. The black woman is both invisible and ubiquitous: never seen in her own right but forever appropriated by the others for their own ends.

Ultimately, though, this mapping of tetrapolar differences is itself a fantasy of universality. Are all the members of each quadrant the same? Where are the nations, the regions, the religions, the classes, the professions? Where are the other races, the interracial subdivisions? How can the human world be totalized, even as a field of divisions? In the following quotation from Zora Neale Hurston's autobiography, we see that even the *same* black woman can express self-division in two completely different ways:

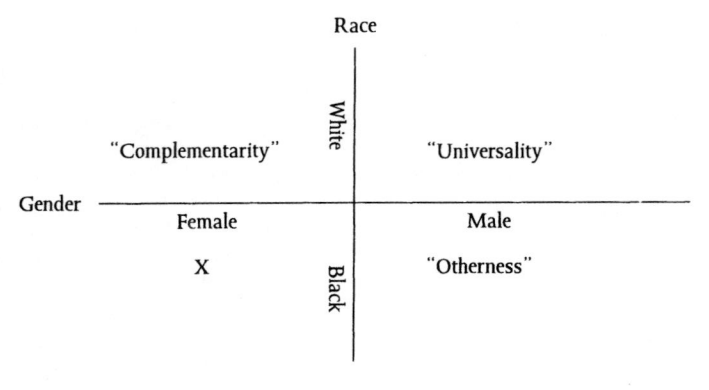

Figure 4

Work was to be all of me, so I said. . . . I had finished that phase of research and was considering writing my first book, when I met the man who
was really to lay me by the heels. . . .

He was tall, dark brown, magnificently built, with a beautifully modeled
back head. His profile was strong and good. The nose and lips were especially good front and side. But his looks only drew my eyes in the beginning.
I did not fall in love with him just for that. He had a fine mind and that in-
trigued me. When a man keeps beating me to the draw mentally, he begins
to get glamorous. . . . His intellect got me first for I am the kind of
woman that likes to move on mentally from point to point, and I like for
my man to be there way ahead of me. . . .

His great desire was to do for me. *Please* let him be a *man!* . . .

That very manliness, sweet as it was, made us both suffer. My career
balked the completeness of his ideal. I really wanted to conform, but it was
impossible. To me there was no conflict. My work was one thing, and he
was all the rest. But I could not make him see that. Nothing must be in
my life but himself. . . . We could not leave each other alone, and we
could not shield each other from hurt. . . . In the midst of this, I received my Guggenheim Fellowship. This was my chance to release him,
and fight myself free from my obsession. He would get over me in a few
months and go on to be a very big man. So I sailed off to Jamaica [and]
pitched in to work hard on my research to smother my feelings. But the
thing would not down. The plot was far from the circumstances, but I
tried to embalm all the tenderness of my passion for him in *Their Eyes Were
Watching God*.[17]

The plot is indeed far from the circumstances, and, what is even more striking, it is lived by what seems to be a completely different woman. While Janie struggles to attain equal respect *within* a relation to a man, Zora readily submits to the pleasures of submission yet struggles to establish the legitimacy of a professional life *outside* the love relation. The female voice may be universally described as divided, but it must be recognized as divided in a multitude of ways.

There is no point of view from which the universal characteristics of the human, or of the woman, or of the black woman, or even of Zora Neale Hurston, can be selected and totalized. Unification and simplification are fantasies of domination, not understanding.

The task of the writer, then, would seem to be to narrate both the appeal and the injustice of universalization, in a voice that assumes and articulates its own, ever differing self-difference. In the opening pages of *Their Eyes Were Watching God* we find, indeed, a brilliant and subtle transition from the seduction of a universal language through a progressive de-universalization that ends in the exclusion of the very protagonist herself. The book begins:

> Ships at a distance have every man's wish on board. For some they come in with the tide. For others they sail forever on the horizon, never out of sight, never landing until the Watcher turns his eyes away in resignation, his drams mocked to death by Time. That is the life of men.
>
> Now, women forget all those things they don't want to remember, and remember everything they don't want to forget. The dream is the truth. Then they act and do things accordingly.
>
> So the beginning of this was a woman, and she had come back from burying the dead. Not the dead of sick and ailing with friends at the pillow and the feet. She had come back from the sodden and the bloated; the sudden dead, their eyes flung wide open in judgment.
>
> The people all saw her come because it was sundown. . . . (p. 9)

At this point Janie crosses center stage and goes out, while the people, the "bander log," pass judgment on her. The viewpoint has moved from "every man" to "men" to "women" to "a woman" to an absence commented on by "words without masters," the gossip of the front porch. When Janie begins to speak, even the universalizing category of "standard English" gives way to the careful representation of dialect. The narrative voice in this novel expresses its own self-division by shifts between first and third person, standard English, and dialect. This self-division culminates in the frequent use of free indirect discourse, in which, as Henry Louis Gates,

Jr., points out,[18] the inside/outside boundaries between narrator and character, between standard and individual, are both transgressed and preserved, making it impossible to identify and totalize either the subject or the nature of discourse.

Narrative, it seems, is an endless fishing expedition with the horizon as both the net and the fish, the big one that always gets away. The meshes continually enclose and let escape, tear open and mend up again. Mrs. Ramsay never finishes the brown stocking.[19] A woman's work is never done. Penelope's weaving is nightly re-unraveled. The porch never stops passing the world through its mouth. The process of de-universalization can never, universally, be completed.

Notes

1. For an excellent discussion of the importance of the metaphor/metonymy distinction, see Maria Ruegg. "Metaphor and Metonymy: the Logic of Structuralist Rhetoric," *Glyph,* 6 (1979).

2. In Roman Jakobson and Morris Halle, *Fundamentals of Language* ('S-Gravenhage: Mouton, 1956).

3. Ibid., 76–77.

4. Roman Jakobson, "Linguistics and Poetics," in *The Structuralists from Marx to Levi–Strauss* (Garden City, NY: Doubleday Anchor, 1972), 95.

5. See George Lakoff and Mark Johnson, *Metaphors We Live By* (Chicago, IL: University of Chicago Press, 1980).

6. Aristotle, *Rhetoric,* III, 1410.

7. Paul de Man, *Allegories of Reading* (New Haven, CT: Yale University Press, 1979), 14.

8. "Folklore Field Notes from Zora Neale Hurston," introduced by Robert Hemenway, *The Black Scholar* 7. 7 (1976), 41–42.

9. First published in 1937; all page references are to the Illini Book Edition (Urbana, IL.: University of Illinois Press, 1978).

10. Erich Auerbach, *Mimesis* (New York: Doubleday Anchor, 1957), 482–483, 488.

11. In *Black American Literature Forum* 15: 4 (1981), 123, 125.

12. W. E. B. Du Bois, *The Souls of Black Folk,* rpt. in *Three Negro Classics* (New York: Avon, 1965), 214–215.

13. James Weldon Johnson, *The Autobiography of an Ex-Colored Man,* rpt. in ibid., 403.

14. Richard Wright, "Between Laughter and Tears," *New Masses,* 5 October 1937, 25–26.

15. Arthur P. Davis, *From the Dark Tower* (Washington, DC: Howard University Press, 1974), 116.

16. Bell Hooks, *Ain't I a Woman* (Boston, MA: South End Press, 1981), 8.

17. Zora Neale Hurston, *Dust Tracks on a Road* (Philadelphia, PA: Lippincott, 1942), 260–288.

18. See Gates's discussion of *Their Eyes Were Watching God* as what he calls (à la Barthes) a "speakerly text," in *The Signifying Monkey* (New York: Oxford University Press, 1985).

19. I wish to thank Patti Joplin of Stanford University for calling my attention to this fact.

Zora Neale Hurston and the Speakerly Text

HENRY LOUIS GATES, JR.

◆   ◆   ◆

Our house stood within a few rods of the Chesa-
peake Bay, whose broad bosom was ever white with
sails from every quarter of the habitable globe.
Those beautiful vessels, robed in purest white, so
delightful to the eye of freemen, were to me so many
shrouded ghosts, to terrify and torment me with
thoughts of my wretched condition. I have often, in
the deep stillness of a summer's Sabbath, stood all
alone upon the lofty banks of that noble bay, and
traced, with saddened heart and tearful eye, the
countless number of sails moving off to the mighty
ocean. The sight of these always affected me powerfully. My thoughts would compel utterance; and
there, with no audience but the Almighty, I would
pour out my soul's complaint, in my rude way, with
an apostrophe to the moving multitude of ships:
"You are loosed from your moorings, and are
free; I am fast in my chains, and am a slave! You
move merrily before the gentle gale, and I sadly before the bloody whip! You are freedom's swift-
winged angels, that fly around the world; I am confined in bands of iron! O that I were free!"
Frederick Douglass, 1845

Ships at a distance have every man's wish on
board. For some they come in with the tide. For others they sail forever on the horizon, never out of
sight, never landing until the Watcher turns his
eyes away in resignation, his dreams mocked to
death by Time. That is the life of men.
Now, women forget all those things they don't
want to remember, and remember everything they

don't want to forget. The dream is the truth. Then
they act and do things accordingly.
                                        Zora Neale Hurston, 1937

I

The eighteenth-century revisions of the trope of the Talking Book that I
traced in chapter 4 and its displacement into tropes of freedom and literacy
in the slave narratives published after 1815 helps us to understand the remarkable degree to which the quest to register a public black voice in Western letters preoccupied the Afro-American tradition's first century. Writing could be no mean thing in the life of the slave. What was at stake for
the earliest black authors was nothing less than the implicit testimony to
their humanity, a common humanity which they sought to demonstrate
through the very writing of a text of an ex-slave's life. In one sense, not
even legal manumission was of more importance to the slave community's
status in Western culture than was the negation of the image of the black
as an absence. To redress their image as a negation of all that was white and
Western, black authors published as if their collective fate depended on
how their texts would be received. It is as difficult to judge how effective
this tacitly political gesture was as it is to judge how the negative image of
the black in Western culture was affected by the publication of black texts.
It seems apparent, however, that the abolition of slavery did not diminish
the force of this impulse to write the race fully into the human community. Rather, the liberation of the slave community and the slow but
steady growth of a black middle class between Reconstruction (1865–1876)
and the sudden ending of the New Negro Renaissance (circa 1930) only
seem to have made this impulse even more intense than it had been in an-
tebellum America. Perhaps this was the case because, once slavery was
abolished, racism assumed vastly more subtle forms. If slavery had been an
immoral institution, it had also been a large, fixed target; once abolished,
the target of racism splintered into hundreds of fragments, all of which
seemed to be moving in as many directions. Just as the ex-slaves wrote to
end slavery, so too did free black authors write to redress the myriad forms
that the fluid mask of racism assumed between the end of the Civil War
and the end of the Jazz Age.
    If the writings of black people retained their implicitly political import
after the war and especially after the sudden death of Reconstruction,
then it should not surprise us that the search for a voice in black letters be-

came a matter of grave concern among the black literati. This concern, as we might expect, led to remarkable polemical debates over the precise register which an "authentic" black voice would, or could, assume. It is also clear that postbellum black authors continued to read and revise the central figures they received from the fragments of tradition that somehow survived the latter nineteenth century's onslaught of de facto and de jure segregation. Zora Neale Hurston's revision of Frederick Douglass's apostrophe to the ships (the epigraphs to this chapter) is only one example of many such instances of a black textual grounding through revision.

Hurston underscores her revision of Douglass's canonical text by using two chiasmuses in her opening paragraphs.[1] The subject of the second paragraph of *Their Eyes Were Watching God* (women) reverses the subject of the first (men) and figures the nature of their respective desire in opposite terms. A man's desire becomes reified onto a disappearing ship, and he is transformed from a human being into "a Watcher," his desire personified onto an object, beyond his grasp or control, external to himself. Nanny, significantly, uses this "male" figure—"Ah could see uh big ship at a distance" (p. 35)—as does Tea Cake, whose use reverses Douglass's by indicating Tea Cake's claim of control of his fate and ability to satisfy Jamie's desire: "Can't no ole man stop me from gittin' no ship for yuh if dat's whut you want. Ah'd git dat ship out from under him so slick til he'd be walkin' de water lak ole Peter befo' he knowed it" (p. 154).

A woman, by contrast, represents desire metaphorically, rather than metonymically, by controlling the process of memory, an active subjective process figured in the pun on (re)membering, as in the process of narration which Janie will share with her friend Phoeby and which we shall "overhear." For a woman, "The dream is the truth"; the truth is her dream. Janie, as we shall see, is thought to be (and is maintained) "inarticulate" by her first two husbands but is a master of metaphorical narration; Joe Starks, her most oppressive husband, by contrast, is a master of metonym, an opposition which Janie must navigate her selves through to achieve self-knowledge. The first sentence ("Now, women forget all those things they don't want to remember, and remember everything they don't want to forget") is itself a chiasmus (women/remember//remember/forget) similar in structure to Douglass's famous chiasmus, "You have seen how a man became a slave, you will see how a slave became a man." Indeed, Douglass's major contribution to the slave's narrative was to make chiasmus the central trope of slave narration, in which a slave-object writes himself or herself into a human-subject through the act of writing. The overarching rhetorical strategy of the slave narratives written after 1845 can be represented as a chiasmus, as repetition and reversal. Hurston, in these enigmatic opening paragraphs, Signifies upon Douglass through formal revision.

This sort of formal revision is one mode of tacit commentary about the shape and status of received tradition. A more explicit mode was the literary criticism published by blacks as a response to specific black texts which, despite great difficulties, somehow managed to be published. While this subject demands a full-length study, I can summarize its salient aspects here. The debate about the register of the black voice assumed two poles. By the end of the Civil War, the first pole of the debate, the value of the representation, of the reality imitated in the text, had been firmly established. Black authors wrote almost exclusively about their social and political condition as black people living in a society in which race was, at best, problematical. By the turn of the century, a second and more subtle pole of the debate had become predominant, and that pole turned upon precisely how an authentic black voice should be represented in print. The proper manner and matter of representation of a black printed voice are not truly separable, of course; these poles of concern could merge, and often did, as in the heated issue of the import of Paul Laurence Dunbar's late nineteenth-century dialect poetry. To understand more fully just how curious were Zora Neale Hurston's rhetorical strategies of revision in *Their Eyes Were Watching God* (1937) and just how engaged in debate these strategies were with the Afro-American tradition, it is useful to summarize the nineteenth-century arguments about representation.

We gain some understanding of this concern over representation by examining *The Anglo-African Magazine,* published in New York by Thomas Hamilton between January 1859 and March 1860. Hamilton, in his introductory "Apology" to the first number, argues what for his generation was self-evident: "[black people], in order to assert and maintain their rank as men among men, must speak for themselves; no outside tongue, however gifted with eloquence, can tell their story." Blacks must "speak for themselves," Hamilton writes, to counter the racist "endeavor to write down the negro as something less than a man."[2] In the second number, W. J. Wilson, in a poem entitled "The Coming Man," defines the presence of the text to be that which separates "the undefinable present," "the dim misty past," and "the unknown future":

> I am resolved. 'Tis more than half my task;
> 'Twas the great need of all my passed existence.
> The glooms that have so long shrouded me,
> Recede as vapor from the new presence,

And the light-gleam—it must be life
So brightens and spreads its rays before,
That I read my Mission as 'twere a book.[3]

Wilson's figure of life as a text to be read, of the race's life as embodied in the book, Frances E. W. Harper elaborated upon in a letter to the editor later that same year. In this letter, we have recorded one of the first challenges to what was then, and has remained, the preoccupation of Afro-American male writers: the great and terrible subject of white racism. "If our talents are to be recognized," Frances Harper writes,

> we must write less of issues that are particular and more of feelings that are general. We are blessed with hearts and brains that compass more than ourselves in our present plight. . . . We must look to the future which, God willing, will be better than the present or the past, and delve into the heart of the world.[4]

Consider the sheer audacity of this black woman, perhaps our first truly professional writer, who could so freely advocate this position in the great crisis year of 1859, which witnessed both John Brown's aborted raid on the Harper's Ferry arsenal and the U.S. Supreme Court's decision to uphold the constitutionality of the Fugitive Slave Act of 1850. Harper, in this statement about representation and in her poems and fictions, demanded that black writers embrace as their subjects "feelings that are general," feelings such as love and sex, birth and death. The debate over the content of black literature had begun, then, as articulated by a black woman writer.

Whereas Harper expressed concern for a new content or "signifier," a content that was at once black, self-contained, and humanly general, the other pole of the debate about representation concerned itself with the exact form that the signifier should take. This concern over what I am calling the signifier occupied, in several ways and for various reasons, the center of black aesthetic theory roughly between the publication of Paul Laurence Dunbar's *Lyrics of Lowly Life* in 1895 and at least the publication in 1937 of Zora Neale Hurston's *Their Eyes Were Watching God*. This debate, curiously enough, returns us in the broadest sense to the point of departure of this chapter, namely the absence and presence of the black voice in the text, that which caused Gronniosaw so much consternation and perplexity. It is not surprising that Dunbar's widely noted presence should engender, in part, the turn of critical attention to matters of language and voice, since it is he who stands, unquestionably, as the most accomplished black dialect poet, and the most successful black poet before Langston Hughes. Nor is it surprising that Hurston's lyrical text should demarcate an ending of this debate, since Hurston's very rhetorical strategy, her invention of what I have chosen to call the speakerly text, seems designed to mediate between, for fiction, what Sterling A. Brown's representation of the black voice mediated between for black poetic diction: namely, a profoundly lyrical, densely metaphorical, quasi-musical, privileged black oral tradition on the one hand, and a received but not yet fully appropriated standard English literary tradition on the other hand. The quandary for the writer was to find a third term, a bold and novel signifier, informed by these two related yet distinct literary languages. This is what Hurston tried to do in *Their Eyes.*

Critics widely heralded Dunbar's black poetic diction, and poets, white and black, widely imitated it. It is difficult to understand the millennarian tones of Dunbar's critical reception. The urgent calls for a black "redeemer-poet," so common in the black newspapers and periodicals published between 1827 and 1919, by the late 1880s were being echoed by white critics. One anonymous white woman critic, for example, who signed herself only as "A Lady from Philadelphia," wrote in *Lippincott's Monthly Magazine* in 1886 that "The Coming American Novelist" would be "of African origin."[5] This great author would be one "With us" but "not of us," one who "has suffered everything a poet, a dramatist, a novelist need suffer before he comes to have his lips anointed." "When one comes to consider the subject," this critic concludes, "there is no improbability to it." After all, she continues, the African "has given us the only national music we have ever had," a corpus of art "distinctive in musical history." He is, moreover, "a natural story-teller,"[6] uniquely able to fabricate what she calls "acts of the imagination," discourses in which no "morality is involved."

> [Why] should not this man, who has suffered so much, who is so easy to amuse, so full of his own resources, and who is yet undeveloped, why should he not some day soon tell a story that shall interest, amuse us, stir our hearts, and make a new epoch in our literature?[7]

Then, in a remarkable reversal, the writer makes an even bolder claim:

> Yet farther: I have used the genetic masculine pronoun because it is convenient; but Fate keeps revenges in store. It was a woman who, taking the wrongs of the African as her theme, wrote the novel that awakened the world to their reality, and why should not the coming novelist be a woman as well as an African? She—the woman of that race—has some claims on Fate which are not yet paid up.

It is difficult to discern which of this critic's two claims is the bolder: that the great American writer would be black or that she would be a black woman. It is not difficult, however, to summarize the energizing effect on our literary tradition which this critic's prediction was to have. Even as late as 1899, W. S. Scarborough would still cite this *Lippincott's* essay to urge black writers to redeem "the race."[8]

W. H. A. Moore, writing about "A Void in Our Literature" in 1890, called for the appearance of a great black poet whose presence would stand as "an indication of the character of [the Afro-American's] development on those lines which determine the capacity of a people." "The Afro-American," he continues,

> has not given to English literature a great poet. No one of his kind has, up to this day, lent influence to the literature of his time, save Phillis Wheatley. It is not to be expected that he would. And yet every fragment, every whispering of his benighted muse is scanned with eager and curious interest in the hope that here may be found the gathered breathings of a true singer.[9]

"The keynote," Moore concludes, "has not yet been struck." To find a poetic diction which reflects "the inner workings of the subject which it seeks to portray," Moore argues, "is the mission of the race." Moore's essay is merely typical of many others published between 1865 and 1930. For example, in 1893, H. T. Johnson, editor of the *Recorder,* outlined the need for race authors to express racial aspirations. Five years later, H. T. Kealing wrote of the unique contributions that only Negro authors could make. The literature of any people, he said, had an indigenous quality, "the product of the national peculiarities and race idiosyncrasies that no alien could duplicate." He called upon the Negro author not to imitate whites, as had been the case hitherto, but to reach "down to the original and unexplored depths of his own being where lies unused the material that is to provide him a place among the great writers." Similarly, Scarborough, speaking at the Hampton Negro Conference in 1899, called for something higher than the false dialect types depicted by white authors; even Chesnutt's and Dunbar's short stories had not gone far enough in portraying the higher aspirations of the race. Only the Negro author could portray the Negro best—his "loves and hates, his hopes and fears, his ambitions, his whole life, in such a way that the world will weep and laugh . . . forgetting completely that the hero and heroine are God's bronze image, but knowing only that they are men and women with joys and sorrows that belong to the whole human family." In the discussion that followed Scarborough's paper, it was agreed that the types portrayed in "vaudeville" were

false. Lucy Laney, principal of the Haines Norman and Industrial Institute,
prefigured a major interest of the 1920s when she spoke of the material for
short stories to be found in the rural South and called upon Negro writers
to go down to the sea islands of Georgia and South Carolina "where they
could study the Negro in his original purity," with a culture and a voice
"close to the African."[10]

Into this black milieu wrote Paul Lawrence Dunbar. Perhaps because we
tend to read Dunbar backwards, as it were, through the poetry of Sterling A.
Brown and the early Langston Hughes, and through the often unfortunate
poetic efforts of Dunbar's less talented imitators, we tend to forget how startling was Dunbar's use of black dialect as the basis of a poetic diction. After
all, by 1895, dialect had come to connote black innate mental inferiority, the
linguistic sign both of human bondage (as origin) and of the continued failure of "improvability" or "progress," two turn-of-the-century keywords.
Dialect signified both "black difference" and that the figure of the black in
literature existed primarily as object, not subject; and even sympathetic
characterizations of the black, such as Uncle Remus by Joel Chandler Harris, were far more related to a racist textual tradition that stemmed from
minstrelsy, the plantation novel, and vaudeville than to representations of
spoken language. As Scarborough summarized the matter:

> Both northern and southern writers have presented Negro nature, Negro
> dialect, Negro thought, as they conceived it, too often, alas, as evolved out
> of their own consciousness. Too often the dialect has been inconsistent, the
> types presented, mere composite photographs as it were, or uncouth speci-
> mens served up so as the humorous side of the literary setting might be
> properly balanced.[11]

This received literary tradition of plantation and vaudeville art, Scarborough concluded, demanded "realism" to refute the twin gross stereotypes
of characterization and the representation of black speech.

For Dunbar to draw upon dialect as the medium through which to
posit this mode of realism suggests a certain boldness as well as a certain
opportunism, two qualities that helped to inform Dunbar's mixed results,
which we know so well, he lamented to his death. Dunbar, nevertheless,
Signified upon the received white racist textual tradition and posited in its
stead a black poetic diction which his more gifted literary heirs would, in
their turn, Signify upon, with often pathetic results. What Sterling A.
Brown would realize in the language of his poetry, Zora Neale Hurston
would realize in the language of her fiction. For, after Dunbar, the two
separate poles of the debate over black mimetic principles, over the shape

of the signifier and the nature of the signified, could no longer be thought of independently. Dunbar's primary rhetorical gesture, as Scarborough concluded in 1899, had been to do just that:

> And here we pause to see what [Dunbar and Chesnutt] have added to our literature, what new artistic value they have discovered. [Both] have followed closely the "suffering side," the portrayal of the old fashioned Negro of "befo' de wah,"—the Negro that [Thomas Nelson] Page and [Joel Chandler] Harris and others have given a permanent place in literature. But they have done one thing more; they have presented the facts of Negro life with a thread running through both warp and woof that shows not only humour and pathos, humility, self-sacrifice, courtesy and loyalty, but something at times of the higher aims, ambition, desires, hopes, and aspiration of the race—but by no means as fully and to as great an extent as we had hoped they would do.[12]

How the black writer represented, and what he or she represented, were now indissolubly linked in black aesthetic theory.

In the curious manner by which one generation's parenthetical concerns come to form the central questions of a subsequent generation's critical debate, Scarborough's judgment that Dunbar's representations of the folk "befo' de wah" were potentially capable of encompassing more than "humour and pathos" became the lynchpin of James Weldon Johnson's attack on dialect as a poetic diction. I have sketched the debate over dialect elsewhere.[13] Suffice it to say here that that great American realist, William Dean Howells, in 1896 thought that Dunbar's dialect verse was a representation of reality, a "portrait . . . undeniably like." The political import of this artistic achievement, Howells maintained, was unassailable: "A race which has reached this effect in any of its members can no longer be held wholly uncivilized; and intellectually Mr. Dunbar makes a stronger claim for the negro than the negro has yet done."[14] By the 1920s, however, dialect was thought to be a literary trap.

A careful study of the aesthetic theories of the New Negro Renaissance suggests strongly that the issue of dialect as an inappropriate literary language seems to have been raised in order for a second poetic diction to be posited in its place. Indeed, we can with some justification set as boundaries of this literary movement James Weldon Johnson's critiques of dialect, which he published in his separate "Prefaces" to the first and second editions of *The Book of American Negro Poetry,* printed in 1923 and 1931, respectively, but also Johnson's "Introduction" to the first edition of Sterling A. Brown's *Southern Road,* printed in 1932.

In his "Preface," Johnson had defined the urgent task of the new black writer to be the "break away from, not Negro dialect itself, but the limitations of Negro dialect imposed by the fixing effects of long convention." And what were these limitations? Said Johnson, "it is an instrument with but two full stops, humor and pathos," repeating and reversing Scarborough's terms. Nine years later, in his second "Preface," Johnson could assert assuredly that "the passing of traditional dialect as a medium for Negro poets is complete." Just one year later, however, Brown's poetry forced Johnson to admit that, although Brown "began writing just after Negro poets had generally discarded conventionalized dialect, with its minstrel traditions of Negro life," he has "infused his [dialect] poetry with genuine characteristic flavor by adopting as his medium the common, racy living speech of the Negro in certain phases of *real* life." Brown's achievement, Johnson acknowledges, is that he has turned to "folk poetry" as a source of a poetic diction, "deepened its meanings and multiplied its implications. . . . In a word, he has taken this raw material and worked it into original and authentic power." Brown's poetry, then, in a remarkable tangible sense, marks the end of the New Negro Renaissance as well as the resolution, for black poetic diction, of a long debate over its mimetic principles.[15]

Brown's achievement in poetry, however, had no counterpart in fiction. True, Jean Toomer's *Cane* can be thought of as a fictional antecedent of Brown's poetic diction; both of those works inform the structure of *Their Eyes Were Watching God.* Yet Toomer's use of the privileged oral voice, and especially its poignant silences, is not without its ironies, since Toomer employs the black oral voice in his text both as a counterpoint to that standard English voice of his succession of narrators but also as evidence of the modernist claim that there had existed no privileged, romantic movement of unified consciousness, especially or not even in the cane fields of a rural Georgia echoing its own swan song. Existence, in the world of *Cane,* is bifurcated, fundamentally opposed, as represented by all sorts of binary oppositions, among these standard English and black speech, as well as black and white, male and female, South and North, textual desire and sensual consummation. Even in that fiction's long, final section, called "Kabnis," in which the place of the narrator becomes that of stage directions in a tragedy, the presence of the oral voice retains its primarily antiphonal function, as in the following exchange among Halsey, Layman, and Kabnis:

> Halsey (in a mock religious tone): Amen t that, brother Layman. Amen (turning to Kabnis, half playful, yet somehow dead in earnest). An Mr. Kabnis, kindly remember youre in th land of cotton—hell of a land. Th white

folks get the boll; th niggers get th stalk. An don't you dare touch th boll, or even look at it. They'll swing y sho. (Laughs)

Kabnis: But they wouldn't touch a gentleman—fellows, men like us three here—

Layman: Nigger's a nigger down this away, Professor. An only two dividins: good an bad. An even they aint permanent categories. They sometimes mixes um up when it comes t lynchin. I've seen um do it.[16]

Toomer's representation of black spoken language, even in this instance, stands essentially as an element of plot and of theme.

Rather than as a self-contained element of literary structure, the oral voice in *Cane* is a motivated sign of duality, of opposition, which Toomer thematizes in each section of his fiction, and specifically in this passage:

Kabnis: . . . An besides, he aint my past. My ancestors were Southern blue-bloods—

Lewis: And black.

Kabnis: Aint much difference between blue an black.

Lewis: Enough to draw a denial from you. Cant hold them, can you? Master; slave. Soil; and the overarching heavens. Dusk; dawn. They fight and bastardize you. The sun tint of your cheeks, flame of the great season's multi-colored leaves, tarnished, burned. Split, shredded: easily burned. No use . . .

His gaze shifts to Stella. Stella's face draws back, her breasts come towards him.

Stella: I aint got nothin f y, mister. Taint no use t look at me. (pp. 217–218)

It would not be until Zora Neale Hurston began to publish novels that Toomer's rhetorical innovation would be extended in black fiction, although the line between Toomer's lyricism and Brown's regionalism is a direct one. Indeed, although Toomer received enthusiastic praise for *Cane*, this praise remained vague and ill defined. Du Bois, for instance, saw the import of the book as its subject matter, which he defined to be male-female sexual relations, which, he protested, were notably absent from the corpus of black fiction. There is not much truly consummated or untroubled sex in *Cane* either, but at least for Du Bois the text treated its possibility. For Du Bois, this stood as *Cane's* significant breakthrough.

By 1923, when Toomer published *Cane*, the concern over the nature and function of representation, of what we might profitably think of as the ideology of mimesis, had focused on one aesthetic issue, which Du Bois would call "How Shall the Negro Be Portrayed?" and which we can, boldly

I admit, think of as "What to do with the folk?" Despite scores of essays, ex-changes, and debates over this problematic of representation, however, by 1929 not only had Toomer's innovations apparently been forgotten, but ironclad "Instructions for Contributors" had been widely circulated among black writers in the "Illustrated Feature Section" of the Negro press. Since these help us to begin to understand the major place of *Their Eyes Were Watching God* in the history of black rhetorical strategies, let me reprint these instructions, written by George S. Schuyler, in full:

> Every manuscript submitted must be written in each-sentence-a-paragraph style.
>
> Stories must be full of human interest. Short, simple words. No attempt to parade erudition to the bewilderment of the reader. No colloquialisms such as "nigger," "darkey," "coon," etc. Plenty of dialogue, and language that is realistic.
>
> We will not accept any stories that are depressing, saddening, or gloomy. Our people have enough troubles without reading about any. We want them to be interested, cheered, and buoyed up; confronted, gladdened, and made to laugh.
>
> Nothing that casts the least reflection on contemporary moral or sex standards will be allowed. Keep away from the erotic! Contributions must be clean and wholesome.
>
> Everything must be written in that intimate manner that wins the reader's confidence at once and makes him or her feel that what is written is being spoken exclusively to that particular reader.
>
> No attempt should be made to be obviously artistic. Be artistic, of course, but "put it over" on the reader so he or she will be unaware of it.
>
> Stories must be swiftly moving, gripping the interest and sweeping on to a climax. The heroine should always be beautiful and desirable, sincere and virtuous. The hero should be of the he-man type, but not stiff, stereotyped, or vulgar. The villain should obviously be a villain and of the deepest-dyed variety: crafty, unscrupulous, suave, and resourceful. Above all, however, these characters must live and breathe, and be just ordinary folks such as the reader has met. The heroine should be of the brown-skin type.
>
> All matter should deal exclusively with Negro life. Nothing will be per-mitted that is likely to engender ill feelings between blacks and whites. The color problem is bad enough without adding any fuel to the fire.[17]

It is precisely these strictures, widely circulated in those very journals in which black authors could most readily publish, which, along with the ex-tended controversy over black oral forms, enable us to begin to understand the black milieu against which Hurston would define herself as a writer of fiction. Here we can only recall, with some irony, W. S. Scarborough's 1899 plea for a great black novelist:

> We are tired of vaudeville, of minstrelsy and of the Negro's pre-eminence in those lines. We want something higher, something more inspiring than that. We turn to the Negro for it. Shall we have it? The black novelist is like the white novelist, in too many instances swayed by the almighty dollar. . . . Like Esau he is ready to sell his birthright for a mess of pottage.
>
> Let the Negro writer of fiction make of his pen and brain all-compelling forces to treat of that which he well knows, best knows, and give it to the world with all the imaginative power possible, with all the magic touch of an artist. Let him portray the Negro's loves and hates, his hopes and fears, his ambitions, his whole life, in such a way that the world will weep and laugh over the pages, finding the touch that makes all nature kin, forgetting completely that hero and heroine are God's bronze images, but knowing only that they are men and women with joys and sorrows that belong alike to the whole human family. Such is the novelist that the race desires. Who is he that will do it? Who is he that can do it?[18]

He that could do it, it seems, turned out to be a she, Zora Neale Hurston.

II

Zora Neale Hurston is the first writer that our generation of black and feminist critics has brought into the canon, or perhaps I should say the canons. For Hurston is now a cardinal figure in the Afro-American canon, the feminist canon, and the canon of American fiction, especially as our readings of her work become increasingly close readings, which Hurston's texts sustain delightfully. The curious aspect of the widespread critical attention being shown to Hurston's texts is that so many critics embracing such a diversity of theoretical approaches seem to find something new at which to marvel in her texts.

My own method of reading *Their Eyes Were Watching God* stems fundamentally from the debates over modes of representation, over theories of mimesis, which as I have suggested form such a crucial part of the history of Afro-American literature and its theory. Mimetic principles can be both implicitly and explicitly ideological, and the explication of Hurston's rhetorical strategy, which I shall attempt below, is no exception. I wish to read *Their Eyes* in such a way as to move from the broadest notion of *what* it thematizes through an ever-tighter spiral of *how* it thematizes, that is, its rhetorical strategies. I shall attempt to show that Hurston's text not only cleared a rhetorical space for the narrative strategies that Ralph Ellison would render so deftly in *Invisible Man*, but also that Hurstons's text is the first example in our tradition of "the speakerly text," by which I mean a text whose rhetorical strategy is designed to represent an oral literary tradition, designed "to emulate the phonetic, grammatical, and lexical patterns of actual speech and produce the 'illusion of oral narration.'"[19] The speakerly text is that text in which all other structural elements seem to be devalued, as important as they remain to the telling of the tale, because the narrative strategy signals attention to its own importance, an importance which would seem to be the privileging of oral speech and its inherent linguistic features. Whereas Toomer's *Cane* draws upon the black oral voice essentially as a different voice from the narrator's, as a repository of socially distinct, contrapuntal meanings and beliefs, a spearkerly text would seem primarily to be oriented toward imitating one of the numerous forms of oral narration to be found in classical Afro-American vernacular literature.

Obviously, I am concerned with what we traditionally think of as matters of voice. "Voice" here connotes not only traditional definitions of "point of view," a crucial matter in the reading of *Their Eyes*, but also the linguistic presence of a literary tradition that exists for us as a written text primarily because of the work of sociolinguists and anthropologists such as Hurston. I am concerned in this chapter to discuss the representation of what we might think of as the voice of the black oral tradition— represented here as direct speech—as well as with Hurston's use of free indirect discourse as the rhetorical analogue to the text's metaphors of inside and outside, so fundamental to the depiction of Janie's quest for consciousness, her very quest to become a speaking black subject. Just as we have begun to think of Hurston as an artist whose texts relate to those of Jean Toomer and Sterling A. Brown, let us round out our survey of the tradition by comparing Hurston's concept of voice with that of Richard Wright and Ralph Ellison.

In *American Hunger* (1977), which along with *Black Boy* (1945) comprises the full text of an autobiography he initially called "The Horror and the Glory," Richard Wright succinctly outlines his idea of the ironic relationship between the individual black talent and an Afro-American cultural tradition ravaged and laid waste to by an omnipresent and irresistible white racism:

What could I dream of that had the barest possibility of coming true? I could think of nothing. And, slowly, it was upon exactly that nothingness that my mind began to dwell, that constant sense of wanting without having, of being hated without reason. A dim notion of what life meant to a Negro in America was coming to consciousness in me, not in terms of external events, lynchings, Jim Crowism, and the endless brutalities, but in terms of crossed-up feelings, of psyche pain. I sensed that Negro life was a sprawling land of unconscious suffering, and that there were but few Negroes who knew the meaning of their lives, who could tell their [own] story.[20]

Wright, as both of his autobiographies seem intent on claiming, certainly counted himself among those few Negroes who could tell not only their own story but also the woeful tale of their pathetic, voiceless black countrymen. If they were signs of the "horror," then his articulated escape was meant to be our "glory."

In his autobiographies and novels, Wright evolved a curious and complex myth of origins of self and race. Whereas a large part of the black autobiographical tradition, as exemplified by Frederick Douglass's three autobiographies, generally depicts a resplendent self as representative of possibilities denied systematically to one's voiceless fellow blacks, Wright's class of ideal individual black selves seems to have included only Wright. *Black Boy,* for example, charts how the boy, Dick, through the key texts of naturalism, gave a shape and a purpose to an exceptional inherent nobility of spirit which emerges from within the chaotic depths of the black cultural maelstrom. Wright's humanity is achieved only at the expense of his fellow blacks, pitiable victims of the pathology of slavery and racial segregation who surround and suffocate him. Indeed, Wright wills this especial self into being through the agency of contrast: the sensitive, healthy part is foregrounded against a determined, defeated black whole. He is a noble black savage, in the ironic tradition of Oroonoko and film characters played by Sidney Poitier—the exception, not the rule.

For Ralph Ellison, Wright's notion of the self and its relation to black culture seemed unduly costly. Indeed, it is this dark and brooding fiction of black culture against which both Ellison and James Baldwin railed, drawing upon a rich body of tropes and rhetorical strategies prefigured, among other places, in Hurston's fictions and critical writings. It is this fiction of obliteration that created the great divide in black literature, a fissure first rendered apparent in the late thirties in an extended debate between Hurston and Wright.

The Hurston-Wright debate, staged not only in the lyrical shape of *Their Eyes Were Watching God* (1937) against the naturalism of *Native Son* (1940) but also in reviews of each other's books, turns between two poles of a problematic of representation—between what is represented and what represents, between the signifier and the signified. Theirs are diametrically opposed notions of the internal structure of the sign, the very sign of blackness.

Hurston rather self-consciously defined her theory of the novel against that received practice of realism which Wright would attempt to revitalize in *Native Son*. Hurston thought that Wright stood at the center of "the sobbing school of Negrohood who hold that nature somehow has given them a low down dirty deal."[21] Against Wright's idea of psychological destruction and chaos, Hurston framed a counternotion which the repressed and conservative maternal figure of *Their Eyes* articulates: "[It] wasn't for me to fulfill my dreams of whut a woman oughta be and to do. Dat's one of de hold-backs of slavery. But nothing can't stop you from wishin'. You can't beat nobody down so low till you can rob 'em of they will." The sign of this transcendent self would be the shaping of a strong, self-reflective voice: "Ah wanted to preach a great sermon about colored women sittin' on high, but they wasn't no pulpit for me. Freedom found me widh a baby daughter in mah arms, so Ah said Ah'd take a broom and a cook-pot and throw up a highway through de wilderness for her. She would expound what Ah felt. But somehow she got lost offa de highway and next thing Ah knowed here you was in de world. So whilst Ah was tendin' you of nights Ah said Ah'd save de text for you."[22] Hurston revoices this notion of the articulating subject in her autobiography, *Dust Tracks on the Road* (1942), in a curious account of her mother's few moments before death: "Her mouth was slightly open, but her breathing took up so much of her strength that she could not talk. But she looked at me, or so I felt, to speak for her. She depended on me for a voice."[23] We can begin to understand how far apart Hurston and Wright stand in the tradition if we compare Hurston's passage about her mother with the following passage from Wright's *Black Boy*, a deathbed revision of Hurston's passage:

> Once, in the night, my mother called me to her bed and told me that she could not endure the pain, that she wanted to die. I held her hand and begged her to be quiet. That night I ceased to react to my mother; my feelings were frozen.[24]

Wright explains that this event, and his mother's extended suffering, "grew into a symbol in my mind, gathering to itself all the poverty, the ignorance, the helplessness; . . . Her life set the emotional tone of my life, colored the men and women I was to meet in the future, conditioned my relation to events that had not happened, determined my attitude to situations and circumstances I had yet to face." If Hurston figures her final moments with her mother in terms of the search for a voice, then Wright, three years later, figures the significance of a similar scene as responsible for a certain "somberness of spirit that I was never to lose." No two authors in the tradition are more dissimilar than Hurston and Wright.

The narrative voice Hurston created, and her legacy to Afro-American fiction, is a lyrical and disembodied yet individual voice, from which emerges a singular longing and utterance, a transcendent, ultimately racial self, extending far beyond the merely individual. Hurston realized a resonant and authentic narrative voice that echoes and aspires to the status of the impersonality, anonymity, and authority of the black vernacular tradition, a nameless, selfless tradition, at once collective and compelling, true somehow to the unwritten text of a common blackness. For Hurston, the search for a telling form of language, indeed the search for a black literary language itself, defines the search for the self. Similarly, for Ellison, the self can emerge only through the will, as signified by the problematical attempt to write itself into being, a unique black self consolidated and rendered integral within a first-person narrative structure.

For Wright, nature was ruthless, irreducible, and ineffable. Unlike Hurston and Ellison, Wright sees fiction not as a model of reality but as a representative bit of it, a literal report of the real. Art, for Wright, always remains referential. His blackness, therefore, can never be a mere sign; it is rather the text of his great and terrible subject. Accordingly, Wright draws upon the voice of the third-person, past-tense authorial mode and various tools of empirical social science and naturalism to blend public with private experience, inner with outer history. Rarely does he relinquish what Roland Barthes calls the "proprietary consciousness," the constant sign of his presence and of some larger context, which the third-person voice inevitably entails. Rather predictably, Wright found Hurston's great novel to be "counter-revolutionary," while Hurston replied that she wrote novels "and not treatises on sociology."

Hurston, Wright, and Ellison's divergent theories of narrative structure and voice, the cardinal points of a triangle of influence, with their attendant ramifications upon the ideology of form and its relation to knowledge and power, comprise a matrix of issues to which subsequent black fictions, by definition, must respond. The rhetorical question that subsequent texts must answer remained the question which the structure of *Their Eyes* answered for Hurston: "In what voice would the Negro speak for her or himself in the language of fiction?" By discussing *Their Eyes'* topoi and fig- ures, its depiction of the relationship among character, consciousness, and setting, and its engagement of shifting points of view, we can begin to un- derstand how primary Hurston's rhetorical strategies remain in this com- pelling text.

On the broadest level, *Their Eyes* depicts the search for identity and self-understanding of an Afro-American woman. This quest for self- knowledge, which the text thematizes through an opposition between the inside and the outside of things, directs attention to itself as a central theme of the novel by certain narrative strategies. I am thinking here espe- cially of the use of the narrative frame and of a special form of plot nega- tion. The tale of Janie Crawford-Killicks-Starks-Woods is narrated to her best friend, Phoeby, while the two sit together on Janie's back porch. We, the readers, "overhear" the tale that Janie narrates to her auditor, whose name we recall signifies the poet. Phoeby, as we might suspect, is an ideal listener: to seduce Janie into narrating her story, Phoeby confesses to her friend, "It's hard for me to understand what you mean, de way you tell it. And then again Ah'm hard of understandin' at times" (p. 19). Phoeby speaks as the true pupil; Janie responds as the true pedagogue:

> "Naw, 'tain't nothin' lak you might think. So 'tain't no use in me telling
> you somethin' unless Ah give you de undersandin' to go 'long wid it. Unless
> you see de fur, a mink skin ain't no different from a coon hide. Looka heah,
> Phoeby, is Sam waitin' on you for his supper?" (p. 19)

At the end of the telling of Janie's tale, an interruption which the text sig- nifies by ellipses and a broad white space (on p. 283), Phoeby, always the per- fect pupil, responds to her teacher as each of us wishes the students to respond:

> "Lawd!" Phoeby breathed out heavily, "Ah done growed ten feet higher
> from jus' listenin' tuh you, Janie. Ah ain't satisfied wid mahself no mo'. Ah
> means tuh make Sam take me fishin' wid him after this. Nobody better not
> criticize yuh in mah hearing." (p. 284)

Such a powerfully transforming tale has effected an enhanced awareness even in Janie's transfixed pupil. And to narrate this tale, Hurston draws upon the framing device, which serves on the order of plot to interrupt the received narrative flow of linear narration of the realistic novel, and which serves on the order of theme to enable Janie to recapitulate, control, and narrate her own story of becoming, the key sign of sophisticated understanding of the self. Indeed, Janie develops from a nameless child, known only as "Alphabet," who cannot even recognize her own likeness as a "colored" person in a photograph, to the implied narrator of her own tale of self-consciousness. This is merely one of Hurston's devices to achieve thematic unity.

Hurston matches the use of the frame with the use of negation as a mode of narrating the separate elements of the plot. The text opens and ends in the third-person omniscient voice, which allows for a maximum of information giving. Its third paragraph commences: "So the beginning of this was a woman and she had come back from burying the dead" (p. 9). By introducing this evidence of the return from burying the dead, Hurston negates her text's themes of discovery, rebirth, and renewal, only to devote the remainder of her text to realizing these same themes. Hurston also draws upon negation to reveal, first, the series of self-images that Janie does not wish to be and, second, to define the matrix of obstacles that frustrate her desire to know herself. The realization of the full text of *Their Eyes* represents the fulfillment of the novel's positive potentialities, by which I mean Janie's discovery of self-knowledge.

How does this negated form of plot development unfold? Hurston rather cleverly develops her plot by depicting a series of intimate relationships in which Janie engages with a fantasy of sexual desire, then with her grandmother, with her first husband (Logan Killicks), her second husband (Joe Starks), and, finally, with her ideal lover, Vergible Woods, "Tea Cake." Her first three relationships are increasingly problematic and self-negating, complex matters which Hurston renders through an inverse relationship between character or consciousness on one hand and setting on the other. If we think about it, Janie comes to occupy progressively larger physical spaces—Nanny's cabin in the backyard of the Washburn's place, Logan Killick's "often-mentioned" sixty acres, and, finally, Joe Starks's big white wooden house, replete with banisters, and his centrally located general store. Indeed, it is fair to say that Mayor Starks owns the town. With each successive move to a larger physical space, however, her housemate seeks to confine Janie's consciousness inversely, seemingly, by just as much. It is only when she eschews what her grandmother had named the "protection" (p. 30) both of material possessions and of rituals of entitlement (i.e., bourgeois marriage) and moves to the swamp, to "the muck," with Vergible "Tea Cake" Woods that she, at last, gains control of her understanding of herself. We can, in fact, conclude that the text opposes bourgeois notions of progress (Killicks owns the only organ "amongst colored folks"; Joe Starks is a man of "positions and possessions") and of the Protestant work ethic, to more creative and lyrical notions of unity. Tea Cake's only possession is a guitar. The relationship between character and setting, then, is ideal for the pedagogical purpose of revealing that character and setting are merely aspects of narrative strategy, and not things in the ordinary sense that we understand a thing to be.

One pleasant way to chart this relationship between consciousness and setting is to examine briefly the metaphor of the tree, which Hurston repeats throughout her text. The use of repetition is fundamental to the process of narration, and Hurston repeats the figure of the tree both to expound her theme of becoming and to render the action of the plot as simultaneous and as unified as possible. In *Dust Tracks on a Road,* Hurston explains that:

> I was only happy in the woods. . . . I made particular friendship with one huge tree and always played about its roots. I named it "the loving pine," and my chums came to know it by that name. (p. 64)

In *Their Eyes,* Janie uses the metaphor of the tree to define her own desires but also to mark the distance of those with whom she lives from these desires. There are well over two dozen repetitions of the figure of the tree in this text. The representation of Janie's narrative to Phoeby commences with the figure of the tree:

> Janie saw her life like a great tree in leaf with the things suffered, things enjoyed, things done and undone. Dawn and doom was in the branches.
> (p. 20)

"Dawn and doom," we are to learn so poignantly, are the true stuff of Janie's tale. "Dawn and doom *was* in the branches," an example of free indirect discourse, reveals precisely the point at which Janie's voice assumes control over the text's narration, significantly in a metaphor of trees. The text describes her own, rather private dawning sexual awareness through lush and compelling tree imagery. Janie longs for an identity with the tree in imagery the text shall echo when she encounters Tea Cake:

> Oh to be a pear tree—*any* tree in bloom! With kissing bees singing of the beginning of the world! She was sixteen. She had glossy leaves and bursting buds and she wanted to struggle with life but it seemed to elude her. Where were the singing bees for her? Nothing on the place nor in her grandma's house answered her. (p. 25)

To "be a pear tree—*any* tree in bloom," which becomes Janie's master trope on her road to becoming, is first stated as she fantasizes under a tree and experiences her first orgasm. That this metaphor returns when she meets Tea Cake echoes the text's enigmatic statement in its second paragraph that, for women, "The dream is the truth." Thus transformed "through pollinated air" (p. 25), Janie experiences her first kiss with the figure she formerly knew as shiftless Johnny Taylor, now "beglamored" even in his rages in her eyes by the splendors of cross-pollination.

This crucial kiss "across the gatepost" establishes the text's opposition between the dream and the truth, already posited in the text's first two paragraphs which, as I said earlier, revise Frederick Douglass's apostrophe to the ships.[25]

The ensuing action, moreover, posits a key opposition for us critics between theory and interpretation. Nanny's discovery of Johnny Taylor's "lacerating her Janie with a kiss" (p. 26) transforms both the event itself and Nanny's physical appearance. For Nanny's reading of the event, her "words," the text tells us, "made Janie's kiss across the gatepost seem like a manure pile after a rain." Nanny's perverse interpretation now transforms her in Janie's eyes into the dreaded figure of Medusa:

> Nanny's head and face looked like the standing roots of some old tree that had been torn away by storm. Foundation of ancient power that no longer mattered. The cooling palma christi leaves that Janie had bound about her grandma's head with a white rag had wilted down and become part and parcel of the woman. Her eyes didn't bore and pierce. They diffused and melted Janie, the room and the world into one comprehension. (p. 26)

When Nanny begins to narrate the story of her oppression in slavery, the narrator informs us that she "thrust back the leaves from her face" (p. 28). "Standing roots from some old tree" is, of course, the negation of the wonderfully lyrical imagery of blossoming pear trees. It is Nanny's "one comprehension" that suffocates, like the stench of the manure pile after a rain. Nanny is truly, as she later says to Janie in her own version of an oral slave narrative (pp. 31–32) delivered just after Janie's sexual experience under the pear tree, a branch without roots, at least the sort of roots that Janie is only just learning to extend.

Afraid that her grandchild will suffer an untimely defoliation, Nanny acts swiftly to gain for her the necessary "protection" to preserve her honor intact. While explaining her dreams for Janie, Nanny tells her that

> when you got big enough to understand things, Ah wanted you to look upon yo'self. Ah don't want yo' feathers always crumpled by folks throwin'

up things in yo' face. And Ah can't die easy thinkin' maybe de menfolks
white or black is making' a spit cup outa you: Have some sympathy fuh me.
Put me down easy, Janie, Ah'm a cracked plate. (p. 37)

So Nanny, the cracked plate, the Medusa figure, forces Janie to marry
Logan Killicks.

As the text states, "The vision of Logan Killicks was desecrating the pear
tree" (p. 28). Logan's framed sixty acres strike Janie as "a lonesome place
like a stump in the middle of the woods where nobody had ever been"
(p. 39), unlike her fecund pear tree. As she complains to Nanny, when after
"the new moon had been up and down three times" and love had not yet
begun, Janie "wants things sweet wid mah marriage lak when you sit
under a pear tree and think. Ah . . ." (p. 43). Love, we learn, never quite
finds its way to Logan Killicks's sixty acres. But even in this confined space,
Janie comes, by negation, to a measure of knowledge, signified in the language of the trees:

> So Janie waited a bloom time, and a green time and an orange time. But
> when the pollen again gilded the sun and sifted down on the world she began
> to stand around the gate and expect things. What things? She didn't know ex-
> actly. Her breath was gusty and short. She knew things that nobody had ever
> told her. For instance, the words of the trees and the wind. (pp. 43–44)

Ultimately, Janie comes to know that "marriage did not make love." As
the text concludes, "Janie's first dream was dead, so she became a woman,"
an echo of the text's opening paragraphs, which figure the opposition between women and men as that between the identity of dream and truth as
a figure for desire (women) and the objectification and personification of
desire onto objects over which one has no control (men).

Janie soon is "liberated" from Logan Killicks by the dashing Joe Starks.
At their first encounter, at the water pump, Joe tells Janie, twice, that he
wishes "to be a big voice" (p. 48) and shares with her his own dreams of
dominance "under the tree [where they] talked" (p. 49). Jody is not yet the
embodiment of Janie's tree, but he signifies the horizon.

> Every day after that they managed to meet in the scrub oaks across the
> road and talk about when he would be a big ruler of things with her reaping
> the benefits. Janie pulled back a long time because he did not represent sun-
> up and pollen and blooming trees, but he spoke for far horizon. (pp. 49–50)

To accept his proposals, Janie must exchange her own master metaphor
for a new master's metaphor: "He spoke for change and chance. Still she

hung back. The memory of Nanny was still powerful and strong" (p. 50). The horizon is not only a key figure in *Their Eyes*, serving to unify it by its repetition in the novel's final paragraph, but it has a central place as well in *Dust Tracks*, Hurston's autobiography:

> I had a stifled longing. I used to climb to the top of one of the huge chinaberry trees which guarded our front gate, and look out over the world. The most interesting thing that I saw was the horizon. Everyway I turned, it was there, and the same distance away. Our house then, was in the center of the world. It grew upon me that I ought to walk out to the horizon and see what the end of the world was like. (p. 44)

With Jody, Janie seeks the horizon. In a burst "of sudden newness and change," she heads south to find her freedom.

> From now on until death she was going to have flower dust and springtime sprinkled over everything. A bee for her bloom. Her old thoughts were going to come in handy now, but new words would have to be made and said to fit them. (pp. 54–55)

But Jody, we learn painfully, is a man of words, primarily, a man of "positions and possessions" (p. 79), a man who "talks tuh unlettered folks wid books in his jaws" (p. 79), "uh man dat changes everything, but nothin' don't change him" (p. 79). For him, Janie is merely a possession: the town's people, we are told, "stared at Joe's face, his clothes and his wife" (p. 57). Just before the lamp-lighting ceremony, where Joe, whose favorite parenthetical is "I god," brings light to the town (purchased from Sears and Roebuck), Tony Taylor welcomes "Brother Starks" to town "and all dat you have seen fit tuh bring amongst us—yo' belov-ed wife, yo' store, yo' land—" (p. 67). Joe, all voice and less and less substance, who had seduced Janie in part by telling her, in an echo of Nanny's desire for Janie to "sit on high," that "A pretty doll-baby lak you is made to sit on de front porch and rock and fan yo' self and eat p'taters dat other folks plant just special for you" (p. 49), not only serves to stifle Janie's potentially emerging voice but chops down the town's virgin trees to build his house and store, in which he keeps Janie imprisoned. That which, for Jody, represents the signs of progress, represents for Janie just another muted, fallen tree.

The text figures Janie's denial of a voice by substituting the metaphor of horizon for Janie's tree metaphor. Only with Tea Cake does Janie's lyrical trope of desire return. Metaphors of silence and the death of flora confirm Janie's sadness and oppression. Joe, having just been elected mayor by acclamation, denies Janie Tony Taylor's request that she address the crowd:

"Thank you fuh yo' compliments, but mah wife don't know nothin' 'bout no speech-makin'. Ah never married her for nothin' lak dat. She's uh woman and her place is in de home." (p. 69)

The text, in Janie's response, conflates the tree imagery with her reactions to Jody's silencing:

> Janie made her face laugh after a short pause, but it wasn't too easy. She had never thought of making a speech, and didn't know if she cared to make one at all. It must have been the way Jody spoke out without giving her a chance to say anything one way or another that took the bloom off of things. (pp. 69–70)

This silencing leads, of course, to a disastrous degeneration; when Janie protests her absence of a voice, Joe responds predictably in a revealing exchange about who is privileged to "tell" what they "see":

> [Joe]: "How come you can't do lak Ah tell yuh?"
>
> [Janie]: "You sho loves to tell me whut to do, but Ah can't tell you nothing' Ah see!"
>
> [Joe]: "Dat's 'cause you need tellin'," he rejoined hotly. "It would be pitiful if Ah didn't. Somebody got to think for women and chillun and chickens and cows. I god, they sho don't think none theirselves."
>
> [Janie]: "Ah knows uh few things, and womenfolks thinks sometimes too!"
>
> [Joe]: "Aw naw they don't. They just think they's thinkin'. When Ah see one thing Ah understands ten. You see ten things and don't understand one." (pp. 110–111)

Their dying relationship soon does. As the narrator tells us, again through the negation of the flowering images:

> The spirit of the marriage left the bedroom and took to living in the parlor.
> . . . The bed was no longer a daisy-field for her and Joe to play in. It was a place where she went and laid down when she was sleepy and tired.
> She wasn't petal-open anymore with him. (p. 111)

And finally, after Joe slaps her:

> She stood there until something fell off the shelf inside her. Then she went inside there to see what it was. It was her image of Jody tumbled down and shattered. But looking at it she saw that it never was the flesh and blood figure of her dreams. Just something she had grabbed up to drape her dreams over. In a way she turned her back upon the image where it lay and looked

further. She had no more blossomy openings dusting pollen over her man, neither any glistening young fruit where the petals used to be. She found that she had a host of thoughts she had never expressed to him, and numerous emotions she had never let Jody know about. Things packed up and put away in parts of her heart where he could never find them. She was saving up feelings for some man she had never seen. She had an inside and an outside now and suddenly she knew how not to mix them. (pp. 112–113)

With this newly defined sense of her inside and her outside, Janie learns to cross deftly that narrow threshold between her two selves:

Then one day she sat and watched the shadow of herself going about tending store and prostrating itself before Jody, while all the time she herself sat under a shady tree with the wind blowing through her hair and her clothes. Somebody near about making summertime out of lonesomeness. (p. 119)

Jody finally dies, just after Janie gains her voice on the porch of the story by Signifyin(g) upon Jody. Jody leaves Janie a handsome legacy and frees her to love again. Eventually she meets Tea Cake, and the text's fecund imagery of her desire returns:

He looked like the love thoughts of women. He could be a bee to a blossom—a pear tree blossom in the spring. He seemed to be crushing scent out of the world with his footsteps. Crushing aromatic herbs with every step he took. Spices hung about him. He was a glance from God. (p. 161)

Unlike Jody, who wanted to be seen as the deliverer of light, Tea Cake is the "glance from God" that reflects upon Janie, who in turn reflects her own inner light back upon him. "Nobody else n earth," Tea Cake tells her, "kin hold uh candle tuh you, baby" (p. 165). Tea Cake negates the terms of the material relationship of "marriage" ordained by Nanny and realized by Logan Killicks and Joe Starks. "Dis ain't no business proposition," Janie tells Phoeby, "and no race after property and titles. Dis is uh love game" (p. 171). Tea Cake not only embodies Janie's tree, he is the woods themselves, the delectable veritable woods, as his name connotes ("Vergible" being a vernacular term for "veritable"). Vergible Tea Cake Woods is a sign of verity, one who speaks the truth, one genuine and real, one not counterfeit or spurious, one not false or imaginary but the thing that in fact has been named. "Veritable," we know, also suggests the aptness of metaphor. Hurston now replaces the figure of the tree as the sign of desire with figures of play, rituals of play that cause Janie to "beam with light" (p. 153).

III

Let us "descend" to a more latent level of meaning by examining the figures of play that recur frequently in Janie's narrative of her life with Tea
Cake. We can consider these figures of play along with the play of voices
that, I wish to argue, make *Their Eyes* an especially rich and complex instance of a multiply vocal text. The mode of narration of *Their Eyes* consists,
at either extreme, of narrative commentary (rendered in third-person
omniscient and third-person restricted voices) and of characters' discourse
(which manifests itself as a direct speech rendered in what Hurston called
dialect). Hurston's innovation is to be found in the middle spaces between
these two extremes of narration and discourse, in what we might think of
as represented discourse, which as I am defining it includes both indirect
discourse and free indirect discourse. It was Hurston who introduced free
indirect discourse into Afro-American narration. It is this innovation,
as I hope to demonstrate, which enables her to represent various traditional modes of Afro-American rhetorical play while simultaneously representing her protagonist's growth in self-consciousness through free
indirect discourse. Curiously, Hurston's narrative strategy depends on the
blending of the text's two most extreme and seemingly opposed modes of
narration—that is, narrative commentary, which begins at least in the diction of standard English, and characters' discourse, which is always foregrounded by quotation marks and by its black diction. As the protagonist
approaches self-consciousness, however, not only does the text use free indirect discourse to represent her development, but the diction of the black
characters' discourse comes to inform the diction of the voice of narrative
commentary such that, in several passages, it is extraordinarily difficult to
distinguish the narrator's voice from the protagonist's. In other words,
through the use of what Hurston called a highly "adorned" free indirect
discourse, which we might think of as a third or mediating term between
narrative commentary and direct discourse, *Their Eyes Were Watching God* resolves that implicit tension between standard English and black dialect, the
two voices that function as verbal counterpoints in the text's opening
paragraphs.

Let us return briefly to the triangle of influence that I have drawn to
connect *Invisible Man, Native Son,* and *Their Eyes Were Watching God.* As I argued
earlier in this chapter, for Hurston the search for a form of narration and
discourse, indeed the search for a black formal language itself, both defines
the search for the self and is its rhetorical or textual analogue. Not only

would Ellison concur, but he would go farther. Ellison's is a literal morality of narration. As he writes in *Invisible Man*, "to retain unaware of one's form is to live death," an idea that Hurston prefigures in *Their Eyes*, from the moment when the child Janie, or "Alphabet," fails to recognize her own image in a group photograph, to the moment in the text when, first, Janie learns to distinguish between her inside and her outside, and when, second, the diction of the black characters' dialect comes to inform heavily the diction of the narrative commentary. We might think of Hurston's formal relation to Wright and Ellison in this way: whereas the narrative strategy of *Native Son* consists primarily of a disembodied, omniscient narrative commentary, similar to the voice that introduces *Their Eyes*, Ellison's first-person narrative strategy in *Invisible Man* revises the possibilities of representing the development of consciousness that Hurston rendered through a dialect-informed free indirect discourse. Wright uses free indirect discourse to some extent in *Native Son*, but its diction is not informed by Bigger's speech. The distinction between figures of speech and figures of thought is one useful way to distinguish between Wright's and Hurston's narrative strategies. The narrative strategies of *Native Son* and *Invisible Man*, then, define the extremes of narrative mode in the tradition, while the narrative strategy of *Their Eyes* partakes of these as well as of a subtle blend of the two. Rhetorically, at least, *Native Son* and *Invisible Man* Signify upon the rhetorical strategies of *Their Eyes Were Watching God.*

Even more curiously, the marvelous potential that *Their Eyes'* mode of narration holds for the representation of black oral forms of storytelling would seem to be remarkably akin to that which Ellison says he is using in his next novel. In an interview with John Hersey, Ellison says that he too has turned away from first-person toward third-person narration "to discover [the text's] most expressive possibilities." As Ellison argues, "I've come to believe that one of the challenges facing a writer who tries to handle the type of materials I'm working with is that of allowing his characters to speak for themselves in whatever artistic way they can." The third person, Ellison concludes, makes it "possible to draw upon broader and deeper resources of American vernacular speech," including multiple narrators and a wide variety of characters.[26] There can be little doubt that this sort of narration, so concerned to represent the sheer multiplicity of American oral narrative forms and voices, is more closely related to the speakerly strategies of *Their Eyes* than it is to most other texts in the Afro-American canon. These are rather large claims to make, but they are firmly supported by the Signifyin(g) strategies of the text itself.

Hurston, whose definition of *signify* in *Mules and Men* is one of the earliest

in the linguistic literature, has made *Their Eyes Were Watching God* into a paradigmatic Signifyin(g) text. Its narrative strategies resolve that implicit tension between the literal and the figurative, between the semantic and the
rhetorical, contained in standard usages of the term *signifying*. *Their Eyes*
draws upon the trope of Signifyin(g) both as thematic matter and as a
rhetorical strategy. Janie, as we shall see, gains her voice within her husband's store not only by daring to speak aloud where others might hear,
but by engaging in that ritual of Signifyin(g) (which her husband had ex-
pressly disallowed) and by openly Signifyin(g) upon the impotency of her
husband, Joe, Mayor, "I god," himself. Janie kills her husband, rhetorically,
by publicly naming his impotence (with her voice) in a public ritual of Sig-
nifyin(g). His image fatally wounded, he soon succumbs to a displaced
"kidney" failure.

　　Their Eyes Signifies upon Toomer's *Cane* in several ways. First, its plot reverses the movement of *Cane's* plot. Whereas the settings of *Cane* move
from broad open fields, through ever-diminishing physical spaces, to a circle of light in a dark and damp cellar (corresponding to the levels of self-
consciousness of the central characters), *Their Eyes'* settings within its embedded narrative move from the confines of Nanny's tiny cabin in the
Washburn's backyard, through increasingly larger physical structures, finally ending "on the Muck" in the Everglades, where she and her lover,
Tea Cake, realize the male-female relationship for which Janie had longed
so very urgently. Similarly, whereas *Cane* represents painfully unconsum-
mated relationships, the agony of which seems to intensify in direct proportion to the diminishment of physical setting, true consummation
occurs in *Their Eyes* once Janie eschews the values implied by material possessions (such as middle-class houses, especially those on which sit idle
women who rock their lives away), learns to play with Tea Cake, and then
moves to the swamp. The trope of the swamp, furthermore, in *Their Eyes*
signifies exactly the opposite of what it does in Du Bois's *Quest for the Silver
Fleece*. Whereas the swamp in Du Bois's text figures an uncontrolled chaos
that must be plowed under and controlled, for Hurston the swamp is the
trope of the freedom of erotic love, the antithesis of the bourgeois life and
order that her protagonist flees but to which Du Bois's protagonists aspire.
Whereas Du Bois's characters gain economic security by plowing up and
cultivating cotton in the swamp, Janie flees the bourgeois life that Du
Bois's characters realize, precisely by abandoning traditional values for
the uncertainties and the potential chaos of the uncultivated, untamed
swamp, where love and death linger side by side. Du Bois's shadowy figure
who seems to dwell in the swamp, we recall, is oddly enough named Zora.

But *Their Eyes* is also a paradigmatic Signifyin(g) text because of its representations, through several subtexts or embedded narratives presented as the characters' discourse, of traditional black rhetorical games or rituals. It is the text's imitation of these examples of traditionally black rhetorical rituals and modes of storytelling that allows us to think of it as a speakerly text. For in a speakerly text certain rhetorical structures seem to exist primarily as representations of oral narration, rather than as integral aspects of plot or character development. These verbal rituals signify the sheer play of black language which *Their Eyes* seems to celebrate. These virtuoso displays of verbal play constitute Hurston's complex response to the New Negro poets' strictures of the use of dialect as a poetic diction. *Their Eyes Were Watching God*'s narrative Signifies upon James Weldon Johnson's arguments against dialect just as surely as Sterling A. Brown's *Southern Road* did. Indeed, we are free to think of these two texts as discursive analogues. Moreover, Hurston's masterful use of free indirect discourse *(style indirect libre)* allows her to Signify upon the tension between the two voices of Toomer's *Cane* by adding to direct and indirect speech a strategy through which she can privilege the black oral tradition, which Toomer found to be problematical and dying.

As I stated earlier, figures of play are the dominant repeated figures in the second half of *Their Eyes,* replacing the text's figures of flowering vegetation, which as we have seen repeat at least two dozen times in the first half of the text. After Janie meets Tea Cake, figures of play supplant those floral figures that appeared each time Janie dreamed of consummated love. Moreover, it is the rhetorical play that occurs regularly on the porch of his store that Janie's husband Jody prevents Janie from enjoying. As the text reads:

> Janie loved the conversation and sometimes she thought up good stories on the mule, but Joe had forbidden her to indulge. He didn't want her talking after such trashy people. "You'se Mrs. Mayor Starks, Janie. I god, Ah can't see what uh woman uh yo' sability would want tuh be treasurin' all dat gum-grease from folks dat don't even own de house dey sleep in. 'Tain't no earthly use. They's jus' some puny humans playin' round de toes uh Time." (p. 85)

When the Signifyin(g) rituals commence—rituals that the text describes as created by "big picture talkers [who] were using a side of the world for a canvas"—Jody forces Janie to retreat inside the store, much against her will.

Eventually, however, this friction ignites a heated argument between the two, the key terms of which shall be repeated, in reverse, when Janie later falls in love with Tea Cake. Their exchange follows:

> "Ah had tuh laugh at de people out dere in de woods dis mornin', Janie. You can't help but laugh at de capers they cuts. But all the same, Ah wish mah people would git mo' business in 'em and not spend so much time on foolishness."
>
> "Everybody can't be lak you, Jody. Somebody is bound tuh want tuh laugh and play."
>
> "Who don't love tuh laugh and play?"
>
> "You make out like you don't, anyhow." (p. 98)

It is this tension between work and play, between maintaining appearances of respectability and control against the seemingly idle, nonquantifiable verbal maneuvers that "produce" nothing, which becomes the central sign of the distance between Janie's unarticulated aspirations and the material aspirations signified by Jody's desire to "be a big voice," a self-designation that Jody repeats with alacrity almost as much as he repeats his favorite parenthetical, "I god."

"Play" is also the text's word for the Signifyin(g) rituals that imitate "courtship," such as the symbolic action executed by Sam Watson, Lige Moss, and Charlie Jones, which the text describes in this way: "They know it's not courtship. It's acting out courtship and everybody is in the play" (p. 105). Play, finally, is the irresistible love potion that Tea Cake administers to Janie. Tea Cake, an apparently unlikely suitor of Joe Starks's widow, since he is a drifter and is generally thought to be "irresponsible," seduces Janie by teaching her to play checkers. Responding to his challenge of a game with "Ah can't play uh lick," Tea Cake proceeds to set up the board and teach Janie the rules. Janie "found herself glowing inside. Somebody wanted her to play. Somebody thought it natural for her to play. That was even nice. She looked him over and got little thrills from every one of his good points" (p. 146). No one had taught her to play in her adulthood. The text repeats Joe's prohibition as Tea Cake's perceptive mode of seduction. As Tea Cake concludes prophetically, "You gointuh be uh good player too, after while." And "after while," Janie and Tea Cake teach other to become "good players" in what the text depicts as a game of love.

This repeated figure of play is only the thematic analogue to the text's rhetorical play, plays of language that seem to be present essentially to reveal the complexity of black oral forms of narration. For *Their Eyes Were Watching God* is replete with storytellers, or Signifiers as the black tradition has named them. These Signifiers are granted a remarkable amount of space in this text to reveal their talents. These imitations of oral narrations, it is crucial to recall, unfold within what the text represents as Janie's framed tale, the tale of her quests with Tea Cake to the far horizon and her lonely return home. This oral narrative commences in chapter 2, while Janie and her friend, Phoeby, sit on Janie's back porch, and "the kissing, young darkness became a monstropolous old thing while Janie talked" (p. 19). Then follow almost three full pages of Janie's direct speech, "while all around the house, the night time put on flesh and blackness" (p. 23). Two paragraphs of narrative commentary follow Janie's narration; then, curiously, the narrative "fades" into "a spring-time afternoon in West Florida," the springtime of Janie's adolescence.

Without ever releasing its proprietary consciousness, the disembodied narrative voice reassumes control over the telling of Janie's story after nine paragraphs of direct discourse. We can characterize this narrative shift as from third person, to "no-person" (that is, the seemingly unmediated representation of Janie's direct speech), back to the third person of an embedded or framed narrative. This device we encounter most frequently in the storytelling devices of film, in which a first-person narrative yields, as it were, to the form of narration that we associate with the cinema. ("Kabnis," we remember, imitates the drama.) *Their Eyes Were Watching God* would seem to be imitating this mode of narration, with this fundamental difference: the bracketed tale, in the novel, is told by an omniscient, third-person narrator who reports thoughts, feelings, and events that Janie could not possibly have heard or seen. This framed narrative continues for the next eighteen chapters, until in chapter 20 the text indicates the end of Janie's storytelling to Phoeby, which we have overheard, by the broad white space and a series of widely spaced ellipses that I mentioned earlier.

This rather unusual form of narration of the tale-within-a-tale has been the subject of some controversy about the success or failure of Janie's depiction as a dynamic character who comes to know herself. Rather than retread that fruitless terrain, I would suggest that the subtleness of this narrative strategy allows for, as would no other mode of narration, the representation of the forms of oral narration that *Their Eyes* imitates so often—so often, in fact, that the very subject of this text would appear to be not primarily Janie's quest but the emulation of the phonetic, grammatical, and lexical structures of actual speech, an emulation designed to produce the illusion of oral narration. Indeed, each of the oral rhetorical structures emulated within Janie's bracketed tale functions to remind the reader that he or she is overhearing Janie's narrative to Phoeby, which unfolds on her porch, that crucial place of storytelling both in this text and in the black community. Each of these playful narratives is, by definition, a tale-within-the-bracketed-tale, and most exist as Significations of rhetorical play rather than events that develop the text's plot. Indeed, these embedded narratives, consisting as they do of long exchanges of direct discourse, often serve as plot impediments but simultaneously enable a multiplicity of narrative voices to assume control of the text, if only for a few paragraphs on a few pages, as Ellison explained his new narrative strategy to John Hersey.

Hurston is one of the few authors of our tradition who both theorized about her narrative process and defended it against the severe critiques of contemporaries such as Wright. Hurston's theory allows us to read *Their Eyes* through her own terms of critical order. It is useful to recount her theory of black oral narration, if only in summary, and then to use this to explicate the various rhetorical strategies that, collectively, comprise the narrative strategy of *Their Eyes Were Watching God.*

Hurston seems to be not only the first scholar to have defined the trope of Signifyin(g) but also the first to represent the ritual itself. Hurston represents a Signifyin(g) ritual in *Mules and Men,* then glosses the word *signify* as a means of "showing off," rhetorically. The exchange is an appropriate one to repeat, because it demonstrates that women most certainly can, and do, Signify upon men, and because it prefigures the scene of Signification in *Their Eyes* that proves to be a verbal sign of such importance to Janie's quest for consciousness:

> "Talkin' 'bout dogs," put in Gene Oliver, "they got plenty sense. Nobody can't fool dogs much."
>
> "And speakin' 'bout hams," cut in Big Sweet meaningly, "if Joe Willard don't stay out of dat bunk he was in last night, Ah'm gonter springle some salt down his back and sugar-cure *his* hams."
>
> Joe snatched his pole out of the water with a jerk and glared at Big Sweet, who stood sidewise looking at him most pointedly.
>
> "Aw, woman, quit tryin' to signify."
>
> "Ah kin signify all Ah please, Mr. Nappy-Chin, so long as Ah know what Ah'm talkin' about."[27]

This is classic Signification, an exchange of meaning and intention of some urgency between two lovers.

I use the word *exchange* here to echo Hurston's use in her essay, "Characteristics of Negro Expression." In this essay Hurston argues that "language is like money," and its development can be equated metaphorically with the development in the marketplace of the means of exchange from bartered "actual goods," which "evolve into coin" (coins symbolizing wealth). Coins evolve into legal tender, and legal tender evolves into "cheques for certain usages." Hurston's illustrations are especially instructive. People "with highly developed languages," she writes, "have words for detached ideas. That is legal tender." The linguistic equivalent of legal tender consists of words such as "chair," which comes to stand for "that-which-we-squat-on." "Groan-causers" evolves into "spear," and so on. "Cheque words" include those such as "ideation" and "pleonastic." *Paradise Lost* and *Sartor Resartus*, she continues, "are written in cheque words!" But "the primitive man," she argues, eschews legal tender and cheque words; he "exchanges descriptive words," describing "one act . . . in terms of another." More specifically, she concludes, black expression turns upon both the "interpretation of the English language in terms of pictures" and the supplement of what she calls "action words," such as "chop-axe," "sitting-chair," and "cook pot." It is the supplement of action, she maintains, which underscores her use of the word "exchange."

Such an exchange, as we have seen, is that between Big Sweet and Joe Willard. As the exchange continues, not only does the characters' language exemplify Hurston's theory, but the definitions of Signifyin(g) that I have been drawing upon throughout this book are also exemplified:

> "See dat?" Joe appealed to the other men. "We git a day off and figger we kin ketch some fish and enjoy ourselves, but naw, some wimmins got to drag behind us, even to de lake."
>
> "You didn't figger Ah was draggin' behind you when you was bringin' dat Sears and Roebuck catalogue over to my house and beggin' me to choose my ruthers. Lemme tell *you* something, *any* time Ah shack up wid any man Ah gives myself de privilege to go wherever he might be, night or day. Ah got de law in my mouth."
>
> "Lawd, ain't she specifyin'!" sniggered Wiley.
>
> "Oh, Big Sweet does dat," agreed Richardson. "Ah knewed she had somethin' up her sleeve when she got Lucy and come along."
>
> "Lawd," Willard said bitterly. "'My people, my people,' as de monkey said. You fool with Aunt Hagar's chillun and they'll sho discriminate you and put yo' name in de streets." (pp. 161–162)

Specifying, putting one's name in the streets, and "as de monkey said" are all figures for Signifyin(g). In *Dust Tracks on a Road*, Hurston even defines specifying as "giving a reading" in the following passage:

> The bookless may have difficulty in reading a paragraph in a newspaper, but when they get down to "playing the dozens" [Signifyin(g)] they have no

equal in America, and, I'd risk a sizable bet, in the whole world. Starting off
in the first by calling you a seven-sided son-of-a-bitch, and pausing to name
the sides, they proceed to "specify" until the tip-top branch of your family
tree has been "given a reading." (p. 217)

The sort of close reading that I am attempting here is also an act of
specifying.

Let me return briefly to Hurston's theory of "Negro Expression" before
turning to explicate rhetorical strategies at work in *Their Eyes Were Watching God*.
Her typology of black oral narration, in addition to "picture" and "action"
words, consists of what she calls "the will to adorn," by which she means the
use of densely figurative language, the presence of "revision," which she defines as "[making] over a great part of the [English] tongue," and the use of
"metaphor and simile," "the double-descriptive," and "verbal nouns." It is
Hurston's sense of revision, defined as "originality [in] the modification of
ideas," and "of language," as well as "reinterpretation," which I have defined in
chapter 2 as the ultimate meaning of the trope of Signifyin(g). By "revision,"
she also means "imitation" and "mimicry," for which she says "The Negro, the
world over, is famous" and which she defines as "an art in itself." The Negro,
she claims, imitates and revises, not "from a feeling of inferiority," rather "for
the love of it." This notion of imitation, repetition, and revision, she maintains,
is fundamental to "all art," indeed is the nature of art itself, even Shakespeare's.

Near the end of her compelling essay, Hurston argues that dialect is
"Negro speech," and Negro speech, she contends throughout the essay, is
quite capable of expressing the most subtle nuances of meaning, despite
"the majority of writers of Negro dialect and the burnt-cork artists." "For-
tunately," she concludes, "we don't have to believe them. We may go
directly to the Negro and let him speak for himself." Using in large part
Hurston's own theory of black oral narration, we can gain some understanding of the modes of narration at work in *Their Eyes* and thereby
demonstrate why I have chosen to call it a speakerly text, a phrase that I
derive both from Roland Barthes's opposition between the "readerly" and
the "writerly" texts—the binarism of which I am here Signifyin(g) upon—
as well as from the trope of the Talking Book, which not only is the Afro-
American tradition's fundamental repeated trope but also is a phrase used
by both Hurston and Ishmael Reed to define their own narrative strategies.

The "white man thinks in a written language," Hurston claims, while
"the Negro thinks in hieroglyphics." By hieroglyphics, she means the
"word-pictures" or the "thought pictures" as she defines these in *Their Eyes*
(p. 81). It is a fairly straightforward matter to list just a few of what we

might think of as Hurston's "figures of adornment," the specifically black examples of figurative language that she labels "simile and metaphor," "double-descriptives," and "verbal-nouns." Karla Holloway lists these as expressed in *Their Eyes:*

1. An envious heart makes a treacherous ear.
2. Us colored folks is branches without roots.
3. They's a lost ball in high grass.
4. She . . . left her wintertime wid me.
5. Ah wanted yuh to pick from a higher bush.
6. You got uh willin' mind, but youse too light behind.
7. . . . . he's de wind and we'se de grass.
8. He was a man wid salt in him.
9. . . . . what dat multiplied cockroach told you.
10. still-bait
11. big-bellies
12. gentlemanfied man
13. cemetary-dead
14. black-dark
15. duskin-down-dark[28]

This list certainly could be extended. Suffice it to say that the diction of both the characters' discourse and the free indirect discourse are replete with the three types of adornment that Hurston argued were fundamental to black oral narration.

In addition to these sorts of figures of adornment, *Their Eyes* is comprised of several long exchanges of direct discourse, which seem to be present in the text more for their own sake than to develop the plot. *Their Eyes* consists of a remarkable percentage of direct speech, rendered in black dialect, as if to display the capacity of black language itself to convey an extraordinarily wide variety of ideas and feelings. Frequently, these exchanges between characters extend for two or three pages, with little or no interruption from the text's narrator. When such narrative commentary does surface, it often serves to function as stage direction rather than as a traditional omniscient voice, as if to underscore Hurston's contention that it is "drama" that "permeates [the Negro's] entire self," and it is the dramatic to which black oral narration aspires. Because, as Hurston writes, "an audience is a necessary part of any drama," these Signifyin(g) rituals tend to occur outdoors, at the communal scene of oral instruction, on the porches of homes and stores.

From the novel's earliest scenes, the porch is both personified and then represented through a series of synecdoches as the undifferentiated "eyes," "mouth," and "ears" of the community. Of these three senses, however, it is the communal speaking voice—"Mouth-Almighty," as the text has it— which emerges early on as the most significant. Indeed, the first time the porch "speaks," the text represents its discourse in one paragraph of "direct quotation" consisting of ten sentences separated only by dashes, as if to emphasize the anonymous if collective voice of the community that the text proceeds to represent in several ways. Against this sort of communal narration the text pits Jody Starks, Janie's second husband, who repeatedly states that he wishes to become "a big voice." This voice, however, is the individual voice of domination. The figure of Jody's big voice comes to stand as a synecdoche of oppression, in opposition to the speech community of which Janie longs to become an integral part.

The representation of modes of black narration begins, as we have seen, with Janie's narration of her story to Phoeby, the framed tale in which most of the novel's action unfolds. Throughout this narrative, the word *voice* recurs with great frequency. Who speaks, indeed, proves to be of crucial import to Janie's quest for freedom, but who sees and who hears at all points in the text remain fundamental as well. Phoeby's "hungry listening," we recall, "helped Janie to tell her story." Almost as soon as Janie's narrative begins, however, Nanny assumes control of the text and narrates the story of Janie's genealogy, from slavery to the present, as Janie listens painfully. This quasi-slave narrative, rendered as a tale-within-a-tale, is one of the few instances of direct speech that serve as a function of the plot. Subsequent speaking narrators assume control of the narrative primarily to demonstrate forms of traditional oral narration.

These double narratives-within-the-narrative begin as soon as Janie and Jody move to Eatonville. Amos Hicks and Joe Coker engage in a brief and amusing exchange about the nature of storytelling generally and about the nature of figurative language specifically, a discussion to which we shall return. Tony Taylor next demonstrates the ironies of speech-making on the day of dedication of Jody's store, a speech that ends with requests that Janie address the community, only to be thwarted by her husband who says that "mah wife don't know nothin' 'bout no speech-makin.'" Jody's harsh actions, the narrator tells us ominously, "took the bloom off of things" for Janie. Subsequent forms of oral narration include "a traditional prayer-poem," a series of speeches, the sung communal poetry of the spirituals, but especially the frontporch Signifyin(g) rituals that serve to impede the plot. The porch is dominated by three narrators. Sam, Lige, and Walter are known as "the ringleaders of the mule-talkers," who sit for hours on the storefront porch and Signify upon Matt Bonner's yellow mule. These exchanges about the mule extend for pages (pp. 81–85, 87–96) and would seem to be present primarily to display the nature of story-telling, allowing a full range of characters' discourse to be heard.

At the end of the second mule Signification, still another tale-within-a-tale-within-a-tale unfolds, which we might think of as the allegory of the buzzards (pp. 96–97). After the second mule tale concludes with his mock funeral and mock eulogy, the disembodied narrator relates the narrative of "the already impatient buzzards," who proceed in ritual fashion to examine and disembowel the mule's carcass. This allegory, of course, serves to mock the preceding mock eulogy, complete with the speaking characters and a patterned oral ritual. This allegory, more especially, shatters completely any illusion the reader might have had that this was meant to be a realistic fiction, even though the text has naturalized the possibility of such an event occurring, if only by representing storytelling in direct speech as its principal mode of narration. Once the reader encounters the allegory of the buzzards, his or her generic expectations have been severely interrupted.

Two pages later, the text returns to more Signifyin(g) rituals, defined by the narrator as "eternal arguments," which "never ended because there was no end to reach. It was a contest in hyperbole," the narrator concludes, "carried on for no other reason" (p. 99). Sam Watson and Lige Moss then proceed to debate, for six pages, the nature of the subject and whether or not "you got to have a subjick tuh talk from, do yuh can't talk" (p. 100), and whether or not these sorts of "readings" have "points" (p. 102). Just as the two Signifiers are about to commence still another oral narration of High John de Conquer tales, three women come walking down the street and thereby generate three pages of rhetorical courtship rituals. At this point in the narrative, as at the beginning of the first mule tale, the omniscient narrator establishes the context by shifting from the past tense to the present tense, then disappears for pages and pages while the characters narrate, underscoring thereby the illusion of overhearing an event.

The most crucial of these scenes of represented speech is the devastating exchange in which Janie first speaks in public against her husband. This exchange is a Signifyin(g) ritual of the first order because Janie Signifies upon Jody's manhood, thereby ending his dominance over her and over the community, and thereby killing Jody's will to live. The exchange is marvelous. Jody begins the fatal confrontation by insulting Janie for improperly cutting a plug of tobacco:

"I god almighty! A woman stay round uh store till she get old as Methusalem and still can't cut a little thing like a plug of tobacco! Don't stand dere rollin' yo' pop eyes at me wid yo' rump hangin' nearly to yo' knees!" (p. 121)

After a short, quick "big laugh," the crowd assembled in the store, "got to thinking and stopped. It was like somebody," the narrative continues, "snatched off part of a woman's clothes while she wasn't looking and the streets were crowded." But most remarkably of all, "Janie took the middle of the floor to talk right into Jody's face, and that was something that hadn't been done before."

Janie, as a startled Jody says, is speaking a new language, "Talkin' any such language as dat." "You de one started talkin' under people's clothes," she retorts. "Not me." Then, indeed, Janie proceeds to talk under clothes, after Jody says:

" 'Tain't no use in getting' all mad, Janie, 'cause Ah mention you ain't no young gal no mo'. Nobody in heah ain't lookin' for no wife outa yuh. Old as you is." (p. 122)

Janie responds:

"Naw, Ah ain't no young gal no mo' but den Ah ain't no old woman neither. Ah reckon Ah looks mah age too. But Ah'm uh woman every inch of me, and Ah know it. Dat's uh whole lot more'n *you* kin say. You big-bellies round here and put out a lot of brag, but 'tain't nothin' to it but yo' big voice. Humph! Talkin' 'bout *me* lookin' old! When you pull down yo' britches, you look lak de change uh life." (pp. 122–123)

"Great God from Zion!" Sam Watson gasped. "Y'all really playin' de dozens tuhnight," the text reads, naming the sort of Signifyin(g) ritual that has occurred. "Wha-whut's dat you said?" Joe challenged, hoping that his ears had fooled him, to which lame retort "Walter taunted" in a synesthesia that the text has just naturalized for us: "You heard her, you ain't blind." Jody, we well know, now thoroughly shattered by the force of Janie's voice, soon succumbs to acute humiliation and his displaced kidney disorder. As he lies dying, Janie contemplates "what had happened in the making of a voice out of a man," the devastating synecdoche that names both Jody's deepest aspiration and his subsequent great fall.

It is striking that Janie gains her voice and becomes a speaking subject inside her husband's store. Not only does she, by speaking, defy his expressed prohibition, but the scene itself is a key repetition of the metaphors of inside and outside, which repeat frequently throughout the text and which, as I hope to show, serve as a thematic, if metaphorical, counterpart to the most striking innovation of *Their Eyes'* narrative strategy, the presence of free indirect discourse.

The repeated metaphors of inside and outside begin in the text's first chapter. Janie narrates her tale, as Phoeby listens, outside on her back porch. Janie's metaphorical and densely lyrical "outside observations," the narrator tells us, "buried themselves in her flesh." After she experiences her first orgasm, then kisses Johnny Taylor, she extends "herself outside of her dream" and goes "inside of the house." As we have seen, it is inside houses in which a series of people (first her grandmother, Nanny; then her first husband, Logan Killicks; then her second husband, Joe Starks) attempt to oppress her and prevent her from speaking and asserting herself. Janie dreams outdoors, in metaphors of flowering springtime, often under pear trees. When Logan insults her, the narrator says that "she turned wrong-side out just standing there and feeling." Jody seduces her with dreams of "far horizons," "under the tree" and outdoors "in the scrub oaks." What Jody speaks out loud and what Janie thinks inside come to represent an opposition of such dimensions that we are not at all surprised when their final confrontation occurs. Janie, we recall, is forced to retreat inside the store when the storytelling rituals commence.

The text represents Janie's crucial if ironic scene of self-discovery rather subtly in this figurative framework of inside and outside. This coming to consciousness is not represented by a speaking scene, however; rather, it is represented in these inside-outside figures. When she finally does speak, therefore, by Signifyin(g) in the store upon Jody's impotence, the gaining of her own voice is a sign of her authority, but not a sign of a newly found unified identity. Janie's speaking voice, rather, is an outcome of her consciousness of division.[29] Indeed, hers is a rhetoric of division.

The text represents this consciousness of division in two scenes that transpire in the chapter that precedes the chapter in which she Signifies upon Jody. The text reads:

> The spirit of the marriage left the bedroom and took to living in the parlor. It was there to shake hands whenever company came to visit, but it never went back inside the bedroom again. So she put something in there to represent the spirit like a Virgin Mary image in a church. The bed was no longer a daisy-field for her and Joe to play in. It was a place where she went and laid down when she was sleepy and tired. (p. 111)

In this passage, Janie's inner feelings, "the spirit of the marriage," are projected onto outer contiguous physical spaces (the bedroom and the parlor). Her inside, in other words, is figured as an outside, in the rooms. Her bed, moreover, ceases to be a place for lovemaking, as signified by both the daisy-field metaphor and the metaphor of play (reminding us, through the repetition, of her central metaphors of dream and aspiration that repeat so often in the novel's first half). The contiguous relation of the bedroom and the parlor, both physical spaces, through which the metaphorical spirit of the marriage now moves, reveals two modes of figuration overlapping in Janie's indirectly reported thoughts for the first time—that is, one mode dependent upon substitution, the other on contiguity.[30] Clearly, the rhetorical relation among "sex" and "spirit of the marriage," and "spirit of the marriage," "bedroom," and "parlor" is a complex one.

Until this moment in the text, Janie's literacy was represented only as a metaphorical literacy. Janie's "conscious life," the text tells us, "had commenced at Nanny's gate," across which she had kissed Johnny Taylor just after experiencing her first orgasm under her "blossoming pear tree in the back-yard." In the moving passage that precedes the event but prepares us for it by describing her increasing awareness of her own sexuality, rendered in free indirect discourse, Janie names her feelings in her first metaphor: "The rose of the world was breathing out smell. It followed her through all her waking moments and caressed her in her sleep" (pp. 23–24). Janie's first language, the language of her own desire, is registered in a lyrical and metaphorical diction found in these passages of free indirect discourse. Janie has mastered, the text tells us early on, "the words of the trees and the wind" (p. 44). In this metaphorical language, "she spoke to falling seeds," as they speak to her, in lyrical metaphors, renaming "the world," for example, "a stallion rolling in the blue pasture of ether." Whereas she speaks, thinks, and dreams in metaphors, the communal voice of the porch describes her in a string of synecdoches, naming parts of her body—such as her "great rope of black hair," "her pugnacious breasts," her "faded shirt and muddy overalls"—as parts standing for the whole (p. 11).

One paragraph later, as a sign that she can name her division, the direction of her figuration reverses itself. Whereas in the first scene she projects her inner feelings onto outer physical space, in this scene she internalizes an outer physical space, her scene of oppression, the store:

> Janie stood where he left her for unmeasured time and thought. She stood there until something fell off the shelf inside her. Then she went inside there to see what it was. It was her image of Jody tumbled down and shattered. But looking at it she saw that it never was the flesh and blood figure

of her dreams. Just something she had grabbed up to drape her dreams over. (p. 112)

Janie has internalized the store through the synecdoche of the shelf.[31] As Barbara Johnson summarizes the rhetorical import of this scene: "These two figural mini-narratives [represent] a kind of chiasmus, or crossover, in which the first paragraph presents an externalization of the inner, a metaphorically grounded metonymy, while the second paragraph presents an internalization of the outer, or a metonymically grounded metaphor. . . . The reversals operated by the chiasmus map out a reversal of the power relations between Janie and Joe."[32] When she soon speaks aloud in public against Jody and thereby redefines their relationship, it is the awareness of this willed figurative division of which her speaking voice is the sign. As the text reads, Janie "found that she had a host of thoughts she had never expressed to him, and numerous emotions she had never let Jody know about. Things packed up and put away in parts of her heart where he could never find them" (p. 112).

Janie is now truly fluent in the language of the figurative: "She had an inside and an outside now and suddenly knew how not to mix them." Three pages before she Signifies upon Jody, the text represents this fluency as follows:

> Then one day she sat and watched the shadow of herself going about tend-
> ing the store and prostrating itself before Jody, while all the time she herself sat
> under a shady tree with the wind blowing through her hair and her clothes.
> Somebody near about making summertime out of lonesomeness. (p. 119)

Janie's ability to name her own division and move the parts simultaneously through contiguous spaces, her newly found and apparently exhilarating double-consciousness, is that crucial event that enables her to speak and assert herself, after decades of being defined almost exclusively by others.

The text prefigures this event. The sign that this consciousness of her own division liberates her speaking voice is Janie's first instance of voicing her feelings within the store, which occurs in the text midway between the slapping scene in which she first internally names her outside and inside (p. 112) and the scene in which she so tellingly Signifies upon Joe (pp. 121–122). Janie speaks after listening in a painful silence as Coker and Joe Lindsay discuss the merits of beating women:

> ". . . Tony love her too good," said Coker. "Ah could break her if she
> wuz mine. Ah'd break her or kill her. Makin' uh fool outa me in front of
> everybody."

> "Tony won't never hit her. He says beatin' women is just like steppin' on
> baby chickens. He claims 'tain't no place on uh woman tuh hit," Joe Lindsay
> said with scornful disapproval, "but Ah'd kill uh baby just born dis mawnin'
> fuh uh thing like dat. 'Taint nothin' but low-down spitefulness 'ginst her
> husband make her do it." (p. 116)

This exchange, of course, refigures the crucial scene in which Joe slaps
Janie because her meal was not well prepared. Joe Lindsay's comparison in
this passage of "beatin' women" and "steppin' on baby chickens" echoes
Joe's proclamation to Janie that "somebody got to think for women and
chillun and chickens and cows," made in their argument about who has
the right "to tell" (pp. 110–111). After Joe Lindsay finishes speaking, and after
his sexist remarks are affirmed as gospel by Jim Stone, Janie—for the first
time—speaks out against the men's opinion about the merits of beatings.
As the text states, "Janie did what she had never done before, that is, thrust
herself into the conversation":

> "Sometimes God gits familiar wid us womenfolks too and talks His in-
> side business. He told me how surprised He was 'bout y'all turning out so
> smart after Him makin' yuh different; and how surprised y'all is goin' tuh
> be if you ever find out you don't know half as much 'bout us as you think
> you do. It's so easy to make yo'self out God Almighty when you ain't got
> nothin' tuh strain against but *women and chickens.*" (p. 117, emphasis added)

Janie reveals God's "inside business" to the superficial store-talkers, warning all who can hear her voice that a "surprise" lay in waiting for those
who see only appearances and never penetrate to the tenor of things. Joe,
we learn just four pages later, is in for the surprise of his life: the killing
timbre of Janie's true inner voice. Joe's only response to this first scene of
speaking is to tell his wife, "You getting' too moufy, Janie," a veritable liter-
alizing of the metaphor of mouth, followed by the ultimate sign of ignoring and circumventing Janie's domain, an order to her to "Go fetch me de
checker-board *and* de checkers." Joe's turn to the male world of play, at
Janie's expense, leads Janie to play the dozens on his sexuality and thus to
his death. These metaphorical echoes and exchanges are deadly serious in
Hurston's text.

Earlier in the narrative, Hicks defined the metaphorical as "co-talkin'"
and says that his is "too deep" for women to understand, which explains,
he says, why "Dey love to hear me talk" precisely "because dey can't understand it. . . . Too much co to it," he concludes (p. 59). As soon as Janie
learns to name her inside and outside and to move between them, as we

have seen, Jody argues that women "need tellin'" because "somebody got to think for women and chillun and chickens and cows" because a man sees "one thing" and "understands ten," while a woman sees "ten things and don't understand one" (pp. 110–111). Jody ironically accuses Janie of failing to understand how one thing can imply or be substituted for ten, thereby arguing that Janie does not understand metaphor, whereas Janie is a master of metaphor whose self-liberation awaits only the knowledge of how to narrate her figures contiguously. It is Jody who has failed to read the situation properly. As a character in *Mules and Men* argues, most people do not understand the nature of the figurative, which he characterizes as expression that "got a hidden meanin', jus' like de Bible. Everybody can't understand what they mean," he continues. "Most people is thin-brained. They's born wid they feet under the moon. Some folks is born wid they feet on de sun and they kin seek out de inside meanin' of words" (pp. 162–163). Jody, it turns out, is both thin-brained and thin-skinned, and proves to have been born with his feet under the moon. He is all vehicle, no tenor. The "inside meanings of words," of course, we think of as the tenor, or inside meaning of a rhetorical figure, while the outside corresponds to its "vehicle." Janie, as the text repeats again and again in its central metaphor for her character, is a child of the sun.

Hurston's use of free indirect discourse is central to her larger strategy of critiquing what we might think of as a "male writing." Joe Starks, we remember, fondly and unconsciously refers to himself as "I god." During the lamp-lighting ceremony (pp. 71–74), as I have suggested earlier, Joe is represented as the creator (or at least the purchaser) of light. Joe is the text's figure of authority and voice, indeed the authority *of* voice:

> "Naw, Jody, it jus' looks lak it keeps us in some way we ain't natural wid one 'nother. You'se always off talkin' and fixin' things, and Ah feels lak Ah'm jus' markin' time. Hope it soons gits over."
>
> "Over, Janie? I god, Ah ain't even started good. Ah told you in de very first beginnin' dat Ah aimed tuh be uh big voice. You oughta be glad, 'cause dat makes uh big woman outa you." (p. 74)

Joe says that "in de very first beginnin'" he "aimed tuh be uh big voice," an echo of the first verse of the Gospel of John: "In the beginning was the Word, and the Word was with God, and the Word was God." Joe, we know, sees himself, and wishes to be seen as the God-figure of his community. The text tells us that when speakers on formal occasions prefaced their remarks with the phrase "Our beloved Mayor," the phrase was equivalent to "one of those statements that everybody says but nobody believes like 'God

is everywhere'" (p. 77). Joe is the figure of the male author, he who has au-
thored both Eatonville and Janie's existences. We remember that when Joe
lights the town's newly acquired lamp, Mrs. Bogle's alto voice sings "Jesus,
the light of the world":

> We'll walk in de light, de beautiful light
> Come where the dew drops of mercy shine bright
> Shine all around us by day and by night
> Jesus, the light of the world. (p. 73)

So, when Janie Signifies upon Joe, she strips him of his hubristic claim to
the godhead and exposes him, through the simile of the "change of life," as
impotent and de/masculated. The revelation of the truth kills him. Janie,
in effect, has rewritten Joe's text of himself, and liberated herself in the
process. Janie writes herself into being by naming, by speaking herself free.
As we shall see in chapter 7, Alice Walker takes this moment in Hurston's
text as the moment of revision and creates a character whom we witness
literally writing herself into being, but writing herself into being in a language that imitates that idiom spoken by Janie and Hurston's black community generally. This scene, this transformation or reversal of status, is
truly the first feminist critique of the fiction of the authority of the male
voice, and its sexism, in the Afro-American tradition.

This opposition between metaphor and metonym appears in another
form as well, that of strategies of tale-telling. Nanny narrates her slave narrative in a linear, or metonymic, manner, with one event following another in chronological order. Janie, by contrast, narrates her tale in a circular, or framed, narrative replete with vivid, startling metaphors. Janie only
liberates herself by selecting alternatives exactly opposed to those advocated by Nanny, eschewing the sort of "protection" afforded by Logan Killicks and so graphically figured for Janie in her grandmother's fantasy of
preaching "a great sermon about colored women sittin' on high." Only
after Janie satisfies Nanny's desire, "sittin' on high" on Joe Starks front
porch, then rejecting it, will she in turn "preach" her own sermon by narrating her tale to Phoeby in a circular, framed narrative that merges her
voice with an omniscient narrator's in free indirect discourse.

IV

If *Their Eyes* makes impressive use of the figures of outside and inside, as well
as the metaphor of double-consciousness as the prequisite to becoming a

speaking subject, then the text's mode of narration, especially its "speaker-liness," serves as the rhetorical analogue to this theme. I use the word *double* here intentionally, to echo W. E. B. Du Bois's metaphor for the Afro-American's peculiar psychology of citizenship and also to avoid the limited description of free indirect discourse as a "dual voice," in Roy Pascal's term.[33] Rather than a dual voice, free indirect discourse, as manifested in *Their Eyes Were Watching God,* is a dramatic way of expressing a divided self. Janie's self, as we have seen, is a divided self. Long before she becomes aware of her division, of her inside and outside, free indirect discourse communi-cates this division to the reader. After she becomes aware of her own divi-sion, free indirect discourse functions to represent, rhetorically, her inter-rupted passage from outside to inside. Free indirect discourse in *Their Eyes* reflects both the text's theme of the doubling of Janie's self and that of the problematic relationship between Janie as a speaking subject and spoken language. Free indirect discourse, furthermore, is a central aspect of the rhetoric of the text and serves to disrupt the reader's expectation of the ne-cessity of the shift in point of view from third person to first within Janie's framed narrative. Free indirect discourse is not the voice of both a charac-ter and a narrator; rather, it is a bivocal utterance, containing elements of both direct and indirect speech. It is an utterance that no one could have spoken, yet which we recognize because of its characteristic "speakerli-ness," its paradoxically written manifestation of the aspiration to the oral.

I shall not enter into the terminological controversy over free indirect discourse, except to refer the reader to the controversy itself.[34] My concern with free indirect discourse, for the purposes of this chapter, is limited to its use in *Their Eyes.*[35] I am especially interested in its presence in this text as an implicit critique of that ancient opposition in narrative theory between showing and telling, between mimesis and diegesis. The tension between diegesis, understood here as that which can be represented, and mimesis, that which Hurston repeats in direct quotations, strikes the reader early on as a fundamental opposition in *Their Eyes.* Only actions or events can be represented, in this sense, while discourse here would seem to be over-heard or repeated. Hurston's use of this form of repetition creates the illu-sion of a direct relationship between her text and a black "real world" (which has led some of her most vocal critics to call this an anthropologi-cal text), while representation of the sort found in narrative commentary preserves, even insists upon, the difference and the very distance between them.

Free indirect discourse, on the other hand, is a third, mediating term. As Michal Ginsberg argues perceptively, "it is a *mimesis* which tries to pass for a *diegesis.*"[36] But it is also, I contend, a diegesis that tries to pass for a mimesis. Indeed, it is precisely this understanding of free indirect discourse that derives from its usage in *Their Eyes Were Watching God,* simply because we are unable to characterize it either as the representation of an action (diegesis) or as the repetition of a character's words (mimesis). When we recall Hurston's insistence that the fundamental indicator of traditional black oral narration is its aspiration to the "dramatic," we can see clearly that her use of free indirect discourse is a profound attempt to remove the distinction between repeated speech and represented events. Here discourse "is not distinct from events." As Ginsberg argues, "Subject and object dissolve into each other. Representation which guaranteed the distance between them is in danger."[37] For Hurston, free indirect discourse is an equation: direct speech equals narrative commentary; representation of an action equals repetition of that action; therefore, narrative commentary aspires to the immediacy of the drama. Janie's quest for consciousness, however, always remains that for the consciousness of her own division, which the dialogical rhetoric of the text—especially as expressed in free indirect discourse—underscores, preserves, and seems to celebrate. It is this theme, and this rhetoric of division, which together comprise the modernism of this text.

A convenient way to think about free indirect discourse is that it appears initially to be indirect discourse (by which I mean that its signals of time and person correspond to a third-person narrator's discourse), "but it is penetrated, in its syntactic and semantic structures, by enunciative properties, thus by the discourse of a character,"[38] and even in Hurston's case by that of characters. In other words, free indirect discourse attempts to represent "consciousness without the apparent intrusion of a narrative voice," thereby "presenting the illusion of a character's acting out his [or her] mental state in an immediate relationship with the reader." Graham Hough defines free indirect discourse as one extreme of "coloured narrative," or narrative-cum-dialogue as in Jane Austen's fictions.[39] Hurston's use of free indirect discourse, we are free to say, is indeed a kind of "coloured narrative"! But Hurston allows us to rename free indirect discourse; near the beginning of her book, the narrator describes the communal, undifferentiated voice of "the porch" as "A mood come alive. Words walking without masters; walking altogether like harmony in a song." Since the narrator attributes these words to "the bander log" (p. 11), or the place where Kipling's monkeys sit, Hurston here gives one more, coded, reference to Signifyin(g): that which the porch (monkeys) has just done is to Signify upon Janie. If Signifyin(g) is "a mood come alive," "words walking without masters," then we can also think of free indirect discourse in this way.

There are numerous indices whereby we identify free indirect discourse in general, among these grammar, intonation, context, idiom, register, and content; it is naturalized in a text by stream of consciousness, irony, empathy, and polyvocality.[40] The principal indices of free indirect discourse in *Their Eyes* include those which "evoke a 'voice' or presence" that supplements the narrator's, especially when one or more sentences of free indirect discourse follow a sentence of indirect discourse. Idiom and register, particularly, Hurston uses as markers of black colloquialism, of the quality of the speakerly informed by the dialect of the direct discourse of the characters. In *Their Eyes*, naturalization would seem to function as part of the theme of the developing but discontinuous self. This function is naturalized primarily by irony, empathy, and polyvocality. When it is used in conjunction with Joe Starks, irony obtains and distancing results; when it is used in conjunction with Janie, empathy obtains and an illustory identification results, an identity we might call lyric fusion between the narrator and Janie. Bivocalism, finally, or the double-voiced utterance, in which two voices co-occur, is this text's central device of naturalization, again serving to reinforce both Janie's division and paradoxically the narrator's distance from Janie. As Ginsberg concludes so perceptively, "Free indirect discourse is a way of expression of a divided self."[41]

Their Eyes employs three modes of narration to render the words or thoughts of a character. The first is direct discourse:

> "Jody," she smiled up at him, "but s'posin—"
> "Leave de s'posin' and everything else to me."

The next is indirect discourse:

> "The vision of Logan Killicks was desecrating the pear tree, but Janie didn't know how to tell Nanny that."

The third example is free indirect discourse. Significantly, this example occurs when Joe Starks enters the narrative:

> Joe Starks was the name, yeah Joe Starks from in and through Georgy. Been workin' for white folks all his life. Saved up some money—round three hundred dollars, yes indeed, right here in his pocket. Kept hearin' 'bout them buildin' a new state down heah in Floridy and sort of wanted to come. But he was makin' money where he was. But when he heard all about 'em makin' a town all outa colored folks, he knowed dat was de place

he wanted to be. He had always wanted to be a big voice, but de white folks had all de sayso where he come from and everywhere else, exceptin' dis place dat colored folks was buildin' theirselves. Dat was right too. De man dat built things oughta boss it. Let colored folks build things too if dey wants to crow over something'. He was glad he had his money all saved up. He meant to git dere whilst de town wuz yet a baby. He meant to buy in big. (pp. 47–48)

I selected this example because it includes a number of standard indices of free indirect speech. Although when read aloud it sounds as if entire sections are in, or should be in, direct quotation, none of the sentences in this paragraph is direct discourse. There are no quotation marks here. The character's idiom, interspersed and contrasted colorfully with the narrator's voice, indicates nevertheless that this is an account of the words that Joe spoke to Janie. The sentences imitating dialect clearly are not those of the narrator alone; they are those of Joe Starks and the narrator. Moreover, the presence of the adverb *here* ("yes, indeed, right here in his pocket") as opposed to *there*, which would be required in normal indirect speech because one source would be describing another, informs us that the assertion originates within and reflects the character's sensibilities, not the narrator's. The interspersion of indirect discourse with free indirect discourse, even in the same sentence, serves as another index to its presence, precisely by underscoring Joe's characteristic idiom, whereas the indirect discourse obliterates it. Despite the third person and the past tense, then, of which both indirect and free indirect discourse consist, several sentences in this paragraph appear to report Joe's speech, without the text resorting to either dialogue or direct discourse. The principal indices of free indirect discourse direct the reader to the subjective source of the statement, rendered through a fusion of narrator and a silent but speaking character.

Exclamations and exclamatory questions often introduce free indirect discourse. The text's first few examples occur when Janie experiences the longing for love, and then her first orgasm:

She saw a dust-bearing bee sink into the sanctum of a bloom; the thousand sister-calyxes arch to meet the love embrace and the ecstatic shiver of the tree from root to tiniest branch creaming in every blossom and frothing with delight. So this was a marriage! . . . Then Janie felt a pain remorseless sweet that left her limp and languid. (p. 24)

Then in the next paragraph:

> She was lying across the bed asleep so Janie tipped on out of the front door.
> Oh to be a pear tree—*any* tree in bloom! With kissing bees singing of the be-
> ginning of the world! She was sixteen. (p. 25)

Unlike the free indirect discourse that introduces Joe, these three sentences retain the narrator's level of diction, her idiom, as if to emphasize
on one hand that Janie represents the potentially lyrical self, but on the
other hand that the narrator is interpreting Janie's inarticulate thoughts
to the reader on her behalf.

This usage remains fairly consistent until Janie begins to challenge, if
only in her thoughts, Joe's authority:

> Janie noted that while he didn't talk the mule himself [Signify], he sat
> and laughed at it. Laughed his big heh, hey laugh too. But then when Lige
> or Sam or Walter or some of the other big picture talkers were using a side
> of the world for a canvas, Joe would hustle her off inside the store to sell
> something. Look like he took pleasure in doing it. Why couldn't he go him-
> self sometimes? She had come to hate the inside of that store anyway. (p. 85)

Here we see Janie's idiom entering, if only in two sentences, the free indirect speech. After she has "slain" Jody, however, her idiom, more and
more, informs the free indirect discourse, in sentences such as "Poor Jody!
He ought not to have to wrassle in there by himself" (p. 129). Once Janie
meets Tea Cake, the reader comes to expect to encounter Janie's doubts
and dreams in free indirect discourse, almost always introduced by the
narrator explicitly as being Janie's thoughts. Almost never, however, curiously enough, does Janie's free indirect discourse unfold in a strictly black
idiom, as does Joe's; rather, it is represented in an idiom informed by the
black idiom but translated into what we might think of as a colloquial
form of standard English, which always stands in contrast to Janie's direct
speech, which is foregrounded in dialect.

This difference between the representations of the level of diction of
Janie's direct discourse and the free indirect discourse that the text asks us
to accept as the figure of Janie's thoughts reinforces for the reader both
Janie's divided consciousness and the double-voiced nature of free indirect
discourse, as if the narrative commentary cannot relinquish its proprietary
consciousness over Janie as freely as it does for other characters. Nevertheless, after Janie falls in love with Tea Cake, we learn of her feelings through
a remarkable amount of free indirect discourse, almost always rendered in
what I wish to call idiomatic, but standard, English.

It is this same voice, eventually, which we also come to associate with that of the text's narrator; through empathy and irony, the narrator begins to read Janie's world and everyone in it, through this same rhetorical device, rendered in this identical diction, even when the observation clearly is not Janie's. The effect is as if the lyrical language created by the indeterminate merging of the narrator's voice and Janie's almost totally silences the initial level of diction of the narrator's voice. Let us recall the narrator's voice in the text's opening paragraph:

> Ships at a distance have every man's wish on board. For some they come in with the tide. For others they sail forever on the horizon, never out of sight, never landing until the Watcher turns his eyes away in resignation, his dreams mocked to death by Time. That is the life of men. (p. 1)

Compare that voice with the following:

> So Janie began to think of Death. Death, that strange being with the huge square toes who lived way in the West. The great one who lived in the straight house like a platform without sides to it, and without a roof. What need has Death for a cover, and what winds can blow against him? (p. 129)

Ostensibly, these are Janie's thoughts. But compare this sentence, which is part of the narrator's commentary: "But, don't care how firm your determination is, you can't keep turning round in one place like a horse grinding sugar cane" (p. 177).

This idiomatic voice narrates almost completely the dramatic scene of the hurricane, where "six eyes were questioning *God.*" One such passage serves as an excellent example of a communal free indirect discourse, of a narrative voice that is not fused with Janie's but which describes events in the idiom of Janie's free indirect discourse:

> They looked back. Saw people trying to run in raging waters and screaming when they found they couldn't. A huge barrier of the makings of the dike to which the cabins had been added was rolling and tumbling forward. . . . The monstropolous beast had left his bed. . . . The sea was walking the earth with a heavy heel. (p. 239)

At several passages after this narration of the hurricane, the interspersed indirect discourse and free indirect discourse become extraordinarily difficult to isolate because of this similarity in idiom:

> Janie fooled around outside awhile to try and think it wasn't so. . . . Well, she thought, that big old dawg with the hatred in his eyes had killed her after all. She wished she had slipped off that cow-tail and drowned then

and there and been done. But to kill her through Tea Cake was too much to bear. Tea Cake, the son of the Evening Sun, had to die for loving her. She looked hard at the sky for a long time. Somewhere up there beyond blue ether's bottom sat He. Was He noticing what was going on around here? . . . Did He *mean* to do this thing to Tea Cake and her? . . . Maybe it was some big tease and when He saw it had gone far enough He'd give her a sign. (pp. 263–264)

Narrative commentary and free indirect discourse, in passages such as this, move toward the indistinguishable. The final instance of free indirect discourse occurs, appropriately enough, in the novel's ultimate paragraph, in which Janie's true figurative synthesis occurs:

> The day of the gun, and the bloody body, and the courthouse came and commenced to sing a sobbing sigh out of every corner in the room; out of each and every chair and thing. Commenced to sing, commenced to sob and sigh, singing and sobbing. Then Tea Cake came prancing around her where she was and the song of the sigh flew out of the window and lit in the top of the pine trees. Tea Cake, with the sun for a shawl. Of course he wasn't dead. He could never be dead until she herself had finished feeling and thinking. The kiss of his memory made pictures of love and light against the wall. Here was peace. She pulled in her horizon like a great fish-net. Pulled it from around the waist of the world and draped it over her shoulder. So much of life in its meshes! She called in her soul to come and see. (p. 286)

Ephi Paul, in a subtle reading of various tropes in *Their Eyes* (in an unpublished essay, "My Tongue Is in My Friend's Mouth"), argues that this "final moment of transcendence" is also a final moment of control and synthesis of the opposed male and female paradigmatic tropes defined in the novel's first two paragraphs:

> The horizon that she learns about from Joe, that helps her rediscover how to "play" again with Tea Cake, has been transformed from the object of a longing gaze to a figurative "fish-net" which an active subject can pull in. While Joe's desires are, like the men of the first paragraph, "mocked to death by Time," Janie's are still alive and thriving: "The kiss of his memory made pictures of love and light against the wall." Janie finds "peace" in "his memory," just as she has always privileged her inward contemplative self over the outer active one. Yet in its own way, Janie's thriving survival of hard time has been an active process of finding a language to name her desire. The horizon as a fish-net seems to signify the synthesis of "men" and "women's" figuration, because the fish-net's "meshes" seem so like the sift-

ing of women's memories—remembering and forgetting all that they want. So Janie has cast her horizon into a sea of possibilities and sorted out her catch of loves, naming them with an even more accurate figuration of desire. She opens her arms to "the waist of the world" and gathers in her satisfactions, rooted in her power of "feeling and thinking" for herself. (pp. 44–45)

This merging of the opposed modes of figuration in the novel's first two paragraphs stands as an analogue of Janie's transcendent moment because of, as Paul argues,

> the male and female modes of figuration (as established in the "paradigm" of its first two paragraphs)—bringing together the horizon of change and the fish-net of memory. In her search for desire and its naming, Janie shifts back and forth between the alienation of the gazing "Watcher" and the empowerment of women believing that "the dream is the truth." She finds her satisfaction only after using Joe's horizon of "change and chance" to transform the desire she experiences alone under the pear tree; she retains the horizon long after she has dismissed Joe, because she can re-figure it to have meaning for herself. (p. 71)

To this I would only add that both the pulling in of her horizon and the calling in of her soul reveal not a unity of self but a maximum of self-control over the division between self and other. Whereas before Tea Cake Janie was forced to send a mask of herself outward, now, at novel's end, she can invite both her horizon (the figure for her desires after meeting Jody) and her soul inside herself "to come and see." She has internalized her metaphors, and brought them home, across a threshold heretofore impenetrable. This self-willed, active, subjective synthesis is a remarkable trope of self-knowledge. And the numerous sentences of free indirect discourse in this paragraph serve to stress this fact of Janie's self-knowledge and self-control. Her invitation to her soul to come see the horizon that had always before been a figure for external desire, the desire of the other, is the novel's sign of Janie's synthesis.

It is because of these dramatic shifts in the idiom in which the voice of the narrator appears that we might think of *Their Eyes* as a speakerly text. For it is clear that the resonant dialect of the character's discourse has come to color the narrator's idiom such that it resembles rather closely the idiom in which Janie's free indirect discourse is rendered. But *Their Eyes* would seem to be a spearkerly text for still another reason. Hurston uses free indirect discourse not only to represent an individual character's speech and thought but also to represent the collective black community's speech and thoughts, as in the hurricane passage. This sort of anonymous, collective, free indirect discourse is not only unusual but quite possibly was Hurston's innovation, as if to emphasize both the immense potential of this literary diction, one dialect-informed as it were, for the tradition, as well as the text's apparent aspiration to imitate oral narration. One example follows:

> Most of the great flame-throwers were there and naturally, handling Big John de Conquer and his works. How he had done everything big on earth, then went up tuh heben without dying atall. Went up there picking a guitar and got all de angels doing the ring-shout round and round de throne . . . that brought them back to Tea Cake. How come he couldn't hit that box a lick or two? Well, all right now, make us know it. (p. 232)

Still another example is even more telling:

> Everybody was talking about it that night. But nobody was worried. The fire dance kept up till nearly dawn. The next day, more Indians moved east, unhurried but steady. Still a blue sky and fair weather. Beans running fine and prices good, so the Indians could be, *must* be, wrong. You couldn't have a hurricane when you're making seven and eight dollars a day picking beans. Indians are dumb anyhow, always were. Another night of Stew Beef making dynamic subtleties with his drum and living, sculptural, grotesques in the dance. (p. 229)

These instances of free indirect discourse are followed in the text by straight diegesis, which retains the dialect-informed echoes of the previous passage:

> Morning came without motion. The winds, to the tiniest, lisping baby breath had left the earth. Even before the sun gave light, dead day was creeping from bush to bush watching man. (p. 229)

There are many other examples of this curious voice (see pp. 75–76, 276). Hurston, in this innovation, is asserting that an entire narration could be rendered, if not in dialect, then in a dialect-informed discourse. This form of collective, impersonal free indirect discourse echoes Hurston's definition of "a mood come alive. Words walking without masters; walking altogether like harmony in a song." The ultimate sign of the dignity and strength of the black voice is this use of a dialect-informed free indirect discourse as narrative commentary beyond that which represents Janie's thoughts and feelings alone.

There are parodoxes and ironies in speakerly texts. The irony of this dialect-informed diction, of course, is that it is not a repetition of a language that anyone speaks; indeed, it can never be spoken. As several other scholars of free indirect discourse have argued, free indirect discourse is speakerless, by which they mean "the presentation of a perspective outside the normal communication paradigm that usually characterizes language."[42] It is literary language, meant to be read in a text. Its paradox is that it comes into use by Hurston so that discourse rendered through direct, indirect, or free indirect means may partake of Hurston's "word-pictures" and "thought-pictures," as we recall she defined the nature of Afro-American spoken language. "The white man thinks in a written language," she argued, "and the Negro thinks in hieroglyphics." The speakerly diction of *Their Eyes* attempts to render these pictures through the imitation of the extensively metaphorical medium of black speech, in an oxymoronic oral hieroglyphic that is meant only for the printed page. Its obvious oral base, nevertheless, suggests that Hurston conceived of it as a third language, as a mediating third term that aspires to resolve the tension between standard English and black vernacular, just as the narrative device of free indirect discourse aspires to define the traditional opposition between mimesis and diegesis as a false opposition. And perhaps this dialogical diction, and this dialogical narrative device, can serve as a metaphor for the critic of black comparative literature whose theoretical endeavor is intentionally double-voiced as well.

If Esu's double voice is figured in *Their Eyes Were Watching God* in the dialogical basis of free indirect discourse, it manifests itself in the fiction of Ishmael Reed in the sustained attempt to critique the strategies of narration central to certain canonical Afro-American texts through parody and pastiche. Like Hurston's text, we may think of Reed's novel as double-voiced, but in an essentially different way. Reed's relation to these authors in the tradition is at all points double-voiced, since he seems to be especially concerned with employing satire to utilize literature in what Frye calls "a special function of analysis, of breaking up the lumber of stereotypes, fossilized beliefs, superstitious terrors, crank theories, pedantic dogmatisms, oppressive fashions, and all other things that impede the free movement . . . of society."[43] Reed, of course, seems to be most concerned with the "free movement" of writing itself. In Reed's work, parody and hidden polemic overlap, in a process Bakhtin describes as follows: "When parody becomes aware of substantial resistance, a certain forcefulness and profundity in the speech act it parodies, it takes on a new dimension of complexity via the tones of the hidden polemic. . . . [A] process of inner dialogization takes place within the parodic speech act."[44] This "internal dialogization" can have curious implications, the most interesting of which perhaps is what Bakhtin describes as "the splitting of double-voice discourse into two speech acts, into two entirely separate and autonomous voices." The clearest evidence that Reed in *Mumbo Jumbo* is Signifyin(g) through parody as hidden polemic is his use of the two autonomous narrative voices in *Mumbo Jumbo*, which Reed employs in the manner of and renders through foregrounding, to parody the two simultaneous stories of detective narration, that of the present and that of the past, in a narrative flow that moves hurriedly from cause to effect. In *Mumbo Jumbo*, however, the second narrative, that of the past, bears an ironic relation to the first narrative, that of the present, because it comments on the other narrative as well as on the nature of its writing itself, in what Frye describes, in another context, as "the constant tendency to self-parody in satiric rhetoric which prevents even the process of writing itself from becoming an oversimplified convention or idea."[45] Reed's rhetorical strategy assumes the form of the relationship between the text and the criticism of that text, which "serves as discourse on that text." If Hurston's novel is a Signifyin(g) structure because it seems to be so concerned to represent Signifyin(g) rituals for their own sake, then Reed's text is a Signifyin(g) structure because he Signifies upon the tradition's convention of representation.

Notes

1. Hurston's revision of Douglass's apostrophe to the sails was suggested to me by Kimberly W. Benston. On chiasmus in *Their Eyes,* see Ephi Paul, "Mah Tongue is in Mah Friend's Mouf," unpublished essay, 10–12.

2. Thomas Hamilton, "Apology," *The Anglo-African Magazine* 1.1 (January 1859): 1.

3. W. J. Wilson, "The Coming Man," *The Anglo-African Magazine* 1.1 (February 1859): 58.

4. Frances E. W. Harper, letter to Thomas Hamilton, dated 1861.

5. A Lady from Philadelphia, "The Coming American Novelist," *Lippincott's Monthly Magazine* xxxvii (April 1886): 440–443.

6. Ibid., 441.

7. Ibid., 443.

8. Ibid. On Scarborough's citation, see note 12 below.

9. W. H. A. Moore, "A Void in Our Literature," *New York Age* 3. 4 (July 5, 1890): 3.

10. *Recorder,* August 1, 1893; *A.M.E. Church Review* xv (October 1898): 629–630. On

Scarborough, see note 11 below. For an excellent discussion of these positions, see August Meier, *Negro Thought in America, 1880–1915: Radical Ideologies in the Age of Booker T. Washington* (Ann Arbor: University of Michigan Press, 1969), 265–266.

11. W. S. Scarborough, "The Negro in Fiction as Portrayer and Portrayed," *Hampton Negro Conference*, No. 3 (Hampton, VA: Hampton Institute, 1899), 65–66.

12. Ibid., 67.

13. See "Dis and Dat: Dialect and the Descent," in Henry Louis Gates, Jr., *Figures in Black* (New York: Oxford University Press, 1986), 167–195.

14. Ibid., 22.

15. Johnson's 1932 comments are found in his "Preface" to Brown's *Southern Road*, reprinted in *The Collected Poems of Sterling A. Brown* (New York: Harper & Row, 1980), 16–17.

16. Jean Toomer, *Cane* (1923; New York: Harper & Row, 1969), 171–172. All subsequent references are to this edition and will be given parenthetically in the text.

17. George Schuyler, "Instructions for Contributors," reprinted in Eugene Gordon, "Negro Fictionist in America," *The Saturday Evening Quill* (April 1929): 20.

18. Scarborough, "The Negro in Fiction," 67.

19. I cite a definition of *skaz* deliberately, for this concept of Russian Formalism is similar to what I am calling the speakerly. See Victor Erlich, *Russian Formalism: History-Doctrine* (Mouton: The Hague, 1969), 238.

20. Richard Wright, *American Hunger* (New York: Harper & Row, 1979), 7.

21. Zora Neale Hurston, "How It Feels to Be Colored Me," *The World Tomorrow* (1928).

22. Zora Neale Hurston, *Their Eyes Were Watching God* (1937; Urbana: University of Illinois, 1978), 31–32. All subsequent references are to this edition and will be given parenthetically in the text.

23. Zora Neale Hurston, *Dust Tracks on a Road: An Autobiography* (Philadelphia: J. D. Lippincott, 1942), 94–95. Subsequent references will be given parenthetically.

24. Richard Wright, *Black Boy* (1945; New York: Harper & Row, 1966), 111.

25. See the epigraphs to this chapter.

26. John Hersey, "Interview with Ralph Ellison," in *The Language of Blackness*, ed. by Kimberly W. Benston and Henry Louis Gates, Jr., forthcoming.

27. Zora Neale Hurston, *Mules and Men: Negro Folktales and Voodoo Practices in the South* (1935; New York: Harper & Row, 1970), 161. Subsequent references will be given parenthetically.

28. The best discussion of the representation of black speech in Hurston's work is Karla Francesca Holloway, *A Critical Investigation of Literary and Linguistic Structures in the Fiction of Zora Neale Hurston*, Ph.D. dissertation, Michigan State University, 1978. See esp. pp. 93–94, and 101.

29. I wish to thank Barbara Johnson of Harvard University for calling my attention to this ironic mode of self-consciousness.

30. In a brilliant analysis of this scene of the novel, Barbara Johnson writes that "The entire paragraph is an externalization of Janie's feelings onto the outer surroundings in the form of a narrative of movement from private to public space. While the whole figure relates metaphorically, analogically, to the marital situation it is designed to express, it reveals the marriage space to be metonymical, a movement through a series of contiguous rooms. It is a narrative not of union but of separation centered on an image not of conjugality but of virginity." See Barbara Johnson, "Metaphor, Metonymy, and Voice in Zora Neale Hurston's *Their Eyes Were Watching God,"* in *Black Literature and Literary Theory,* ed. by H. L. Gates, Jr. (New York: Methuen, 1984), 205–219.

31. Cf. Johnson: "Janie's 'inside' is here represented as a store that she then goes in to inspect. While the former paragraph was an externalization of the inner, here we find an internalization of the outer; Janie's inner self *resembles* a store. The material for this metaphor is drawn from the narrative world of continguity; the store is the place where Joe has set himself up as lord, master, and proprietor. But here, Jody's image is broken, and reveals itself never to have been a metaphor, but only a metonymy, of Janie's dream: 'Looking at it she saw that it never was the flesh and blood *figure* of her dreams. Just something to drape her dreams over.'" Ibid.

32. Ibid.

33. See Roy Pascal, *The Dual Voice: Free Indirect Discourse and Its Functioning in the Nineteenth-Century European Novel* (Totowa, NJ: Rowman and Littlefield, 1977), 1–33.

34. See Brian McHale, "Free Indirect Discourse: A Survey of Recent Accounts," *PTL* 3 (1978): 249–287, for an excellent account of the controversy. I think the most lucid study is Michel Peled Ginsberg, "Free Indirect Discourse: Theme and Narrative Voice in Flaubert, George Eliot, and Verga," Ph.D. dissertation, Yale University, 1977. See also Stephen Ullmann, *Style in the French Novel* (Cambridge: Cambridge University Press, 1957).

35. In a sequel to this book, I would like to compare Hurston's use of free indirect discourse to that of other writers, especially Virginia Woolf.

36. Ginsberg, "Free Indirect Discourse," 34.

37. Ibid., 35.

38. Oswald Ducrot and Tzvetan Todorov, *Encyclopedic Dictionary of the Sciences of Language,* trans. by Catherine Porter (Baltimore: Johns Hopkins University Press, 1979), 303.

39. See Graham Hough, "Narration and Dialogue in Jane Austen," *The Critical Quarterly* xii (1970); and Pascal, *The Dual Voice,* 52.

40. McHale, "Free Indirect Discourse," 264–280.

41. Ginsberg, "Free Indirect Discourse," 23.

42. Janet Holmgren McKay, *Narration and Discourse in American Realistic Fiction* (Philadelphia: University of Pennsylvania Press, 1982), 19.

43. Northrop Frye, *Anatomy of Criticism: Four Essays* (Princeton, NJ: Princeton University Press, 1957), 233.

44. Mikhail Bakhtin, "Discourse Typology in Prose," 190.

45. Frye, *Anatomy of Criticism,* 234.

The Politics of Fiction, Anthropology, and the Folk

Zora Neale Hurston

HAZEL V. CARBY

◆   ◆   ◆

THE WORK OF Zora Neale Hurston, in particular the novel *Their Eyes Were Watching God,* has been the object of more than a decade of critical attention. But, in addition to the critical consideration of Hurston's writings, her work has received the level of institutional support necessary for Hurston to enter the American literary mainstream. Two examples of this support would be the special Hurston seminar held at the Modern Language Association annual conference in 1975 and the award of two grants from the National Endowment for the Humanities to Robert Hemenway to write Hurston's biography. Hurston's work has also received institutional support from publishers: The rights to reprint *Their Eyes Were Watching God* in a paperback edition were leased to the University of Illinois Press by Harper and Row, but the 1978 Illinois edition has been so profitable that Harper and Row refused to renew leasing contracts and is reprinting *Their Eyes, Jonah's Gourd Vine, Mules and Men,* and *Tell My Horse* themselves with Henry Louis Gates as series editor. During the years between Hemenway's biography and the new Harper and Row/Gates monopoly of Hurston, there have been a variety of anthologies and collections of Hurston's essays and short stories, and in 1984, a second edition of Hurston's autobiography, *Dust Tracks on a Road,* was published.[1]

As academics we are well aware that we work within institutions that police the boundaries of cultural acceptability and define what is and what is not "literature": Our work as teachers and as critics creates, maintains, and sometimes challenges boundaries of acceptability. Graduate students tell me that they teach *Their Eyes Were Watching God* at least once a semester; it is a text that is common to a wide variety of courses in African American Studies, American Studies, English, or Women's Studies. It is frequently the case that undergraduates in the Humanities may be taught the novel as many as four times, or at least once a year during their undergraduate careers. Traditions, of course, are temporal, and are constantly being fought over and renegotiated. Clearly, a womanist- and feminist-inspired desire to recover the neglected cultural presence of Zora Neale Hurston initiated an interest in her work, but it is also clear that this original motivation has become transformed. Hurston is not only a secured presence in the academy; she is a veritable industry, and an industry that is very profitable. The new Harper and Row edition of *Their Eyes* sold its total print run of 75,000 in less than a month.[2] The *New York Times* of February 4, 1990, published an article on Hurston called "Renaissance for a Pioneer of Black Pride" in which it was announced that a play based on Hurston's life and entitled "Zora Neale Hurston: A Theatrical Biography" was opening in New York, and that another play, "Mule Bone," a collaboration with Langston Hughes, is scheduled to open this summer.[3] On February 14, 1990, the Public Broadcasting System, in their prestigious American Playhouse series, broadcast "Zora is My Name" starring Ruby Dee in a dramatization of selections from *Mules and Men* and *Dust Tracks*. Although it could be said that Hurston has "arrived" as a contemporary, national, cultural presence, I await one further development: the announcement of a Hollywood movie.

I am as interested in the contemporary cultural process of the inclusion of Hurston into the academy as I am interested in her writing. I wonder about the relation between the cultural meanings of her work in the 1920s and 1930s and the contemporary fascination with Hurston. How is she being reread, now, to produce cultural meanings that this society wants or needs to hear? Is there, indeed, an affinity between the two discrete histories of her work? Certainly, I can see parallels between the situation of black intellectuals in the 1920s and 1930s, described now as a "Renaissance," and the concerns of black humanists in the academy in the 1980s. Literary histories could doubtless be written about a "renaissance" of black intellectual productivity within the walls of the academy in the post-civil rights era of the twentieth century.

Their Eyes Were Watching God now, of course, has a cultural existence outside of the realm of African American Studies and independent of scholars of the field, but how tenuous is this presence? Does the current fascination of the culture industry for the cultural production of black women parallel the white fascination for African American peoples as representatives of the exotic and primitive in the 1920s?[4] And will the current thirst for the cultural production of black women evaporate as easily? Will the economic crisis of the late 1980s and early 1990s be used, in a future literary history, to mark the demise of the black intellectual presence in the academy in the same way as the 1929 stock market crash has been used by literary historians to mark the death of the Harlem Renaissance? If there is a fragile presence of black peoples in universities, is our cultural presence secure or only temporarily profitable? With or without reference to our contemporary economic conditions, it is startlingly obvious that current college enrollment figures reveal a sharp fall in the numbers of black graduate students, figures which would seem to confirm the tenuous nature of our critical presence. But what I find most intriguing is the relation between a crisis of representation that shaped cultural responses to black urban migration after World War I and the contemporary crisis of representation in African American humanist intellectual work that determines our cultural and critical responses, or the lack of response, to the contemporary crisis of black urban America.[5]

However, let me make a theoretical intervention here. Edward Said has asserted that it is "now almost impossible . . . to remember a time when people were *not* talking about a crisis in representation," and he points to the enormous difficulties of uncertainty and undecidability that are a consequence of transformations "in our notions of formerly stable things such as authors, texts and objects."[6] In an attempt to be as specific as I can about the particular crisis of representation in black cultural production out of which, I am going to argue, Hurston's work emerges, I will try to define some terms.

The subaltern group that is the subject of Hurston's anthropological and fictional work is represented as the rural black folk. However, the process of defining and representing a subaltern group is always a contentious issue, and is at the heart of the crisis of representation in black intellectual thought in both historical moments.[7] The dominant way of reading the cultural production of what is called the Harlem Renaissance is that black intellectuals assertively established a folk heritage as the source of, and inspiration for, authentic African American art forms. In African American Studies the Harlem Renaissance has become a convention particularly for literary critics, but it is, as is the case with all literary histories, an imagined or created historical perspective that privileges some cultural developments while rendering other cultural and political histories invisible. The dominance of this particular literary history in our work, as opposed to organizing a history around a Chicago Renaissance, for example, has uncritically reproduced at the center of its discourse the issue of an authentic folk heritage. The desire of the Harlem intellectuals to establish and re-present African American cultural authenticity to a predominantly white audience was a mark of a change from, and confrontation with, what were seen by them to be externally imposed cultural representations of black people produced within, and supported by, a racialized social order. However, what was defined as authentic was a debate that was not easily resolved and involved confrontation among black intellectuals themselves. Alain Locke, for example, who attempted to signal a change or a break in conventions of representation by calling his collection of the work of some Harlem intellectuals *The New Negro,* assumed that the work of African American intellectuals would be to raise the culture of the folk to the level of art.[8] Locke's position has been interpreted by contemporary critics as being very different from, if not antagonistic to, the dominant interpretation of the work of Hurston, who is thought to reconcile the division between "high and low culture by becoming Eatonville's esthetic representative to the Harlem Renaissance."[9]

In 1934, Hurston published an essay called "Spirituals and Neo-Spirituals" in which she argues that there had "never been a presentation of genuine Negro spirituals to any audience anywhere." What was "being sung by the concert artists and glee clubs [were] the works of Negro composers or adaptors *based* on the spirituals."

> Glee clubs and concert singers put on their tuxedos, bow prettily to the audience, get the pitch and burst into magnificent song—but not *Negro* song. . . . let no one imagine that they are the songs of the people, as sung by them.[10]

Hurston was concerned to establish authenticity in the representation of popular forms of folk culture and to expose the disregard for the aesthetics of that culture through inappropriate forms of representation. She had no problem in using the term "the people" to register that she knew just who they were. But critics are incorrect to think that Hurston reconciled "high" and "low" forms of cultural production. Hurston's criticism were not reserved for the elitist manner in which she thought the authentic culture of the people was reproduced. The people she wanted to represent she defined as a rural folk, and she measured them and their cultural forms against an urban, mass culture. She recognized that the people whose culture she rewrote were not the majority of the population, and that the cultural forms she was most interested in reproducing were not being maintained. She complained bitterly about how "the bulk of the population now spends its leisure in the motion picture theatres or with the phonograph and its blues." To Hurston, "race records" were nothing more than a commercialization of traditional forms of music, and she wanted nothing more to do with them.[11]

Understanding these *two* aspects of Hurston's theory of folk culture is important. When Hurston complained about the ways in which intellectuals transformed folk culture by reproducing and reinterpreting it as high culture, she identified a class contradiction. Most African American intellectuals were generations removed from the "folk" they tried to represent. Their dilemma was little different from debates over proletarian fiction in the Soviet Union, in Europe, in the Caribbean, and in North America generally: debates that raged over the question of how and by whom should "the people," the masses of ordinary people, be portrayed.[12] Hurston identified herself as both an intellectual and as a representative figure from the folk culture she reproduced and made authentic in her work. However, asserting that she *was* both did not resolve the contradictions embedded in the social meanings of each category. When Hurston complained about "race records" and the commercialization of the blues, she failed to apply her own analysis of processes of cultural transformation. On the one hand, she could argue that forms of folk culture were constantly reworded and remade when she stated that "the folk tales" like "the spirituals are being made and forgotten every day."[13] But, on the other hand, Hurston did not take seriously the possibility that African American culture was being transformed as African American peoples migrated from rural to urban areas.

The creation of a discourse of "the folk" as a *rural* people in Hurston's work in the 1920s and 1930s displaces the migration of black people to cities. Her representation of African American culture as primarily rural and oral is Hurston's particular response to the dramatic transformations within black culture. It is these two processes that I am going to refer to as Hurston's discursive displacement of contemporary social crises in her writing. Hurston could not entirely escape the intellectual practice that she so despised, a practice that reinterpreted and redefined a folk consciousness in its own elitist terms. Hurston may not have dressed the spirituals in tuxedos but her attitude toward folk culture was not unmediated; she did have a clear framework of interpretation, a construct that enabled her particular representation of a black, rural consciousness.

Gayatri Spivak has pointed to an important dilemma in the issue of representing the subaltern. She sees "the radical intellectual in the West" as being caught either "in a deliberate choice of subalternity, granting to the oppressed . . . that very expressive subjectivity which s/he criticizes [in a post-structuralist theoretical world]" or, instead she faces the possibility of a total unrepresentability.[14] I don't know if the choice is always as bleak as Spivak claims, or is quite so simple and polarized. Langston Hughes, for example, in his use of the blues to structure poetry, represented a communal sensibility embedded in cultural forms and reproduced social meaning rather than individual subjectivity. In his blues poetry, the reader has access to a social consciousness through the reconstruction and representation of nonliterary, contemporary cultural forms that embodied the conditions of social transformation. Hurston, by contrast, assumed that she could obtain access to, and authenticate, an individualized social consciousness through a utopian reconstruction of the historical moment of her childhood in an attempt to stabilize and displace the social contradictions and disruption of her contemporary moment.

The issue of representing the subaltern, then, not only involves the relation of the intellectual to the represented, but also the relation of the intellectual to history. In Hurston's work, the rural black folk become an aesthetic principle, a means by which to embody a rich oral culture. Hurston's representation of the folk is not only a discursive displacement of the historical and cultural transformation of migration, but also is a creation of a folk who are outside of history. Hurston aggressively asserted that she was not of the "sobbing school of Negrohood"—in particular, to distinguish her work from that of Richard Wright—but she also places her version of authentic black cultural forms outside of the culture and history of contestation that informs his work. What the *New York Times* has recently called Hurston's "strong African-American sensibility" and is generally agreed to be her positive, holistic celebration of black life, also needs to be seen as a representation of "Negroness" as an unchanging, essential entity, an essence so distilled that it is an aesthetic position of blackness.

Hurston was a central figure in the cultural struggle among black intellectuals to define exactly who the people were that were going to become the representatives of the folk. Langston Hughes shaped his discursive category of the folk in direct response to the social conditions of transformation, including the newly forming urban working class and "socially dispossessed," whereas Hurston constructed a discourse of nostalgia for a rural community.[15] In her autobiographical writings, Hurston referenced the contradictory nature of the response of the black middle class and urban intellectuals to the presence of rural migrants to cities. In an extract written six months after completion of *Their Eyes Were Watching God,* Hurston describes this response:

> Say that a brown young woman, fresh from the classic halls of Barnard College and escorted by a black boy from Yale, enters the subway at 50th Street. They are well-dressed, well-mannered and good to look at . . .
>
> . . . the train pulls into 72nd Street. Two scabby-looking Negroes come scrambling into the coach. . . . but no matter how many vacant seats there are, no other place will do, except side by side with the Yale-Barnard couple. No, indeed! Being dirty and smelly, do they keep quiet otherwise? A thousand times, No! They woof, bookoo, broadcast. . . .
>
> Barnard and Yale sit there and dwindle and dwindle. They do not look around the coach to see what is in the faces of the white passengers. They know too well what is there. . . . "That's just like a Negro." Not just like *some* Negroes, mind you, no, like all. Only difference is some Negroes are better dressed. Feeling all of this like rock-salt under the skin, Yale and Barnard shake their heads and moan, "My People, My People!" . . .
>
> Certain of My People have come to dread railway day coaches for this same reason. They dread such scenes more than they do the dirty upholstery and other inconveniences of a Jim Crow coach. They detest the forced grouping. . . . So when sensitive souls are forced to travel that way they sit there numb and when some free soul takes off his shoes and socks, they mutter, "My race but not My taste." When somebody else eats fried fish, bananas, and a mess of peanuts and throws all the leavings on the floor, they gasp, "My skinfolks but not my kinfolks." And sadly over all, they keep sighing, "My People, My People!"[16]

This is a confrontation of class that signifies the division that the writer as intellectual has to recognize and bridge in the process of representing the people. It is a confrontation that was not unique to Hurston as intellectual, but it was one that she chose to displace in her decision to recreate Eatonville as the center of her representation of the rural folk.

The Eatonville of *Their Eyes Were Watching God* occupies a similar imaginative space to the mountain village of Banana Bottom in Claude McKay's novel of the same name published four years earlier.[17] McKay's Jamaican novel, set in the early 1900s, recreates the village where he grew up. Much of the argument of *Banana Bottom* emerges in the tension between attempts by missionaries to eradicate black cultural forms and the gentler forms of abuse present in white patronage of black culture. Against these forms of exploitation McKay reconstructs black culture as sustaining a whole way of life. But it is a way of life of the past, of his formative years, a place that the intellectual had to leave to become an intellectual and to which he does not return except in this Utopian moment. Eatonville, likewise, is the place of Hurston's childhood, a place to which she returns as an anthropologist. As she states in her introduction to *Mules and Men,* she consciously returns to the familiar,[18] and she recognizes that the stories she is going to collect, the ones she heard as a child, are a cultural form that is disappearing.[19]

In returning to and recreating the moment of her childhood, Hurston privileges the nostalgic and freezes it in time. Richard Wright, in his review of *Their Eyes Were Watching God,* accused Hurston of recreating minstrelsy. Though this remark is dismissed out of hand by contemporary critics, what it does register is Wright's reaction to what appears to him to be an outmoded form of historical consciousness. Whereas Wright attempted to explode the discursive category of the Negro as being formed, historically, in the culture of minstrelsy, and as being the product of a society structured in dominance through concepts of race, Hurston wanted to preserve the concept of Negroness, to negotiate and rewrite its cultural meanings, and, finally, to reclaim an aesthetically purified version of blackness. The consequences for the creation of subaltern subject positions in each of their works are dramatically different. The antagonism between them reveals Wright to be a modernist and leaves Hurston embedded in the politics of Negro identity.

Eatonville, as an anthropological and fictional space, appears in Hurston's work before her first anthropological expedition in 1927.[20] Not all the stories and anecdotes in *Mules and Men* originated from her research, and many appeared in different versions in different texts.[21] Rather than being valued primarily as a mode of scholarly inquiry, anthropology was important to Hurston because it enabled her to view the familiar and the known from a position of scientific objectivity, if not distance. She could not see her culture for wearing it, she said: "It was only when I was off in college, away from my native surroundings, that I could see myself like somebody else and stand off and look at my garment. Then I had to have the spy-glass of Anthropology to look through at that."[22] Anthropology, then, is seen by Hurston as providing a professional point of view. Ethnography becomes a tool in the creation of her discourse of the rural folk that displaces the antagonistic relations of cultural transformation.[23]

George Marcus and Michael Fischer have described the ways in which anthropology "developed the ethnographic paradigm" in the 1920s and 1930s. "Ethnographies as a genre," they argue, "had similarities with traveler and explorer accounts, in which the main narrative motif was the romantic discovery by the writer of people and places unknown to the reader."[24] Hurston shares this romantic and, it must be said, colonial imagination. Her representation of Eatonville in *Mules and Men* and in *Their Eyes Were Watching God* is both an attempt to make the unknown known and a nostalgic attempt to preserve a disappearing form of folk culture.[25] Marcus and Fischer argue that there are three dimensions to the criticism and ethnography offered of Western civilization:

> [T]hey—primitive man—have retained a respect for nature, and we have lost it (the ecological Eden); they have sustained close, intimate, satisfying communal lives, and we have lost this way of life (the experience of community); and they have retained a sense of the sacred in everyday life, and we have lost this (spiritual vision).[26]

Whereas the other students of Franz Boas, Margaret Mead and Ruth Benedict, turned to societies outside of Europe and North America to point to what the West had lost but the cultural "other" still retained, Hurston's anthropological work concentrated upon the cultural "other" that existed within the racist order of North America.

In 1935, Ruth Benedict published *Patterns of Culture*, in which she asserted that black Americans were an example of what happens "when entire peoples in a couple of generations shake off their traditional culture and put on the customs of the alien group. The culture of the American Negro in northern cities," she continued, "has come to approximate in detail that of the whites in the same cities."[27] With this emphasis in the school of anthropological thought that most influenced Hurston, anthropology provided her with not only a "spyglass" but with a theoretical paradigm that directed her toward rural, not urban, black culture and folk forms of the past, not the present.

Hurston, like Benedict, was concerned with the relationships among the lives and cultures that she reconstructed and her own search for a construction of the self.[28] She lived the contradictions of the various constructions of her social identity and rewrote them in *Their Eyes Were Watching God*. Her anthropological "spyglass," which she trained on the society that produced her, allowed her to return to that society in the guise of being a listener and a reporter. In her fictional return, Hurston represents the tensions inherent in her position as an intellectual—in particular as a writer—in antagonistic relation to her construction of the folk as community. It is in this sense that I think Hurston is as concerned with the production of a sense of self as she is with the representation of a folk consciousness through its cultural forms. Both, I would argue, are the motivating forces behind the use of anthropological paradigms in Hurston's work. But it is the relation and tension between the two, particularly the intellectual consciousness and the consciousness of the folk, that is present in the fictional world of *Their Eyes Were Watching God,* which is written between her two books of anthropology, *Mules and Men* and *Tell My Horse.* In this novel, we can see how Hurston brings into being a folk consciousness that is actually in a contradictory relation to her sense of herself as an intellectual.

Throughout the 1930s, Hurston is in search of a variety of formal possibilities for the representation of black rural folk culture. She produced three musicals—*From Sun to Sun, The Great Day,* and *Singing Steel*—because she was convinced that folk culture should be dramatized. She returned to fiction as a form after a gap of six years when she wrote "The Gilded Six Bits" in 1933, and *Jonah's Gourd Vine,* which was published in 1934. Then Hurston seriously considered pursuing a Ph.D. degree at Columbia in anthropology and folklore. After finalizing all the arrangements for the publication of *Mules and Men,* however, Hurston accompanied Alan Lomax on a trip to collect folk music for the Library of Congress in 1935. That fall she joined the Federal Theatre Project and was prominent in organizing its Harlem unit as well as producing a one-act play, "The Fiery Chariot." Between 1936 and 1938, Hurston spent a major part of her time in the Caribbean collecting material on voodoo practices. She spent six months in Jamaica, and *Their Eyes Were Watching God* was written while she was in Haiti.[29] In *Their Eyes* she reproduces Eatonville from a distance which is both geographical and metaphorical and politically inscribed with issues of gender and class. Hurston's work during this period, then, involves an intellectual's search for the appropriate forms in which to represent the folk and a decision to rewrite the geographical boundaries of representation by situating the southern, rural folk and patterns of migration in relation to the Caribbean rather than the northern states.

Henry Louis Gates, Jr. has explored in the great detail matters of voice in *Their Eyes Were Watching God* in relation to a politics of identity by tracing Hurston's construction of a protagonist engaged in a search "to become a speaking black subject."[30] On the other hand, Mary Helen Washington and Robert Stepto have both raised intriguing questions about Janie's *lack* of voice in the text. Washington relates this silencing of a female protagonist to her reading of *Jonah's Gourd Vine* and concludes that "Hurston was indeed ambivalent about giving a powerful voice to a woman like Janie who is already in rebellion against male authority and against the roles prescribed for women in a male dominated society."[31] However, both sides of this debate about the speaking or silent subject exist within the same paradigm of voice. I wish to introduce an alternative paradigm that suggests ways in which *Their Eyes Were Watching God* is a text concerned with the tensions arising from Hurston's position as writer in relation to the folk as community that she produces in her writing. In other words, I want to concentrate upon the contradictions that arise in the relation between writer, as woman and intellectual, and her construction of subaltern subject positions rather than remain within critical paradigms that celebrate black identity.

The two chapters that frame the story of Janie's life and are central to arguments about the ways in which Hurston prepares the fictional space in which Janie can tell her own story actually detail the antagonistic relation between Janie, as a woman alone, and the folk as community. The community sits "in judgment" as the figure of Janie, the protagonist, walks through the town to her house. This walk can be seen as analogous to crossing a stage and "running the gauntlet." Oral language, as it was embodied in the folktale in *Mules and Men,* was a sign of an authentic culture that enabled a people to survive and even triumph spiritually over their oppression. In the opening chapter of *Their Eyes Were Watching God,* however, oral language is represented as a "weapon," a means for the destruction and fragmentation of the self rather than a cultural form that preserves a holistic personal and social identity. Questions become "burning statements," and laughs are "killing tools" (p. 2). Janie has broken the boundaries of social convention and becomes the accused. She doesn't act appropriate for her age, which is "way past forty" (p. 3). (Hurston was forty-five years old at the time the text was written, but on various occasions took between seven and nineteen years off her age.)[32] Also inappropriate are the class codes that Janie threatens in her behavior and in her dress: as a middle-class widow she should not have associated with the itinerant Tea Cake; and as a middle-class woman, her "faded shirt and muddy overalls" are a comforting sign to the folk as community who can ease their antagonism and resentment with the thought that maybe she will "fall to their level someday" (p. 11).

Hurston increases the tension between her protagonist and the community to which she returns through a series of binary oppositions between the intellect, or mind, and speech. The process of the analysis by the anthropological self in *Mules and Men* is reversed by the creator of fiction in *Their Eyes Were Watching God.* In the former, the oral tale is a sign of a whole healthy culture and community; in the latter, the individual functions of speaking are isolated and lack a center. Janie responds to her victimization through synecdoche. The community is indicted as a "Mouth Almighty," a powerful voice that lacks intellectual direction. Far from being spiritually whole, the folk who are gathered on the porch are reduced to their various body parts: In each, an "envious heart makes a treacherous ear" (p. 5).[33] This is the context that determines Janie's refusal to tell her story directly to the community, a refusal that distinguishes her story from the directly told and shared folktale. In the process of transmitting Janie's story, Hurston requires an instrument of mediation between her protagonist and the folk, and it is Janie's friend Pheoby who becomes this mediator. When Janie decides to tell her story through her friend—"Mah tongue is in mah friend's mouf" (p. 5), she says—Hurston creates a figure for the form of the novel, a fictional world that can mediate and perhaps resolve the tension that exists in the difference between the socially constructed identities of "woman" and "intellectual" and the act of representing the folk.[34]

Hurston's particular form of mediation appears to be an alternative version of the anthropological spyglass that she needed to create a professional point of view between her consciousness of self and the subjects she was reproducing. Janie's definite refusal to tell her tale directly, as in a folktale, distinguishes not only her story from other stories that are communally shared, but also her position from that of the folk as community. Hurston's position as intellectual is reproduced as a relation of difference, as an antagonistic relationship between Janie and the folk. The lack in the folk figures, the absence of mind, or intellectual direction in the porch sitters, is symbolically present when Janie mounts her own porch.

In *Mules and Men,* the porch is the site for the expression of the folktale as an evocation of an authentic black culture. In *Their Eyes Were Watching God,* the porch is split and transformed. Whereas in *Mules and Men* the anthropological self is positioned on a figuratively unified porch, primarily as a listener and a recorder, in *Their Eyes Were Watching God* the anthropological role of listener is embedded in the folk as community and the role of recorder situated in the mediator—Pheoby/the text. In the novel, then, a listening *audience* is established for the narrative self, whereas in *Mules and Men* Hurston constructs a listening *anthropological subject.* It is Janie who can address and augment the lack in the folk as community and Janie who can unify the division between mind and mouth. Janie, of course, is placed in the subject position of intellectual and has the desire to "sit down and tell [the folk] things." Janie, as intellectual, has traveled outside of the community and defines herself as "a delegate to de big 'ssociation of life" (p. 6); her journey is the means by which knowledge can be brought into the community. As intellectual she creates subjects, grants individual consciousness, and produces understanding—the cultural meanings without which the tale is useless to the community—"taint no use in me telling you somethin' unless Ah give you de understandin' to go 'long wid it," Janie tells Pheoby. The conscious way in which subjectivity is shaped and directed is the act of mediation of the writer; it is this sense in which Pheoby becomes both Hurston's instrument of mediation and her text in an act of fictionalization.

The second part of the frame in the last chapter of *Their Eyes Were Watching God* opens with the resolution of the tension, division, and antagonism that are the subject of the opening chapter. The pattern of division of the first part of the frame is repeated: Janie is verbally condemned by the folk as community because she killed Tea Cake. The folk "lack" the understanding of the reasoning behind Janie's actions, but this deficiency is compensated for only through Janie's defense of herself in a court of law. The folk on the muck finally end their hostility to Janie when Sop explains that Tea Cake went crazy and Janie acted to protect herself. Reconciliation, then, between the position of intellectual and the folk as community takes place through acts of narration. The discursive unity that is maintained in the framing of the text prefigures the possibility for reconciliation between the position of Janie, as both intellectual and woman, and the folk as community when Pheoby provides them with the understanding of Janie's life through what will be another act of narration. *Their Eyes Were Watching God,* as such an act of narration itself, offers a resolution to the tension between Hurston, as intellectual, as writer, and the people she represents. In a paragraph that reproduces the tension in relation of the intellectual to the folk Hurston specifies the source of antagonism between Janie and the community as being a lack of knowledge.

> Now, Pheoby, don't feel too mean wid de rest of 'em 'cause dey's parched up from not knowin' things. Dem meatskins is *got* tuh rattle tuh make out they's alive. Let 'em consolate theyselves wid talk. 'Course, talkin' don't amount tuh uh hill uh beans when yuh can't do nothin' else. And listenin' tuh dat kind uh talk is jus' lak openin' yo' mouth and lettin' de moon shine down yo' throat. It's uh known fact, Pheoby, you got tuh *go* there tuh *know* there. Yo' papa and yo' mama and nobody else can't tell yuh and show yuh. Two things everybody's got tuh do fuh theyselves. They got tuh go tuh God, and they got tuh find out about livin' fuh theyselves. (p. 183)

The passage that I have quoted here is the final paragraph in Janie's story. It gains authority from claiming the tone of the preacher and the pedagogue, and at the same time it evokes the dilemma of the intellectual. Hurston's journey away from the community that produced her and that she wants to reproduce has provided her with a vision of an alternative world. Although it is not actually present in the text, the novel ends with the possibility that that history could be brought into the community and suggests that Pheoby/the text is the means for accomplishing the transformation necessary to reconcile difference. However, as a woman and as an intellectual, Hurston has to negotiate both gendered and classed constructions of social identity and subjectivities.

Critics often forget that Janie is a protagonist whose subject position is defined through class, that she can speak on a porch because she *owns* it. The contradictions between her appearance in overalls, a sign of material lack, and the possession of nine hundred dollars in the bank are important. Hurston's anthropological trips for *Mules and Men* were financed by a patron, Mrs. Osgood Mason, to whom she dedicates the text. The folklore material that Hurston had collected she could not freely utilize as she wished: Mason had made it abundantly clear that she claimed proprietary ownership of all of that ethnographic material. Hurston traveled to Jamaica and Haiti on her own Guggenheim grant, and, when she was writing *Their Eyes,* she must have pleasured in the sense that no one else could claim ownership of her words and her work. However, the problem is that providing her protagonist with the financial independence that Hurston herself must have found necessary in order to occupy a position from which to write reinforces the division between Janie and her community. The text here echoes Janie's grandmother's demand for a place like the white woman's, a place on high. The fact that Janie does indeed mount and own her porch enables the story, but also permeates it with a bourgeois discourse that differentiates her from the folk as community.

But this intellectual and property owner is also a woman, and thus the problem of representation here is also a question of how a woman can write her story within a site that is male-dominated and patriarchally defined. In *Mules and Men,* Hurston addresses the social constitution of gender roles in particular tales and through brief narratives that describe the relations among the tale-tellers on the porch, but she does not inscribe a concern with gender within the terms of the professional role of the anthropologist itself.[35] However, the role of listener had its limitations. Hurston's conscious reversal of the role of anthropologist reveals the contradictions inherent in the processes through which an intellectual, an intellectual who is also a woman, can instruct a community about what is outside of its social consciousness. This is the problem that frames the novel. The final metaphor of the horizon as a "great fish-net" with "so much of life in its meshes" (p. 184) that Janie pulls in and drapes around herself is an appropriate image for a writer who can recreate and represent a social order in her narrative. But what this metaphor also confirms is the distance between the act of representation and the subjects produced through that act of representation. The assertion of autonomy implicit in this figuration of a discourse that exists only for the pleasure of the self displaces the folk as community utterly and irrevocably.

I have suggested ways in which the narrative strategies of *Mules and Men* and *Their Eyes Were Watching God* are different and yet similar in that they both evoke the romantic imagination so characteristic of ethnography in the 1930s. If, as Marcus and Fischer suggest, the main narrative motif of ethnography is the "romantic discovery by the writer of people and places unknown to the reader," then *Mules and Men* both discovers the rural folk and acts to make known and preserve a form of culture that embodies a folk consciousness. The folk as community remain the "other" and exist principally as an aesthetic device, a means for creating an essential concept of blackness. The framing of that novel is the process of working out, or mapping, a way of writing and discovering the subject position of the intellectual in relation to what she represents.

Hurston's journey to Jamaica and two trips to Haiti produced *Tell My Horse*, a text that Robert Hemenway has dismissed as Hurston's "poorest book." Hemenway argues that Hurston "was a novelist and folklorist, not a political analyst or traveloguist."[36] I would agree that Hurston's overtly political comments in *Tell My Horse* are usually reactionary, blindly patriotic, and, consequently, superficial. The dominant tendency in Hurston scholarship has been to ignore or dismiss as exceptional some of her more distasteful political opinions but, as Marcus and Fischer have explained, the ethnology and travelogue share a romantic vision (and I would add a colonial or imperial vision), making *Tell My Horse* not an exception to Hurston's work at this moment in her life but an integral part of it. In the second chapter of Part Two of *Mules and Men*, the section entitled "Hoodoo," Hurston shifts away from a concern to record and preserve a particular form of black culture, the folktale, and toward a desire to create the boundaries of a cultural world in a relation of difference to the dominant culture. The geographical boundaries of Hurston's black folk are rural, but their Southernness is not defined through a difference to Northernness as much as it is related to cultural practices and beliefs of the Caribbean. This shift is clear when Hurston, the anthropologist, moves from Florida to New Orleans and seeks to become a pupil of a "hoodoo doctor."[37]

In her introduction to *Mules and Men*, Hurston explains that she chose

Florida as a site for the collection of folklore not only because it was familiar but because she saw Florida as "a place that draws people . . . Negroes
from every Southern state . . . and some from the North and West. So I
knew it was possible for me to get a cross section of the Negro South in one
state."³⁸ In the section of *Mules and Men* that is situated in Louisiana, we can
see a shift in Hurston's work to a stress on a continuity of cultural beliefs
and practices with beliefs and practices in the Caribbean. In *Their Eyes Were
Watching God* this system of reference is continued through the way in
which Hurston discursively displaces the urban migration of black people
in the continental United States. In her novel, as in *Mules and Men,* migration is from the Southern states further south to Eatonville, Florida. Migration in a northerly direction is undertaken only by the Barbadians who
join Janie and Tea Cake on the "muck." After the completion of her novel,
Hurston continued her search for an appropriate vehicle for the expression
of black culture in *Tell My Horse*—a first-person account of her travels in
Jamaica and Haiti. Part Three of *Tell My Horse* completes the journey, initiated in *Mules and Men,* in search of the survival of the ritual and practices of
Vodoun.³⁹

The geographic boundaries that enclose *Their Eyes Were Watching God* en-
large our understanding of the metaphoric boundaries of self and community. The discourse of the folk, which I have argued is irrevocably displaced
in the figuration of a discourse of individualized autonomy existing only for
the pleasure of the self, is dispersed and fragmented in a narrative of
Hurston's personal initiation into African religious practices in the diaspora.
Hurston does not return again to a romantic vision of the folk. Her next
book, *Moses, Man of the Mountain,* is an extension of her interest in the relations
between and across black cultures because it rewrites in fictional terms the
worship of Moses and the worship of Damballah that had first interested
her in Haiti.⁴⁰ This figuration of Moses/Damballah also transforms questions about the relation of the intellectual to the folk as community into an
exploration of the nature of leaders and leadership. The intricate inquiry
into the construction of subject positions, as writer, as woman, and as intellectual, is also not repeated. In *Dust Tracks on a Road,* an apparently autobiographical act, Hurston ignores her earlier attempts to represent the complexity of the relationship between public and private constructions of the
self. She continues, however, to displace the discourse of a racial social order
and maintains the exclusion of the black subject from history. This is the
gesture that eventually wins her the recognition and admiration of the
dominant culture in the form of the Anisfield-Wolf Award for the contribution of *Dust Tracks on a Road* to the field of race relations.⁴¹

We need to return to the question why at this particular moment in our society, *Their Eyes Were Watching God* has become such a privileged text. Why is there a shared assumption that we should read the novel as a positive holistic celebration of black life? Why is it considered necessary that the novel produce cultural meanings of authenticity, and how does cultural authenticity come to be situated so exclusively in the rural folk?

I would like to suggest that, as cultural critics, we could begin to acknowledge the complexity of our own discursive displacement of contemporary conflict and cultural transformation in the search for black cultural authenticity. The privileging of Hurston at a moment of intense urban crisis and conflict is, perhaps, a sign of that displacement: large parts of black urban America under siege; the number of black males in jail in the 1980s doubled. The news media have recently confirmed what has been obvious to many of us for some time—that one in four young black males are in prison, on probation, on parole, or awaiting trial, and young black children face the prospect of little, inadequate, or no health care. Has *Their Eyes Were Watching God* become the most frequently taught black novel because it acts as a mode of assurance that, really, the black folk are happy and healthy?

Richard Wright has recently been excluded from contemporary formations of the African-American canon because he brought into fictional consciousness the subjectivity of a *Native Son* created in conditions of aggression and antagonism,[42] but, perhaps, it is time that we should question the extent of our dependence upon the romantic imagination of Zora Neale Hurston to produce cultural meanings of ourselves as native daughters.

Notes

1. I would like to thank Richard Yarborough for his helpful suggestions and corrections made to an earlier version of this manuscript. The editions cited in the text are as follows: Robert E. Hemenway, *Zora Neale Hurston: A Literary Biography* (Urbana: University of Illinois Press, 1977); Zora Neale Hurston, *Their Eyes Were Watching God* (New York: Harper and Row, 1990); Hurston, *Dust Tracks on a Road* (New York: Harper and Row, 1990); Hurston, *Mules and Men: Negro Folktales and Voodoo Practices in the South* (New York: Harper and Row, 1990); Hurston, *Tell My Horse* (New York: Harper and Row, 1990).

2. Personal communication with Henry Louis Gates, Jr. (February 1990).

3. Rosemary L. Bray, "Renaissance for a Pioneer of Black Pride," *New York Times* (February 4, 1990).

4. A more detailed consideration of this parallel would need to examine what

Nelson George calls "selling race." The ability of the record industry to market and make a profit from "black talent performing black music" in the 1920s could be interestingly compared to the highly profitable publishing of the work of black women writers, the Book of the Month Club's distribution of Alice Walker's novel *The Color Purple* and the subsequent film of the same name, and the success of Spike Lee's *She's Gotta Have It* and *School Daze.* See Nelson George, *The Death of Rhythm and Blues* (New York: Pantheon, 1988), 8–9.

    5. Hazel V. Carby, *Reconstructing Womanhood: The Emergence of the Afro-American Woman Novelist* (New York: Oxford University Press, 1987), 163–166.

    6. Edward W. Said, "Representing the Colonized: Anthropology's Interlocutors," *Critical Inquiry* 15 (Winter 1989): 205–206.

    7. See Gayatri Chakravorty Spivak, *In Other Worlds: Essays in Cultural Politics* (New York: Methuen, 1987), 197–221. Spivak identifies and elaborates upon the concern of the work of subaltern studies with change as "confrontations rather than transition" and the marking of change through "function changes in sign systems." This rather awkward phrase, "function changes in sign systems," becomes in the process of Spivak's analysis the somewhat shorter phrase "discursive displacements."

    8. See, for example, Hemenway, *Zora Neale Hurston,* 50.

    9. Ibid., 56.

    10. Hurston, "Spirituals and Neo-Spirituals," in *The Sanctified Church* (Berkeley, CA: Turtle Island, 1981), 80–81.

    11. Hemenway, *Zora Neale Hurston,* 92.

    12. See Hazel V. Carby, "Proletarian or Revolutionary Literature: C. L. R. James and the Politics of the Trinidadian Renaissance," *South Atlantic Quarterly* 87 (Winter 1988): 39–52.

    13. Hurston, "Spirituals and Neo-Spirituals," 79.

    14. Spivak, *In Other Worlds,* 209.

    15. See Ralph Ellison, "Recent Negro Fiction," *New Masses* 40 (August 5, 1941): 22–26.

    16. Hurston, *Dust Tracks on a Road,* 292–294.

    17. Claude McKay, *Banana Bottom* (New York: Harper & Row, 1933).

    18. Hurston, *Mules and Men,* 17–19.

    19. Ibid., 24.

    20. See Hurston, "The Eatonville Anthology," *Messenger* 8 (Sept., Oct., Nov., 1926): 261–262, 297, 319, 332.

    21. See Arnold Rampersad's comments in his introduction to the new edition of *Mules and Men* (New York: Harper and Raw, 1990), xxii–xxiii.

    22. Hurston, *Mules and Men,* 17.

    23. See Hemenway, *Zora Neale Hurston,* 221, who calls this reconstruction of Eatonville idealized but feels that Hurston chose to assert positive images "because

she did not believe that white injustice had created a pathology in black behavior."
I remain unconvinced by this argument because it simplifies to a level of binary oppositions between positive and negative images what are very complex processes of
representation. It is interesting that Hemenway seems to realize this inadequacy in
the next paragraph when he raises but cannot resolve the problem of "professional
colonialism" in Hurston's anthropological stance.

24. George E. Marcus and Michael E. Fischer, *Anthropology as Cultural Critique: An
Experimental Moment in the Human Sciences* (Chicago: University of Chicago Press, 1986),
129, 24.

25. Hurston's desire to make black people and culture known is evident in letters she wrote to James Weldon Johnson. See Zora Neale Hurston to James Weldon
Johnson, January 22, 1934, in which she complains that the J. B. Lippincott Company
is "not familiar with Negroes"; and May 8, 1934, in which she says about the review
of *Jonah's Gourd Vine* in the *New York Times* that she "never saw such a lack of information about us." Both letters are in the James Weldon Johnson Collection, Beinecke
Library, Yale University.

26. Marcus and Fischer, *Anthropology as Cultural Critique*, 129.

27. Ruth Benedict, *Patterns of Culture* (Boston: Houghton Mifflin, 1934), 13.

28. See Margaret Mead's introduction to *Patterns of Culture*, written in 1958, which
opens the 1959 edition, ix.

29. Hemenway, *Zora Neale Hurston*, 184–185, 202–227, 230.

30. Henry Louis Gates, Jr., *The Signifying Monkey: A Theory of Afro-American Literary
Criticism* (New York: Oxford University Press, 1988), 170–216.

31. Mary Helen Washington, *Invented Lives: Narratives of Black Women 1860–1960* (New
York: Doubleday, 1987), 245. Washington's re-reading of *Their Eyes Were Watching God* is
an admirable analysis of the ways in which this text has been romanticized, and ini-
tiates the important work of comparative analysis across texts. It was this essay that
first encouraged and inspired me to follow her lead and think seriously of the relations between Hurston's texts. See also Robert Stepto, *From Behind the Veil: A Study of
Afro-American Narrative* (Urbana: University of Illinois Press, 1979), 164–167.

32. See Hemenway's introduction to the second edition of *Dust Tracks on a
Road*, xi.

33. I am grateful to Richard Yarborough for pointing out to me that of course,
this aphorism is itself drawn from oral tradition. My emphasis is that in its applica-
tion at this point in the novel, it stresses division.

34. I am implicitly arguing, therefore, that it is necessary to step outside questions of voice and issues of third-person (as opposed to first-person) narration in
order to understand why Hurston needs an instrument of mediation between the
teller of the tale and the tale itself.

35. This may have been because other women like Mead and Benedict were also

using the role of anthropologist as a position from which to accumulate knowledge that was both authoritative and scientific. But this is just a guess. The relations among these three anthropologists have not been explored, as far as I know, but a comparative examination of the nature of their work would seem to be an interesting area for future study.

36. Hemenway, *Zora Neale Hurston,* 248–249.

37. Hurston, *Mules and Men,* 239.

38. Ibid., 17.

39. It would be fruitful to explore the relationship between Hurston's interest in and use of the Caribbean in these years with the cultural production of intellectuals who turned to the Caribbean, in particular the island of Haiti, as a source for an alternative revolutionary black history. I am thinking here, among other works, of the production of the play *Toussaint L'Ouverture* by C. L. R. James, which opened in London in March 1936 starring Paul Robeson, and the publication, in 1938, of *Black Jacobins;* Jacob Lawrence's series of paintings on Touissaint L'Ouverture, 1937–38; Langston Hughes's *Troubled Island* written for, but never produced by, the Federal Theatre; and the New York Negro Federal Theatre production of *Macbeth,* often referred to as the "voodoo" *Macbeth,* directed by Orson Welles in 1936. Other black units in the Federal Theatre performed *Black Empire,* by Christine Ames and Clarke Painter, and *Haiti,* by William Du Bois, a journalist for the *New York Times.*

40. Hurston, *Tell My Horse,* 139–140.

41. Hemenway, introduction to Hurston, *Dust Tracks,* ix.

42. See Henry Louis Gates, Jr., *The Signifying Monkey: A Theory of Afro-American Literary Criticism,* 118–120 and 181–184.

The Erotics of Talk

"That Oldest Human Longing" in
Their Eyes Were Watching God

CARLA KAPLAN

◆　◆　◆

"Mah tongue is in mah friend's mouf"
—*Their Eyes Were Watching God*

"That Oldest Human Longing"

Reduced to its basic narrative components, Zora Neale Hurston's *Their Eyes Were Watching God* is the story of a young woman in search of an orgasm. From the moment Janie is "summoned to behold a revelation" and witnesses the "panting," "frothing," "ecstatic," "creaming" fulfillment of a blossoming pear tree,[1] her quest is set; she wants, as she puts it, "tuh utilize mahself all over" (p. 169). The novel was written in a cultural context of multiple sanctions against any representation of black female sexuality.[2] Nonetheless, Hurston's description of Janie's "revelation" is one of the sexiest passages in American literature:

> It was a spring afternoon in West Florida. Janie had spent most of the day under a blossoming pear tree in the back-yard. . . . She was stretched on her back beneath the pear tree soaking in the alto chant of the visiting bees, the gold of the sun and the panting breath of the breeze when the inaudible voice of it all came to her. She saw a dust-bearing bee sink into the sanctum of a bloom; the thousand sister-calyxes arch to meet the love embrace and the ecstatic shiver of the tree from root to tiniest branch creaming in every blossom and frothing with delight. . . . Janie felt a pain remorseless sweet that left her limp and languid. (pp. 23–24)[3]

But Janie's chances of fulfillment seem very attenuated. As her grand-mother describes it, all Janie can expect is to tote "de load" and bear "de burden": "De nigger woman is de mule uh de world so fur as Ah can see" (p. 29).

Not surprisingly, Janie does not see herself as the possible agent of the ecstacy she has witnessed, but rather as a fairy tale or modern romance heroine, "looking, waiting, breathing short with impatience" (p. 25) for her prince—or in this case her bee—to come. But Janie mistakes the nature of the "revelation" she has been "summoned to behold." Mistakenly con-cluding, after watching the pear tree's "creaming" and "frothing," that "this was a marriage!" (p. 24), Janie is married three times: first to Logan Killicks, a man whose head is "long one way" and "flat on de sides" and "whose toe-nails look lak mule foots" (p. 42), but who happens to possess sixty acres, a mule, and an organ (musical); second, to Jody Starks, who "did not represent sun-up and pollen and blooming trees, but . . . spoke for the far horizon" (p. 50); and third, to Vergible "Tea Cake" Woods, a gambler who plays guitar, is twelve years younger than Janie, and "looked like the love thoughts of women" (p. 161). Tea Cake, Janie decides, "could be a bee to a blossom—a pear tree blossom in the spring" (p. 161).

As the novel opens, this third marriage has ended in tragedy and Janie has just settled down on her porch, back home, to tell her story to her best friend Pheoby Watson. This conversation, in which "Pheoby's hungry listening helped Janie to tell her story" (p. 23), is the frame that opens and closes the novel and its most lyrical scene. The meaning of Janie's pear tree "revelation," it turns out, is not marriage or a husband or sex, but talk itself, the experience of conversation, the act of storytelling and self-narration. It is only in telling her story to Pheoby that Janie finally is able to satisfy "that oldest human longing—self revelation" (p. 18). Only in tell-ing her story to Pheoby does she fulfill her quest for the satisfaction she be-held under the pear tree.[4] Telling her story to Pheoby supplies the erotic fulfillment Janie misunderstands as "marriage," and in this sense Pheoby, whose "hungry listening helped Janie to tell her story," is the "bee" to Janie's "blossom."

"Hungry Listening"

Why does Hurston begin her novel with a woman awakening to her sexuality—an extremely bold move in a context in which black woman's sexuality, as Gloria Naylor puts it, had been "deadened to the point of invisibility"[5] by white racist stereotypes of licentiousness and promiscuity as well as by black admonitions to counter such stereotypes with images of asexual purity—and then rewrite desire itself as the desire to tell one's story? Why does she foreground female sexuality only to represent "the oldest human longing" as the longing to talk? Is the figuration of Pheoby as Janie's "bee" a lesbian alternative to romantic ideology and heterosexual narrative teleology or simply a sororal, asexual bond? Is Hurston participating in the long history of silencing black women's sexuality by displacing it onto safer, more legitimate, less controversial pleasures? Or is she eroticizing narration and conversation?

Some critics might respond that narrative is always already eroticized, that it has the form of sexual desire, or that narrative is always a search for a fit listener. As Mikhail Bakhtin, for example, puts it, "this orientation toward the listener is usually considered the basic constitutive feature of rhetorical discourse."[6] In Charles Taylor's argument, recognition from others not only "meets a vital human need" but is a particular feature of modern society. Our specifically *modern* preoccupation with identity, he writes, inflects demands for recognition in particularly pressing ways: "The thesis is that our identity is partly shaped by the recognition of its absence, often by the misrecognition of others, and so a person or group can suffer real damage, real distortion, if the people or society around them mirror back to them a confusing, or demeaning, or contemptible picture of themselves. Non- or misrecognition can inflict harm, can be a form of oppression, imprisoning someone in a false, distortive and reduced mode of being."[7]

Following Taylor's argument, one would expect that misrecognized and demeaned social groups—blacks, women, Asians, Latinos, lesbians and gays, and others—would be particularly invested in narrative as a means of reconstructing damaged identities. And indeed, critics of African American, Asian American, Latin American, gay, and women's writing often advance this argument, sometimes in broad claims for the therapeutic and revolutionary potential of narrative self-revelation.[8]

Hurston's construction of sexual desire as a longing to talk, of "that oldest human longing" as "self-revelation" (p. 18), seems to value narrative accordingly, as a means of recognition and identity-formation.

Most critics argue that *Their Eyes Were Watching God* is about Janie's acquisition of voice and that her trajectory from silence to speech demonstrates how self-narration can generate recognition and constitute subjectivity.[9] Houston Baker, for example, argues that Janie acquires a "blues" voice.[10] Henry Louis Gates, Jr. describes the novel as the story of "the quest of a

silent black woman . . . to find a voice."¹¹ Similarly, Barbara Johnson
has advanced a reading of Janie's voice which maps her self-articulation in
terms of a "division into inside and outside,"¹² a thesis Karla Holloway
shares in her argument that "Janie gains her voice from the available voice
of the text and subsequently learns to share it with the narrator."¹³ And
Susan Lanser maintains that "Hurston's novel is indeed a record of Janie
Crawford's struggle to find voice and through voice an identity."¹⁴

Janie never does *acquire* a voice, however, but had one, in fact, all along.
She is a "born orator" (p. 92), an able preacher, and she is also adept at
using words as a "weapon" when she wants to. Indeed, when she tells Jody
that "when you pull down yo' britches, you look lak de change uh life"
(p. 123), her words prove lethal. The number of times when Janie is violently silenced by others testifies to the power, both potential and real, of
her voice. Nor does telling her story develop or enable Janie's voice; such
telling is only the final instance of verbal skills Janie displays throughout
the novel. Hurston's conception of narrative's social and psychological status is a very skeptical one. She does not represent narrative as constitutive
of social or personal identity. And for her, its salutary psychosocial outcome is always contingent and circumscribed, never guaranteed.

While contingency may seem implicit in the very idea that the narrative
or dialogic encounter serves a *need,* it is often taken for granted, as I have argued elsewhere,¹⁵ that the interactive reading or listening process itself
transforms its readers or listeners, that narrative has the means, as Hans
Robert Jauss put it, "to create an interlocutor capable of understanding."¹⁶

But feminist and African American fiction, I would contend, often seeks
to dramatize its *lack* of listeners, the impossibility of finding competent—let
alone ideal—interlocutors and therefore the impossibility of satisfying a
"longing" for talk. When Janie pines for a "kissing bee" what she is really
longing for is that elusive but necessary listener: "She was seeking confirmation of the voice and vision, and everywhere she found and acknowledged
answers. A personal answer for all other creations except herself. She felt an
answer seeking her, but where? When? How? . . . She had glossy leaves
and bursting buds and she wanted to struggle with life but it seemed to
elude her. Where were the singing bees for her? Nothing on the place nor in
her grandma's house answered her" (pp. 24–25).

The provision of Janie's ideal listener in Pheoby's "hungry listening,"
the description of Janie and Pheoby as "kissin'-friends," (p. 19) does more
than simply substitute a lesbian erotic for the heterosexual formula of narrative erotics—"tumescence and detumescence," "tension and resolution," "intensification to the point of climax and consummation"¹⁷—

which many consider basic to all narrative. It frees Janie from either the juridical/attestory narrative position typical of slave narratives trying to win the approval of hostile, usually uncomprehending listeners or the seductive narrative position typical of white women's romances which seek to captivate their listeners as their heroines seek to captivate the hero. And it inscribes the novel's various historical and implied readers into its form, highlighting disjunctions between implied and ideal readers.

"Why Don't They Come Kiss and Be Kissed?"

Janie's refusal of attestory or seductive narrative positions is initially evident in her refusal to tell her story to one of the novel's potential audiences: the townspeople who are crowded eagerly on their porches, sitting in "judgment" like "lords of sounds and lesser things," passing "nations through their mouths" (p. 10), hoping to hear what happened to Janie since she left town with Tea Cake. The townspeople, or as Janie calls them, "Mouth-Almighty," use their mouths as weapons to chew up, "gnaw on," (p. 17) and "swallow and relish" (p. 10) all the unkind thoughts they can. As Pheoby leaves "Mouth-Almighty" to welcome Janie home and bring her some dinner, she feels them "pelting her back with unasked questions. They hoped the answers were cruel and strange" (p. 14). "Ah don't mean to bother wid tellin' 'em nothing," Janie declares to Pheoby. "Tain't worth de trouble" (p. 17). She reiterates this important resolve to keep her story to herself midway through the novel, when she declares, "Ah ain't puttin' it in de street. Ah'm tellin' *you*" (p. 172, italics in original), and again when she finishes telling her story to Pheoby. While she feels some sympathy, she says, for how "parched up [they are] from not knowin' things" (p. 285), she warns Pheoby not to waste her breath on people whose conversation is all one-sided, people who are, literally, all talk: "Dem meatskins is *got* tuh rattle tuh make out they's alive," she says to Pheoby. "Let 'em consolate theyselves wid talk" (p. 285).

Janie's response to the way "Mouth-Almighty" "made burning statements with questions, and killing tools out of laughs" (p. 10) is to ask Pheoby "if they wants to see and know why they don't come kiss and be kissed? Ah could then sit down and tell 'em things" (p. 18). This kiss metaphor is one of the novel's central tropes.[18] It not only makes talk and sex coterminous but at the same time encodes the practices of discursive reciprocity that define what we might call the ethos of this novel's erotics of talk. In a stunning reversal of standard literary practice, Hurston resituates narrative reliability in terms of the reader rather than the narrator and makes fidelity to this discursive ethos an implicit principle of readerly competence.[19]

Hurston relies on this trope particularly strongly in the beginning of the novel to set up the social and discursive situations within which Janie must operate. Nanny, for example, articulates her anxieties about Janie's marital expectations through the metaphor of the kiss, or better, the difference between different kinds of kisses: "'Humph!'" Nanny says, "'don't 'spect all dat tuh keep up. He ain't kissin' yo' mouf when he carry on over yuh lak dat. He's kissin' yo' foot and 'tain't in uh man tuh kiss foot long. Mouf kissin' is on uh equal and dat's natural but when dey got to bow down tuh love, dey soon straightens up'" (p. 40–41).

Pheoby and Janie, moreover, are "kissin'-friends" (p. 19). And it is in the opening stages of Janie telling Pheoby her story that this important trope is first worked out. The darkness surrounding the porch is "kissing," the bees are "kissing bees," and Janie expresses her trust in Pheoby's ability to speak for her with the metaphor "mah tongue is in mah friend's mouf" (p. 17). This figuration goes beyond "female bonding"[20] to suggest not only the intimate familiarity of their friendship and its erotic tracings, but also both the intimacy and eros necessary for a successful discursive "self revelation." It is hard to imagine a more apt expression for an eroticized image of competent listening and satisfying talk.

Because the townspeople don't understand "mouf kissin" and don't know enough to "kiss and be kissed," they cannot possibly be competent listeners for Janie. The ethos of reciprocity and equality Hurston expresses in the trope of "mouf kissin" helps explain why if the oldest human longing is self-revelation we have a story about a character distinguished by her *lack* of listeners and her *refusal* to tell her own story. Whereas Pheoby's "hungry listening" helps Janie to tell her story and earns Pheoby the right to hear it, this novel sees something shameful in telling a story to hostile or incompetent audiences.

The figure of Annie Tyler haunts this novel—although she is a relatively minor character—because she represents the sexual and verbal humiliation Janie manages to escape. Having left town a widow (like Janie) and gone off (like Janie) with a much younger man, Annie Tyler returns a ruined woman:

> Hair all gray and black and bluish and reddish in streaks. All the capers that cheap dye could cut was showing in her hair. Those slippers bent and griped just like her work-worn feet. The corset gone and the shaking old

woman hanging all over herself. Everything that you could see was hanging. Her chin hung from her ears and rippled down her neck like drapes. Her hanging bosom and stomach and buttocks and legs that draped down to her ankles. She groaned but never giggled.

She was broken and her pride was gone, so she told those who asked what had happened.

. . . They put her to bed and sent for her married daughter from up around Ocala to come see about her. The daughter came as soon as she could and took Annie Tyler away to die in peace. (pp. 178–179, my italics)

Telling her story is the *sine qua non* of her shame and collapse. Rather than constitute subjectivity, in other words, self-revelation may destroy it and even lead to death. Staging one's private misery in public is nothing but self-abasement and self-destruction. The fact that Annie Tyler never actually appears in the novel but is only described in the third person only renders her discursive self-erasure more complete. No longer having a voice of her own, she is nothing but a tale told by others. Janie and Pheoby both recognize Janie's vulnerability to Annie Tyler's fate. "Ah sho would hate tuh see her come up lak Mis' Tyler," Pheoby declares. "Janie, you be keerful 'bout dis sellin' out and goin' off wid strange men. Look what happened tuh Annie Tyler. . . . It's somethin' tuh think about" (p. 172).

Hurston privileges dialogue and storytelling at the same time as she represents and applauds Janie's *refusal* to speak. She valorizes and eroticizes self-narration at the same time as she underscores what may be the impossibility of its fulfillment (given how rarely—if ever—listeners as ideal as Pheoby are available). To understand the seeming paradoxes of this erotics of talk, we need to situate it within the representational cultural politics to which it responded and in which it sought to intervene.

"Colored Women Sittin' on High"

Although *Their Eyes Were Watching God* has always been taken as ahistorical and set in a vague and undetermined/undeterminable past,[21] the conversation between Janie and Pheoby takes place at a very precise historical moment: the opening years of the Harlem Renaissance. Surprisingly, no critic has ever dated the novel's story, even though the clues to its historical moment are not particularly obscure. On the contrary, they are ones that Hurston should have safely been able to predict many readers would notice.

In the second chapter, Nanny, who grew up in slavery, relates her own family history to Janie and describes how her master left to join the Civil War when Leafy (Janie's mother) was just a week old. He departs just after Sherman's troops have invaded Atlanta: 1864. Seventeen years later, Leafy is raped, and still seventeen, gives birth to Janie: 1881 or 1882. Since Janie is sixteen when Nanny tells her story, it is 1897 or 1898 when Janie's "conscious life" begins. She is forty when she returns home: 1921 or 1922, the *anni mirabiles* of the Harlem Renaissance (as well as of modernism), the two years which saw the founding of Marcus Garvey's African Orthodox Church, the opening of the first all-black play, "Shuffle Along," the establishment of the Pan-African Congress, approval by the House of Representatives of the nation's first anti-lynching legislation, and the publication of *Harlem Shadows, The Book of American Negro Poetry, Bronze*, and Carter Woodson's *The Negro in Our History*, only one year before the publication of *Cane* and *The Philosophy and Opinions of Marcus Garvey*, and three years before the publication of *The New Negro*, and *Color*, among other significant works.

While the rural setting of the novel makes its relationship to the central literary and political preoccupations of the Harlem Renaissance seem oblique or tangential, its treatment of desire and voice responds to that movement's most central debates. The boldness with which Hurston represents female desire was transgressive in a context in which black publication guidelines warned that nothing liable to add fuel to racist stereotypes of wanton licentiousness and primitivism would be printed: "nothing that casts the least reflection on contemporary moral or sexual standards will be allowed. Keep away from the erotic! Contributions must be clean and wholesome."[22] While a number of Harlem Renaissance male writers and artists—Claude McKay, Jean Toomer, Langston Hughes, Bruce Nugent, Wallace Thurman, and Aaron Douglas, for example—did explore questions of sexuality, admonitions against its representation were much more rigorously applied to the work of black women. "Racist sexual ideologies," Hazel Carby writes, "proclaimed the black woman to be a rampant sexual being, and in response black women writers either focused on defending their morality or displaced sexuality onto another terrain."[23] By insisting on Janie's right to erotic pleasure, Hurston takes on this complex politics of sexuality.

She is even more critical, however, of the Harlem Renaissance's politics of voice, the idea that literature and the arts offered African Americans their best means of advancement and social protest, the recognition, as one *Negro World* article put it in 1921, that "the history and literature of any race are the credentials on which that race is admitted to the family of civilized men and are the indications of its future possibilities."[24]

Much of the coherence of the Harlem Renaissance as a literary-political movement was due to such shared assumptions about the role of black arts. In 1926, for example, when W. E. B. Du Bois addressed the NAACP on the "Criteria of Negro Art," he began by remarking that "a group of radicals trying to bring new things into the world, a fighting organization which has come up out of the blood and dust of battle, struggling for the right of black men to be ordinary human beings" did not "turn aside [from its mission] to talk about Art.'" On the contrary, he argued, Art was an important part of their arsenal.[25] "After trying religion, education, politics, industrial, ethical, economic, [and] sociological approaches," James Weldon Johnson wrote, "through his artistic efforts the Negro is smashing [the race barriers] faster than he has ever done through any other method"[26]

To suggest, in this context, that "talkin' don't amount tuh uh hill uh beans when you can't do nothin' else" (p. 285), that narrative and self-revelation "'tain't worth de trouble" was to subvert the entire representational agenda behind the cultural politics of African American activism from the early 1920s through the 1930s and beyond. While this view of art as a political weapon was most powerfully articulated in the postwar rhetoric of the Harlem Renaissance, its roots go much father back, originating in pre-emancipation debates over literacy and in the postenlightenment emphasis on writing as the "sign of [human] reason," as Gates put it.[27] "If blacks could write and publish imaginative literature, then they could, in effect, take a few 'giant steps' up the chain of being in an evil game of 'Mother, May I?'"[28] Hurston's challenge to the value and status of self-revelation as a means of social transformation was tantamount to heresy. It strikes directly at the two available political models of African American resistance.

Influential works like W. E. B. Du Bois's "Returning Soldiers," with its call to "return fighting," and Claude McKay's "If We Must Die," with its admonition that even if black men are "pressed to the wall" and "far outnumbered" they should die "fighting back," helped construct what I would call the contestational aesthetic of the Harlem Renaissance, an art and rhetoric based not only on the belief that letters and literacy would serve—as they indisputably did—as effective tools of social liberation, but also on themes, images, metaphors, and discourses drawn directly from combat and warfare and dependent upon a grounding in normative masculinity, often specifically drawn from the riveting martial imagery of the returning, triumphant, black 369th regiment.

This rhetoric, while clearly empowering in many ways, put radical black women in a very difficult position. On the one hand, they were accused by their contemporaries of holding back black militancy through their "genteel" or feminine commitment to respectability, manners, and propriety. Langston Hughes, for example, in "The Negro Artist and the Racial Mountain," one of the period's most influential essays on art and politics, makes a brilliant and compelling case for aesthetic self-determination. But when Hughes goes on to imagine the impediments to this agenda, it is the figure of a woman, specifically a "Philadelphia Club-woman," whose girlish fears and lack of masculine courage stand in the way of its realization. "Oh, be respectable, write about nice people, show how good we are," she whines to Hughes's imaginary black male artist.[29] By the same token, should a black woman desire to show her radical credentials in print, to indicate her own refusal to be bamboozled by white values and standards, the "martial and manly" rhetoric of fighting back would hardly have stood her in good stead.[30]

This is not to say of course that there isn't a vital, militant black feminism going back through the 1800s. Hurston is not only aware of this vibrant tradition, her characterization of Nanny parodies it nearly as derisively (if for different reasons) as did some of her male colleagues. As Janie's erotics of talk stages a rejection of the contestational aesthetic of Harlem Renaissance artists, writers, and intellectuals, her repudiation of Nanny's politics also rejects available models of black feminist resistance which developed or depended upon a contestational discursive aesthetic, implicitly and paradoxically implicating an entire black feminist tradition characterized by organizations like the National Association of Colored Women and the Black Women's Club Movement in the antifemale and antierotic strains she discerns in Harlem Renaissance political discourse.

Although Nanny advises Janie to marry a man she does not love, to face the fact that, as a black woman, she is "de mule uh de world" and should "leave things de way dey is. Youse young yet. No tellin' whut mout happen befo' you die. Wait awhile, baby. Yo' mind will change" (p. 43), she is not simply an accommodationist or conservative. In fact, more than anything else, Nanny wants to be an activist and spokeswoman for the rights of black women. "Ah wanted to preach a great sermon about colored women sittin' on high," she tells Janie, "but they wasn't no pulpit for me. . . . Ah said Ah'd save de text for you. Ah been waitin' a long time, Janie, but nothin' Ah been through ain't too much if you just take a stand on high ground lak Ah dreamed" (pp. 31–32). Some critics have suggested that Nanny's "stand on high ground" is mere materialsism, a matter of parlors and pianos not pulpits and politics. But it is no mistake that Hurston has

Nanny's rhetoric resonate so strongly with Hughes's fiery and militant call
to self-determination, to "stand on top of the mountain, free within ourselves." Nanny's position, however unrealizable, is a feminist alternative to
the male radicalism of African American cultural politics of the 1920s.

Nanny's history as a black slave woman gives her a particular purchase on
sexual abuse and romantic ideology, issues central to the black feminism she
would have "preached" had there been a pulpit for her. Nanny was raped by
her white slave master, and Leafy, Janie's mother, was raped by a black
schoolteacher.[31] Given this history, Nanny, not surprisingly, fears for Janie's
safety and longs to see her protected from "de menfolks white or black . . .
makin' a spit cup outa" her (p. 37). Nanny's view of marriage is practical and
unsentimental: a man with "a house bought and paid for and sixty acres uh
land" (p. 41) is better than one with nothing. Her view of love is a straightforward, witty, and tough-minded repudiation of heterosexual romantic ideology. Love, she argues, is a myth, a form of social control, a tool of the patriarchy to trick women into compliance with their own subordination: *"Dat's
de very prong all us black women gits hung on. Dis love!* Dat's just whut's got us uh
pullin' and uh haulin' and sweatin' and doin' from can't see in de mornin'
till can't see at night" (p. 41, my italics). While slavery, not love, has turned
Nanny into a "cracked plate" (p. 37) and an "old tree that had been town
away by storm" (p. 26), romance is implicated in the structures of oppression
that ensure that "de white man is de ruler of everything [and] De nigger
woman is de mule uh de world" (p. 29). So Nanny tries to raise Janie to be a
feminist activist like Harriet Tubman, Sojourner Truth, Anna Julia Cooper,
Mary McLeod Bethume, or Ida B. Wells-Barnett, a woman who can "preach"
in public about the rights and dreams of black women. But Janie rejects this
idea, just as she does the contestational aesthetic of the Harlem Renaissance.
She repudiates her grandmother's life and values and looks back only in resentment, refusing even to visit her grandmother's grave.

Janie's politics of voice can seem downright reactionary. Whereas both
Nanny and the community view voice as a mode of negotiating into and
within the public sphere, Janie's view of voice seems private and personal,
even privatistic. Throughout the novel she consistently chooses not to
fight back with her voice. In general, "Janie took the easy way away from a
fuss. She didn't change her mind but she agreed with her mouth" (p. 99).
When Janie witnesses the townsmen cruelly taunting the yellow mule
with whom she had often identified, for example, she "wanted to fight
about it. . . . A little war of defense for helpless things was going on inside her. . . . 'But Ah hates disagreement and confusion, so Ah better
not talk. It makes it hard tuh git along'" (p. 90). Hurston also relates that

"the years took all the fight out of Janie's face, no matter what Jody did, she said nothing" (p. 118). Janie chooses not to fight back with her voice, however, because in her view, "it didn't do her any good" (p. 111).

Hurston could not have been unaware that this skeptical representation of the politics of voice was controversial. In a passage from *Mules and Men,* her earlier anthropological collection, Hurston describes such self-censorship as a racial strategy, one which she clearly endorses as a form of self-protection (in this case, from a metaphorical rape):

> The Negro, in spite of his open-faced laughter, his seeming acquiescence, is particularly evasive. You see we are a polite people and we do not say to our questioner, "Get out of here!" We smile and tell him or her something that satisfies the white person because, knowing so little about us, he doesn't know what he is missing. The Indian resists curiosity by a stony silence. The Negro offers a feather bed resistance. That is, we let the probe enter, but it never comes out. It gets smothered under a lot of laughter and pleasantries.
>
> The theory behind our tactics: "The white man is always trying to know into somebody else's business. All right, I'll set something outside the door of my mind for him to play with and handle. He can read my writing but he sho' can't read my mind. I'll put this play toy in his hand, and he will seize it and go away. Then I'll say my say and sing my song."[32]

Having gotten rid of an inept, hostile audience, the speaker can now "say my say and sing my song." But to whom? Some critics would argue that she can now turn to "say" and "sing" to the black community which observes the speaker's strategy and whose collective voice she has ostensibly taken over in her adoption of the pronoun "we." What I want to stress here, however, is not only the way this passage renders public speech as meaningless nonsense but also the relatively inconsequential role it assigns to *any* listener. The speaker of this passage, like Janie, needs a competent listener to hear—but not constitute—her song; her song exists independent of either the misrecognitions or recognitions of its possible listeners.

Is this simply an apolitical, individualistic aesthetic that Janie embodies? Many of Hurston's critics have argued as much, from Richard Wright's claim that "her novel carries no theme, no message, no thought"[33] to Hazel Carby's assessment of Hurston's as a "limited vision, a vision which in its romantic evocation of the rural and the folks avoids some of the most crucial and urgent issues of cultural struggle."[34] But I think Hurston was challenging—not simply ignoring—the idea of politics to which such assessments appeal. For her, as Marcuse puts it, "the fight for Eros is the *politi-*

cal fight."³⁵ Janie rejects her grandmother (and, impliticly, the cultural politics of many of her contemporaries) because Nanny gives up on female desire. Nanny, as Janie describes it, had taken the horizon—or desire itself—and "pinched it in to such a little bit of a thing that she could tie it about her granddaughter's neck tight enough to choke her" (p. 138). Such erotic erasure has no place in Janie's political economy. Nor, more paradoxically, does self-revelation to hostile or antagonistic audiences. But even this position is not the disengagement and resignation it seems. Susan Lanser identifies what she calls "self-silencing" as a "willful [albeit often staged] refusal to narrate" that refuses the compromises embedded in narrative conventions, protects narrators or characters from "direct contact with an unfriendly or uncomprehending readership," and indicts the audience to which the narrator will not speak as unreliable, unworthy, or otherwise inadequate.³⁶ Building on Lanser's description of the subversive imperatives of "self-silencing," I want to argue that Janie's various refusals of public voice, self revelation, and fighting back do constitute an important form of political protest.

"The Understandin' To Go 'Long Wid It"

Let us turn to the one other instance in the novel where Janie indulges, as she does in her conversation with Pheoby, in "self revelation" and attempts to tell her story to others. Juxtaposing these two scenes helps explain why Hurston seems at once to privilege narration and doubt its social or personal value. The trial scene destabilizes narrative's privileged status as a personal or social "talking cure" by first elevating its importance and then, ironically, undercutting its effectiveness. Janie must here tell her story to save her life, but she knows that her storytelling may beget misrecognition and alienation. Just as much as the framing conversation between Janie and Pheoby, the trial scene serves as a microcosm for the novel as a whole, an allegory of the dilemma Janie faces in seeking the audience with whom she might satisfy her longing for self-revelation.

Janie finds herself in a Southern courtroom, on trial for Tea Cake's murder, facing two hostile audiences. The black community is there, "with their tongues cocked and loaded. . . . They were all against her, she could see. So many were there against her that a slap from each one of them would have beat her to death. She felt them pelting her with dirty thoughts" (p. 275). The white community is also there with its all-male jury—"twelve strange men who didn't know a thing about people like Tea

Cake and her were going to sit on the thing" (p. 274)—and its female observers who are not authorized to pass judgment, impose sentence, or dispense sympathy: "it would be nice if she could make *them* know how it was instead of those menfolks" (p. 275).

Janie is silent throughout most of the trial, merely looking on as a series of white men tell her story for her. First, "the sheriff took the stand and told how Janie had come to his house with the doctor and how he found things when he drove out to hers. Then they called Dr. Simmons and he told about Tea Cake's sickness and how dangerous it was. . . . Then the strange white man that was going to talk for her got up there" (pp. 276–277). By the time Janie herself is called to the stand, her testimony has already been undercut.

Janie is trapped. And she knows it. She has no alternative but to testify to these "twelve strange men": "They all leaned over to listen while she talked. . . . She didn't plead to anybody. She just sat there and told and when she was through she hushed" (p. 278).[37]

In this representation of Janie's trial, Hurston enacts the social history of African American voice. Janie is silent, like African Americans denied the right to testify, vote, or learn to read and write. And Janie also speaks, taking on the role of post-Reconstruction blacks who agitated and argued on their own behalf. Why, then, is Janie's testimony rendered only in the narrator's summary and not directly, in the first person, in her own dramatic voice?[38] Hurston is having it both ways here. By having Janie deliver her testimony in court, she acknowledges the relatively recent historical amelioration of the most overt and brutalizing forms of enforced African American silence. By also opting not to render Janie's voice directly at this most crucial of narrative moments—Janie's very life and freedom are, after all, on the line here—Hurston is suggesting that black female voice is still constrained, although perhaps now in more covert, complex, and less absolute ways.

The largest problem Janie faces is that whatever she says to the jury, however she chooses to structure her "self revelation," she knows they lack the necessary "understandin' to go 'long wid it" (p. 19) and that without that understanding "self revelation" just "tain't worth de trouble" and wouldn't, as she considered earlier, "do her any good." Since she and the jury lack shared values, she can only attempt to open their horizons through narrative, approximating experience with story. But this dialogic back and forth cannot function in what is, for Janie, a closed circle: without common experiences her audience/jury cannot understand her story; her story is the only tool she has to provide a sense of commonality. Narrative, in this situation, can neither close the gap between worlds nor break the closed circle of necessity/inadequacy in which it circulates.

While the jury does acquit Janie, it is entirely unclear whether her story has been decisive in that outcome. After she finishes testifying, there is no response from anyone in the courtroom: "She had been through for some time before the judge and the lawyer and the rest seemed to know it. But she sat on in that trial chair until the lawyer told her she could come down" (p. 278). Either the courtroom has been moved to silence by Janie's story or they have been paying no attention to her at all, having already made up their minds based on the testimony of the string of white men who precede—and authorize—Janie's speech.

Is Janie's paradoxical double bind intrinsic to all narrating situations or, rather, is the dubious heuristic value of her testimony a function of its reception context? Immediately following the courtroom scene, Hurston returns us to the framing conversation between Janie and Pheoby in order to juxtapose their nonjuridical dialogue to the juridical one we have just witnessed and to contrast the strong effect Janie's story has had on Pheoby with the dubious effect it had in court. But the topic, at this point, of Janie and Pheoby's conversation is, appropriately enough, the singular importance *and* the dubious value of talk.

> "Lawd!" Pheoby breathed out heavily. . . . "Ah ain't satisfied wid mahself no mo'. Ah means tuh make Sam take me fishin' wid him after this. Nobody better not criticize yuh in mah hearin'."
>
> "Now, Pheoby, don't feel too mean wid de rest of 'em 'cause dey's parched up from not knowin' things. Dem meatskins is *got* tuh rattle tuh make out they's alive. Let 'em consolate theyselves wid talk. 'Course, talkin' don't amount tuh uh hill uh beans when yuh can't do nothin' else. And listenin' tuh dat kind uh talk is jus' lak openin' yo' mouth and lettin' de moon shine down yo' throat. It's uh known fact, Pheoby, you got tuh *go* there tuh *know* there. Yo' papa and yo' mama and nobody else can't tell yuh and show yuh. Two things everybody got tuh do fuh theyselves. They got tuh go tuh God, and they got tuh find out about livin' fuh theyselves.' (pp. 284–285)

You can't, Janie concludes, approximate experience with story. Janie does not respond to Pheoby's "hungry listening" by reaffirming the positive effects of storytelling. On the contrary, in spite of the way the story has affected Pheoby's growth, self-esteem, and feelings of worth, Janie reiterates the message of her courtroom scene: that narrative is mostly a waste of breath, that there is no real relation between storytelling and experience, that narrative cannot substitute for experience and perhaps doesn't even count *as* experience, since you have to *"go* there tuh *know* there."

But shouldn't we read this statement ironically? Janie's staged self-silencing, after all, occurs within a text that *does* tell her story, which is not silent, which in fact delivers Janie's self-revelation to a larger reading public. Doesn't this publicity affirm the very value of narrative that Janie seems to want to shut down? Is Hurston representing the efficacy of narration or, ultimately, its uselessness? The likelihood or the unlikelihood of black female satisfaction through "self revelation"?

Robert Stepto argues that frame structures demonstrate the reading models that readers are meant to adapt and that, as such, they interpolate their readers into the text:

> Framed tales by their nature invent storylisteners within their narra-
> tives and storyreaders, through their acts of reading, may be transformed
> into storylisteners. In tale after tale, considerable artistic energy is brought
> to the task of persuading the reader to constitute himself as a listener, the
> key issue affecting that activity being whether the reader is to pursue such
> self-transformations in accord with or at variance with the model of the lis-
> tener found within the narrative itself. (p. 312)

Ideal listeners such as Pheoby, then, are there as heuristic models for the reader; they teach us what we need to learn and how we ought to read. This account not only assumes the constitutive dynamics of storytelling; it has its own erotic appeal. If the activity of reading can make us better listeners (even if we begin badly), then we, like Pheoby, can come "kiss and be kissed." We, like Pheoby, will have Janie's tongue in our mouth. Talk will be more than simply an empty longing. It will amount to more than "uh hill uh beans."

But are we, as Stepto's model suggests, really meant to identify with Pheoby? Is any (or every) reader capable of being the ideal listener for whom this text has been waiting, the "bee" to this textual "blossom"? Or are we, instead, like Janie's various courtroom audiences, either inaccessible, incompetent, or somehow antagonistic? Are we meant to discover that we are probably as unteachable as they? These are difficult questions. Hurston structures an ambiguity into the novel's relation to its reader by deliberately juxtaposing audiences and portraying the only ideal audience as a virtual mirror of Janie herself. The framing device Hurston uses gives the entire novel the quality of, as Lorranie Bethel puts it, an "overhead conversation."[39] While we can hear Janie's story, in other words, we do so in the form of a reminder that *we* are *not* its ideal audience, that it is not addressed to us, that we are not having a conversation with Janie, and that we, unlike Pheoby (and apparently regardless of whoever "we" in fact happen to be), do not have our tongue in either Janie's or Hurston's mouth.

"With Their Tongues Cocked and Loaded"

"Women writers," Tania Modleski writes, "have always had their own way of 'evening things up'" through a "hidden, but ubiquitous plot of revenge that . . . protest[s] against the authority of fathers and husbands."⁴⁰ Both of Janie's first two husbands are punished for being bad listeners, as well as for being unable to arouse or sustain Janie's desire. Janie's "revenge" on Logan Killicks is relatively mild; she simply walks away from him, after telling him, "you ain't done me no favor by marryin' me" (p. 53).⁴¹ Jody, who "never was the flesh and blood figure of her dreams[,] just something she had grabbed up to drape her dreams over" (p. 112), receives harsher treatment for making her tie up her hair so none of the other men can appreciate it, making her work in the store, beating her, and isolating her from the town's verbal play and "lying" sessions. But Jody's greatest crime is in becoming deaf to Janie and refusing to listen to her. This, Janie tells him, is why he has "got" to die: "now you got tuh die tuh find out dat you got tuh pacify somebody besides yo'self if you wants any love and any sympathy in dis world. You ain't tried tuh pacify *nobody* but yo'self. Too busy listening tuh yo' own big voice" (p. 133).

The novel's dramatic and vivid revenge on Tea Cake, the very embodiment of the "love thoughts of women," has baffled many readers. Initially, Tea Cake encourages both talk and play. Janie and Tea Cake "run" their "conversation from grass roots tuh pine trees" (p. 160); they talk about everything from checkers to passenger trains, from Janie's good looks to Tea Cake's past loves. When Tea Cake taught Janie to play checkers, she "found herself glowing inside. Somebody wanted her to play. Somebody thought it was natural for her to play" (p. 146).

But Hurston's description of their romance is double-edged. Within the positive and sometimes even idyllic depictions of Janie and Tea Cake's love affair there is also something suffocating, almost sinister: "Janie awoke next morning by feeling Tea Cake *almost kissing her breath away.* Holding her and caressing her *as if he feared she might escape* his grasp" (p;. 162, my italics); "Janie looked down on him and felt a *self-crushing love*" (p. 192, my italics); "He seemed to be *crushing* scent out of the world with his footsteps. *Crushing* aromatic herbs with every step he took" (p. 161, my italics). While the life

Tea Cake and Janie share on the muck is often glorious, it is not shared equally: *"Tea Cake's house* was a magnet. . . . Janie stayed home and boiled big pots of black-eyed peas and rice. Sometimes baked big pans of navy beans with plenty of sugar and hunks of bacon laying on top. That was something Tea Cake loved" (p. 197, my italics).

Increasingly, Tea Cake attempts to speak for Janie, to *tell* her what her own desires are. But Janie's tongue isn't in Tea Cake's mouth. When he speaks Janie's desires for her, he often gets them wrong. And his inability— or refusal—to listen makes him dangerous. When the Seminole Indians correctly read the natural signs of the impending flood, Tea Cake discounts them. "Indians don't know much uh nothin', tuh tell de truth," he declares (p. 231). Once they are already trapped by the flood waters, Janie cautions against leaving the house, but Tea Cake "stunned the argument with half a word" (p. 237), and consequently they venture out into the floodwaters which are ultimately responsible for Janie's accident, Tea Cake's rabies, and his subsequent death.

At the emotional register, Tea Cake's death is of course a tragedy. But within the narrative logic of this novel, Tea Cake's death also liberates Janie to continue her quest and, ultimately, to satisfy her "oldest human longing—self revelation" with someone who *can* listen. As yet another in a long succession of failed listeners, his death is part of what we might call this poetic novel's erotic justice.

In representing Janie's desperate—and largely unfulfilled—need for a listener, Hurston dramatizes the impossibility of the social situation she depicts, resisting what Fredric Jameson has described as literature's ideological task: "inventing imaginary or formal 'solutions' to unresolvable social contradictions."[42] Whereas Houston Baker chides critics for failing "to provide the kind of comprehensive hearing offered by Pheoby,"[43] I am suggesting that Hurston very deliberately figures Pheoby's "comprehensive listening" as a hard act to follow. The presence of multiple—and mostly failed—listeners in the novel reminds us that there are also multiple narratees, implied readers, and historical readers. And there is no reason to assume, out of hand, that all of these are either successful or ideal. Any given reader may as easily resemble "Mouth Almighty" as Pheoby.

This is, of course, not to say that there aren't now and haven't been readers very much like Pheoby. But remembering that Hurston allegorizes such a reader as not only black, female, from the same background as Janie and with similar experiences, but also as operating from a position of sympathy (Pheoby's "hungry listening"), sensuality and erotic openness to Janie ("mah tongue is in mah friend's mouf"), generosity and nurturance

(Pheoby's "mulatto rice"), protectiveness ("nobody better not criticize yuh in mah hearing") and, finally, discursive passivity (the willingness to remain a listener, not to demand an exchange of places, not to insist on telling her own story as well), we must conclude that her depiction is an exaggerated idealization, just as all objects of romantic desire and fantasy are exaggerated and idealized. But it is also, like most, an idealization with political bite, coming as it does from a black woman writer who we know had such good reasons to distrust her own reception and to doubt the motives of her audience(s), as much when they chose to celebrate her as when they chose to vilify her.

To say that Hurston's allegory of intersubjective understanding (as I read the framing conversation) has political bite is not to say that it is politically unambiguous. On the contrary. Eroticizing Janie and Pheoby's dialogue seems to affirm storytelling, narration, and communication in just the way we might expect from an anthropologist and writer who devoted so much of her life to documenting African American discursive, dialogic, and narrative practices.[44] But at the same time, Hurston's construction of ideal listening as virtual mirroring seems essentialistic, seems to suggest that she either could not imagine communicability across differences or that she could not imagine (or locate) the nurturant, sympathetic community in which such communication might be possible, conclusions which resonate with her eventual withdrawal from her own community and, finally, from publicity and writing itself—her apparent decision to live out her life in near isolation and cultural exile.[45] The frame, then, not only gives shape to aesthetic and political questions of rhetoric and reception which we can now recognize as reflecting back on the aesthetic and political debates of the Harlem Renaissance, it also embodies a paradoxical political position generally associated with the reclusive, diffident, self-isolating Hurston of the fifties, not the exuberant cultural radical of the twenties or thirties.

Perhaps it is in consideration of the possible homology between the implied reader and "Mouth Almighty" that Janie's repudiation of both the Eatonville and "muck" (or Everglades) communities has been so hard for critics to accept. If Janie will not speak to them, then is Hurston also rejecting us, keeping us at bay as Janie distances herself from "Mouth Almighty"? This homology is potentially very unsettling; it reverses the conventional problem of narrative authority by asking whether the reader is authorized and competent to *listen,* instead of whether the narrator is authorized to speak. The question of narratee-authority is potentially so troubling because it raises a further question: if we *don't* have the "understandin' to go long wid" the story we are reading, if we, like the community, can't tell a

"mink skin" from a "coon hide" (p. 19), then where would we get that authority? Can we, to reverse Ross Chambers's problematic formulation that
narrators "earn the authority to narrate in the very act of storytelling,"[46]
earn the authority to *hear* in the very act of storylistening?

The answer would be "yes" if we could convince ourselves that Janie
and her community are reconciled and that, if only symbolically, she does
"reveal" herself to them. And critics again and again try to return Janie to
her community. "Janie's voice," Nellie McKay argues, "emerges from the
community she helps to form and . . . [which] also forms her."[47] "Janie
has come home to tell her story," Priscilla Wald writes.[48] Janie "learns to be
one of the people," claims Elizabeth Meese.[49] Both Robert Hemenway and
Barbara Christian describe Janie's psychological maturation in terms of her
reintegration into communal life. "Janie's 'blossoming,'" writes Hemenway, "refers personally to her discovery of self and ultimately to her meaningful participation in black tradition."[50] According to Christian, "Janie
Stark is not an individual in a vacuum. She is an intrinsic part of a community, and she brings her life and its richness, joys, and sorrows back to it."[51]
Baker, who initially argues against "romantic readings of *Their Eyes Were
Watching God,*" also writes that Janie "returns to the communal landscape
. . . as a storyteller and blues singer par excellence . . . returns to sing
to an exclusively black audience."[52] Even Mary Helen Washington, who argues, as I noted earlier, that Janie is "outside of the folk community," sees a
potential for Janie's reintegration into her community by virtue of her
very rejection of it: "Janie has, of course," Washington argues, "reformed
her community by her resistance to its values."[53]

This "of course," I am suggesting, is precisely what Hurston puts in
question in *Their Eyes Were Watching God* through the text's admonition *not* to
assume that verbal resistance leads ineluctably to the reformation or transformation it seeks. The reconciliation of Janie and her community argued
for by contemporary critics derives, I think, from our own nostalgia and
longing for forms of communal life. As critic Jean E. Kennard would have
it, texts should "satisfy us" and "comfort us by providing that sense of
community we read for in the first place."[54] But reading *Their Eyes Were
Watching God* as a story of communal reintegration and reconciliation mediated through the positivity of love and voice occludes the ways in which
Hurston's revision of the romance narrative (denying Janie her conventional hero-lover and granting her a heroine-listener instead) works to
deepen rather than reduce the contradictions cutting across it.

There is a laudable political agenda behind such romanticizing readings—a desire to see narrative, dialogue, and conversation not only as

forms of personal and social recognition but also as means of social transformation. If the community—and by extension the reader—remains
unchanged by her life and her story, after all, in what sense can Janie's resistance (or Hurston's) be called effective? The problem is that Janie's community *doesn't* change and that Janie (and perhaps Hurston) believes that
hearing her story won't help.

And the problem this raises is not only moral but methodological as
well. How, in recuperating this novel, can we avoid assuming that we are
already its reconstituted, transformed, ideal reader—even as we effectively
read and analyze its longing for just such a reception? How can we avoid
romanticizing away its narrative skepticism and distrust of discourse in the
name of our own emancipatory project and in implicit historicization of
our own recuperation of that very message?

In contrast to John Callahan's claim that "Hurston invites her readers
to respond as listeners and participants in the storytelling,"[55] I'd suggest
that only by including oneself in Hurston's blanket indictment, assuming
that one is, for whatever reason, a different reader than Hurston's idealized, eroticized, and romanticized projection, can one learn to listen, learn
to listen differently, and to help—thereby—create the very conditions
under which Janie's black female longing for narration and self-revelation
might, someday, be satisfied.

Notes

1. Zora Neale Hurston, *Their Eyes Were Watching God* (Urbana: Univ. of Illinois
Press, 1978), 24. Future references are to this edition and will be cited parenthetically.

2. See Mary Dearborn, *Pocohontas's Daughters: Gender and Ethnicity in American Culture*
(New York: Oxford Univ. Press, 1986); Gloria T. Hull, *Color, Sex, and Poetry: Three Women
Writers of the Harlem Renaissance* (Bloomington: Indiana Univ. Press, 1987); Deborah E.
McDowell, "Introduction," *Quicksand* and *Passing* (New Brunswick: Rutgers Univ.
Press, 1986), xii; Hazel V. Carby, *Reconstructing Womanhood: The Emergence of the Afro-
American Woman Novelist* (New York: Oxford Univ. Press, 1987), 176. During the period
in which Hurston is writing, black women, Hull writes, had to be "especially care-
ful to counter negative stereotypes of themselves as low and sluttish" (p. 12).

3. For an entirely different reading of this passage, see Houston A. Baker, Jr.'s
argument that the novel is really about economics, not sexuality or desire at all:
"the pear tree metaphor is a deceptively prominent construction in *Their Eyes Were
Watching God*; it leads away from the more significant economic dimensions of the
novel" (*Blues, Ideology, and Afro-American Literature: A Vernacular Theory* [Chicago: Univ. of
Chicago Press, 1984], 57).

4. Janie's gradual improvement in choice of lovers is measured, however, by their successively improved conversation. Whereas Johnny Taylor, Janie's first kiss, doesn't speak and Logan Killicks soon "stopped speaking in rhymes to her" (p. 45), the first sign of love between Janie and Jody is a conversation: "they sat under the tree and talked" (p. 49). Tea Cake is distinguished by his witty banter and his encouragement of Janie's talk and laughter. As she later tells Pheoby, "he done taught me de maiden language all over" (p. 173).

5. Gloria Naylor, "Love and Sex in the Afro-American Novel," *The Yale Review* 78 (Autumn 1988): 19–31.

6. M. M. Bakhtin, "Discourse in the Novel," *The Dialogic Imagination*, ed. Michael Holquist (Austin: Univ. of Texas Press, 1981), 280. See also Hans Robert Jauss, *Question and Answer: Forms of Dialogic Understanding*, ed. and trans. Michael Hays (Minneapolis: Univ. of Minnesota Press, 1989). According to Peter Brooks, *Reading for the Plot: Design and Intention in Narrative* (New York: Vintage, 1985), 53–54, "the desire to be heard, recognized, understood . . . to captivate a possible listener" is the "motor" or motivating force of storytelling.

7. Charles Taylor, "The Politics of Recognition," Working Papers and Proceedings of the Center for Psychosocial Studies (Chicago: Center for Psychosocial Studies, 1992), 1–2.

8. See, for example, Joanne Frye, *Living Stories, Telling Lives: Women and the Novel in Contemporary Experience* (Ann Arbor: Univ. of Michigan Press, 1986), and Jay Clayton, "The Narrative Turn in Recent Minority Fiction," *American Literary History* 2 (Fall 1990): 375–393. Houston A. Baker, Jr., drawing on the work of Michael Awkward, puts this tendency in historical context by reading the need "for a participatory expressive return to wholeness or, in Awkward's term '(comm)unity,'" as a response, in part, to being the "split subject of slavery's 'othering'" *(Workings of the Spirit: The Poetics of Afro-American Women's Writing* [Chicago: Univ. of Chicago Press, 1992], 63).

Bruce Robbins has recently argued that there is a basic "antinarrativism" in contemporary theory. See his "Death and Vocation: Narrativizing Narrative Theory," *PMLA* 107 (January 1992): 38–50.

9. See, however, Mary Helen Washington, "'I love the Way Janie Crawford Left Her Husbands': Hurston's Emergent Female Hero," in *Invented Lives: Narratives of Black Women, 1860–1960* (New York: Doubleday, 1987), 237–254; Mary Helen Washington, "Foreword," *Their Eyes Were Watching God* (New York: Harper and Row, 1990); and Michael Awkward, "'The Inaudible Voice of it All': Silence, Voice, and Action in *Their Eyes Were Watching God,"* in his *Inspiring Influences: Tradition, Revision, and Afro-American Women's Novels* (New York: Columbia Univ. Press, 1989).

Both Washington's and Awkward's readings of voice include important debates with other critics over the meaning of Hurston's rhetorical strategies for suggesting rather than directly rendering Janie's voice. See, especially, Henry Louis Gates,

Jr., "Zora Neale Hurston and the Speakerly Text," in his *The Signifying Monkey: A Theory of African-American Criticism* (New York: Oxford Univ. Press, 1988), and Robert Stepto, *From Behind the Veil: A Study of Afro-American Narrative* (Urbana: Univ. of Illinois Press, 1979), 164–167.

  10. Baker, *Blues, Ideology, and Afro-American Culture*, 58–59.

  11. Henry Louis Gates, Jr., *The Signifying Monkey*, 169, 202.

  12. Barbara Johnson, "Metaphor, Metonymy, and Voice in *Their Eyes Were Watching God*," in *Black Literature and Literary Theory*, ed. Henry Louis Gates, Jr., (New York: Methuen, 1984), 212.

  13. Karla F. C. Holloway, *The Character of the Word: The Texts of Zora Neale Hurston* (New York: Greenwood, 1987), 40.

  14. Susan Lanser, *Fictions of Authority: Women Writers and Narrative Voice* (Ithaca: Cornell Univ. Press, 1992), 201–202.

  15. Carla Kaplan, "Narrative Contracts and Emancipatory Readers: *Incidents in the Life of a Slave Girl*," *Yale Journal of Criticism* 6 (Spring 1993): 93–119. See also my *The Erotics of Talk: Women's Writing and Feminist Paradigms* (New York: Oxford University Press, 1996).

  16. Hans Robert Jauss, *Toward an Aesthetic of Reception*, trans. Timothy Bahti (Minneapolis: Univ. of Minnesota Press, 1982), 21.

  17. Robert Scholes, *Fabulation and Metafiction* (Urbana: Univ. of Illinois Press, 1979), 26.

  18. "The kiss" has been brilliantly explored by Catherine Stimpson as a "staple of lesbian fiction," a particularly strong and resilient symbol because it can neither "wholly reveal" nor "wholly deny, lesbian eroticism." See "Zero Degree Deviancy: The Lesbian Novel in English," in her *Where the Meanings Are: Feminism and Cultural Spaces* (New York: Methuen, 1988), 99, 103.

  While the friendship between Janie and Pheoby has received substantial critical attention, few critics have commented on Hurston's explicitly lesbian eroticizing of that friendship and of their storytelling exchange. See, however, Lorraine Bethel, "'This Infinity of Conscious Pain': Zora Neale Hurston and the Black Female Literary Tradition," in *All the Women Are White, and All the Blacks Are Men, But Some of Us Are Brave: Black Women's Studies*, ed. Gloria T. Hull, Patricia Bell Scott, and Barbara Smith (New York: Feminist Press, 1982), 187.

  On this discursive ethos, see also John Callahan, *In the African-American Grain: The Pursuit of Voice in Twentieth-Century Black Fiction* (Urbana: Univ. of Illinois Press, 1984).

  19. Robert Stepto provides a compelling analysis of the status of "unreliability" and "competence" in the African American literary tradition. Readers familiar with Stepto's argument will trace its resonance throughout my own. See his "Distrust of the Reader in Afro-American Narratives," *Reconstructing American Literary History*, ed. Sacvan Bercovitch (Cambridge: Harvard Univ. Press, 1986). Where Stepto argues that African American writers often invoke a "discourse of distrust" aimed at

their readers in place of the more conventional posture of intimacy and familiarity, I am arguing that alongside a longing for discursive intimacy in women's writing we may also find an even more profoundly critical "distrust of discourse." For a more extended discussion of this "distrust of discourse," see my "Narrative Contracts and Emancipatory Readers." On reliability as a category of readerly, as well as narratorial, competence, see also Susan Lanser, *Fictions of Authority.*

20. Nellie McKay, "'Crayon Enlargements of Life': Zora Neale Hurston's *Their Eyes Were Watching God* as Autobiography," in *New Essays on "Their Eyes Were Watching God,"* ed. Michael Awkward (Cambridge: Cambridge Univ. Press, 1990), 62.

21. It has long been a critical commonplace to view *Their Eyes Were Watching God* as ahistorical, as Hortense Spillers puts it, a "timeless current . . . [of] ahistorical, specifically rustic, image clusters." Or as Hazel Carby puts it, a "limited vision, a vision which in its romantic evocation of the rural and the folk avoids some of the most crucial and urgent issues of cultural struggle." Susan Willis makes a more pointed accusation, charging Hurston with a "utopian betrayal of history's dialectic." See Hortense J. Spillers, "A Hateful Passion, A Lost Love," in *Feminist Issues in Literary Scholarship,* ed. Shari Benstock (Bloomington: Indiana Univ. Press, 1987), 195; Hazel Carby, *Reconstructing Womanhood: The Emergence of the Afro-American Woman Novelist* (New York: Oxford Univ. Press, 1987), 175; and Susan Willis, *Specifying: Black Women Writing the American Experience* (Madison: Univ. of Wisconsin Press, 1987), 48.

Wahneema Lubiano argues, as I do, that such a romanticizing reading "leaves out a necessary historicizing of Hurston and her deliberate interventionary project," a historicizing she does not there attempt. See her "Constructing and Reconstructing Afro-American Texts: The Critic as Ambassador and Referee," *American Literary History* 1 (Summer 1989): 433–447. See also Missy Dehn Kubitschek, "'Tuh de Horizon and Back': The Female Quest in *Their Eyes Were Watching God,"* *Black American Literature Forum* 17 (Fall 1983): 109–115; reprinted in *Zora Neale Hurston's "Their Eyes Were Watching God,"* ed. Harold Bloom (New York: Chelsea, 1987), 13–19.

22. George Schuyler, "Instructions for Contributors," as cited by Henry Louis Gates, Jr., *The Signifying Monkey,* 179.

23. Carby, *Reconstructing Womanhood,* 176. See also Ann Allen Shockley, *Afro-American Women Writers, 1746–1933* (New York: New American Library, 1988), 401–412.

24. William Ferris, "The Arts and Black Development," *Negro World,* 30 April 1921, as quoted in *Voices of a Black Nation: Political Journalism in the Harlem Renaissance,* ed. Theodore G. Vincent and Robert Chrisman (San Francisco: Ramparts Press, 1973), 327.

25. W. E. B. Du Bois, "Criteria of Negro Art," published text of address to the Chicago Conference of the National Association for the Advancement of Colored People, *The Crisis,* October 1926, 290–297. Taking this quotation out of context and misassigning it to Du Bois himself, David Levering Lewis concludes that Du Bois

was disappointed with the direction of Negro arts and that by midcentury, "the old warrior was not in the mood for art" *(When Harlem Was in Vogue* [New York: Oxford Univ. Press, 1979], 177).

26. James Weldon Johnson, "Race Prejudice and the Negro Artist," *Harper's,* November 1928, quoted in Lewis, *When Harlem Was in Vogue,* 193.

27. Henry Louis Gates, Jr., *Figures in Black: Words, Signs and the 'Racial' Self,* (New York: Oxford Univ. Press, 1987), 6.

28. Henry Louis Gates, Jr., "Writing 'Race' and the Difference It Makes," *Critical Inquiry* 12 (Autumn 1985): 8.

29. Langston Hughes, "The Negro Artist and the Racial Mountain," *The Nation,* 23 June 1926, 692–694; reprinted in *Voices from the Harlem Renaissance,* ed. Nathan Irvin Huggins (New York: Oxford Univ. Press, 1976), 305–309.

30. I am not suggesting that black women's resistance was, in any sense, less forceful, effective, or determined than that of black men, only that the prevailing political-aesthetic *rhetoric* did not lend itself to women's issues or their voices. On black women's political participation during this period, see Rosalyn Terborn-Penn, "Discontented Black Feminists: Prelude and Postscript to the Passage of the Nineteenth Amendment," in *Decades of Discontent: The Women's Movement, 1920–1940,* ed. Lois Scharf and Joan M. Jensen (Boston: Northeastern Univ. Press, 1983), 261–278; Paula Giddings, *When and Where I Enter: The Impact of Black Women on Race and Sex in America* (New York: Bantam, 1984); Nancy F. Cott, *The Grounding of Modern Feminism* (New Haven: Yale Univ. Press, 1987); Darlene Clark Hine, ed., *Black Women in United States History,* 4 vols. (New York: Carlson, 1990); Dorothy Salem, *To Better Our World; Black Women in Organized Reform, 1890–1920* (New York: Carlson, 1990); and Darlene Clark Hine, ed., *Black Women's History: Theory and Practice,* 2 vols. (New York: Carlson, 1990).

31. Few historical figures are more glorified in nineteenth- and early twentieth-century black American literature than the Reconstruction schoolteacher. In making Janie's father not simply a racist but a Reconstruction schoolteacher as well, Hurston seems to suggest that rape is a transhistorical fact of life, at least for black women. That he apparently tries later, unsuccessfully, to find Leafy and marry her only deepens this scathing portrayal, given this novel's critique of the institution of marriage.

32. Zora Neale Hurston, *Mules and Men* (Bloomington: Indiana Univ. Press, 1978), 4–5. For a different discussion of this passage, see Barbara Johnson, "Thresholds of Difference: Structures of Address in Zora Neale Hurston," *Critical Inquiry* 12 (Autumn 1985): 280.

33. Richard Wright, "Between Laughter and Tears," review of *Their Eyes Were Watching God, New Masses,* 5 October 1937, 22–25; Darwin T. Turner, *In a Minor Chord* (Carbondale: Southern Illinois Univ. Press, 1971), 92, 98, 111.

34. Carby, *Reconstructing Womanhood,* 175.

35. Herbert Marcuse, *Eros and Civilization: A Philosophical Inquiry into Freud* (Boston, Beacon, 1974), xxv.

36. Lanser, *Fictions of Authority*, 201.

37. Janie's testimony has particularly strong symbolic resonance given, on the one hand, a history of legal prohibitions against black Americans testifying on their own behalf, and, on the other, a tradition of cultural practices, such as "call and response" and "testifying" grounded in the importance of individual and communal rites of testimony. As Geneva Smitherman points out, "testifying" and "call and response" are performative rituals of recognition; they dramatize the constitutive force of a reception context, and they enact the conferral and confirmation of both individual and collective identity. As Barbara Bowen puts it, "'call and response' is the drama of finding authority through communal voice." See Geneva Smitherman, *Talkin and Testifyin: The Language of Black America* (Boston: Houghton Mifflin, Co., 1977), 150; Barbara Bowen, "Untroubled Voice: Call and Response in *Cane*," in *Black Literature and Literary Theory*, ed. 1985. See also Mae Gwendolyn Henderson, "Speaking in Tongues: Dialogics, Dialectics, and the Black Woman Writer's Literary Tradition," in *Changing Our Own Words: Essays on Criticism, Theory, and Writing by Black Women*, ed. Cheryl A. Wall (New Brunswick: Rutgers Univ. Press, 1989), 21–22, 24.

38. As I indicated earlier (n. 10), this is a lively and important debate among Hurston scholars. While it is not practical for me to rehearse this debate here, the interested reader might see, among others, Washington, Awkward, Lanser, McKay, Callahan, Gates, in "Zora Neale Hurston and Speakerly Text," Stepto, in *From Behind the Veil*, Bernard Bell, in *The Afro-American Novel and Its Tradition* (Amherst: Univ. of Massachusetts Press, 1987).

39. Bethel, 180.

40. Tania Modleski, *Loving with a Vengeance: Mass-Produced Fantasies for Women* (New York: Methuen, 1984), 16, 25.

41. See also Mary Helen Washington, "'I Love the Way.'"

42. Fredric Jameson, *The Political Unconscious: Narrative as a Socially Symbolic Act* (Ithaca: Cornell Univ. Press, 1981), 79.

43. Baker, *Workings of the Spirit*, 64.

44. See, especially, "Characteristics of Negro Expression," *Mules and Men, Tell My Horse*, and *Mule Bone*.

45. See Robert Hemenway, *Zora Neale Hurston: A Literary Biography* (Urbana: Univ. of Illinois Press, 1977), 319–348.

46. Chambers, *Story and Situation*, 214.

47. McKay, 56–57.

48. Priscilla Wald, "'Becoming Colored': The Self-Authorized Language of Difference in Zora Neale Hurston," *American Literary History* 2 (Spring 1990): 79–100.

49. Meese, 53.

50. Robert E. Hemenway, *Zora Neale Hurston,* 239.

51. Barbara Christian, *Black Women Novelists* (Westport, CT: Greenwood, 1980), 57.

52. Houston Baker, *Blues, Ideology, and Afro-American Literature,* 60, 59. Kubitschek, who also wants to challenge "the common critical portrait of Zora Neale Hurston . . . [as] a romantic elitist," romanticizes community as well. "The novel," Kubitschek writes, "strongly implies communal enjoyment of, and benefit from, the quester's prize. . . . [Janie is] the successful quester returning with a boon for her community. . . . an artist who enriches Eatonville by communicating her understanding. . . . [The] critical frame story concerns her return to community and the resultant possibility for communal as well as personal growth" (pp. 19–22).

53. "'I Love the Way,'" 250.

54. Jean E. Kennard, "Convention Coverage or How to Read Your Own Life," *New Literary History* 13 (Autumn 1981): 86.

55. Callahan, 118.

Vodou Imagery, African American Tradition, and Cultural Transformation in Zora Neale Hurston's *Their Eyes Were Watching God*

DAPHNE LAMOTHE

◆ ◆ ◆

ZORA NEALE HURSTON wrote *Their Eyes Were Watching God* in 1937 while in Haiti collecting folklore on Vodou.[1] A year later, she published *Tell My Horse*, which documents the findings from that expedition. While the history of these publications suggests that, for Hurston, folklore and fiction converge in Haiti, few critics have adequately explored that juncture. Most acknowledge Hurston's interest in Haitian Vodou, but their analyses of the impact of this belief system on her work frequently do not extend beyond perfunctory glosses. A notable exception is Ellease Southerland's essay "The Influence of Voodoo on the Fiction of Zora Neale Hurston," published in the 1979 collection *Sturdy Black Bridges*.[2] Southerland's article makes an important contribution to readings of Hurston's integration of folklore and fiction. The essay discusses the appearance and significance of various "voodoo" signs, symbols, and rituals in Hurston's fiction; and more specific to this paper, it identifies the use of Vodou symbolism in *Their Eyes Were Watching God* very early in the history of the novel's criticism. But Southerland does not cite her sources for certain voodoo rituals, or for the significance of various numbers and colors that appear repeatedly in Hurston's fiction. Her analysis therefore seems based on anecdotal evidence, and it ignores the cultural distinctions amongst Haitian, Louisiana, and other kinds of voodoo and hoodoo. These aspects of the essay contribute to the failure, or refusal, of succeeding generations of literary critics to further examine the cultural influences that Southerland found in *Their Eyes Were Watching God.* Some—although certainly not all—critics have categorized Hurston's study and incorporation of Vodou as an intriguing curiosity, perhaps considering it to fall within the purview of anthropology and not literature. Reading the novel within such narrow parameters, however, has resulted in a general inability on the part of Hurston's readers to identify the extent to which her use of Vodou ethnography in her literature enables her exploration of female empowerment and African American cultural identity.

In this paper, I focus specifically on Hurston's use of Haitian Vodou imagery in *Their Eyes Were Watching God,* and I argue that the folklore enables her confrontation of various kinds of social and personal transformation. Her use of Vodou imagery enables her to analyze the relationship among migration, culture and identity that lies at the heart of the African Diaspora. In contrast to those critics who read Hurston's use of folk culture, such as Vodou, as a sign of nostalgia, I view it as her means of comprehending transformation. Within traditional cultural forms lies a structure that encourages and enables dynamic change. Therefore, Hurston's reluctance to abandon African American tradition does not signal a rejection of modernity; rather, it becomes a vehicle for her to acknowledge modernity.

I concern myself here specifically with Vodou because *Their Eyes Were Watching God* alludes to similarities between the protagonist, Janie Killicks Starks Wood, and the Vodou goddess Ezili. Janie's physical appearance, her romantic relationships, and her interactions with the Eatonville community mirror in a multitude of ways the characteristics of that spirit (Iwa). These allusions are so embedded into the foundation of the narrative that they are virtually invisible, compelling us to ask what it was about Hurston's experiences in Haiti that compelled her to relate Vodou to her characters. Perhaps her instinct as a folklorist and writer led her to a cultural experience in which the self-expression of a displaced people comes to the fore. Perhaps because she was raised in the self-contained all-black community of Eatonville, Florida, she looked to a belief system that addressed black people's capacity for self-determination. Hurston found in Haitian Vodou a syncretic cultural production that spoke to both of those interests and more. Her anthropological research revealed that the ways in which Haitian people worked out their political, social, and psychic conditions in the spiritual plane resonated with the concerns and experiences of African Americans in the United States. Because the Vodou gods' and goddesses' appearances and actions speak to the concerns and experiences of

their worshippers, one finds that Vodou alludes to the heroic and the re-
bellious; reflects mundane jealousies, desires and hierarchies; illustrates the
ravages of slavery on a collective consciousness; and provides a means of
self-expression for that same collective.

Hurston was very aware of Haiti's symbolism for African Americans,
and implicit references to its significance are scattered throughout the text.
For example, Joe Starks dreams of a place where he can be a "big voice" and
settles on Eatonville because "de white folks had all de sayso where he
come from and everywhere else, exceptin' dis place dat colored folks was
buildin' theirselves" (p. 27). This reference to a place where black people
live independent of white authority alludes to post-Revolution Haiti, the
first black independent republic in the Western hemisphere; and it underscores the revolutionary notion of a town in the United States built and
run by black people. Nanny makes a similar allusion to the black republic
and the collective desire for autonomy and empowerment. She dreams of
"some place way off in de ocean where de black man is in power," revealing Haiti's significance as a place where the potential for black autonomy
has been realized (p. 14).

Nanny's musings also address a desire for female empowerment. For it
is in that "place way off in de ocean" that she also imagines that a black
woman might not have to be "de mule uh de world" (p. 14). Anthropologist Karen McCarthy Brown writes in *Mama Lola* about the possibilities for
empowerment afforded to Haitian women by Vodou:

> The adaptability of Vodou over time, and its responsiveness to other cul-
> tures and religions; the fact that it has no canon, creed, or pope; the multi-
> plicity of its spirits; and the intimate detail in which those spirits reflect the
> lives of the faithful—all these characteristics make women's lives visible
> within Vodou in ways they are not in other religious traditions, including
> those of the African homeland. This visibility can give women a way of
> working realistically and creatively with the forces that define and confine
> them.[3] (p. 221)

Through the use of a Vodou subtext, Hurston comments on and rebels
against the forces that "define and confine" black women as sexual beings, work horses, and mothers. She also uses Vodou philosophy to shed
light on the characters' views on poverty, class, community, and displacement. Building on the work of those critics who investigate the political
implications of Hurston's cultural work, I argue that her use of Vodou
imagery provides her with a vehicle for political engagement and social
commentary.

Folklore, Literature, and the Lure of the Primitive

In order to fully comprehend the significance of the text's Vodou imagery, it is crucial to understand the context in which Hurston wrote. I believe she submerged the Vodou images in the novel beneath more accessible folk images of the black South in a dual effort to conform to and resist popular demands for the primitive. Unlike the performance of the dozens, the telling of folk tales and other aspects of African American folk culture that the reader can easily identify and separate from the plot, Hurston's use of Vodou is not as easily discerned. Its presence in the text has no stylistic markers, nor can we categorize the Vodou elements as mere ornaments for the central narrative.[4] Hurston's more obvious use of African American folk culture made her vulnerable to criticisms of pandering to the then popular taste for "the minstrel stereotypes of the lazy, sensual, ignorant, laughing darky. . . ."[5] As one of the stars of the Harlem Renaissance, courted and funded by white benefactors, Hurston juggled her literary aspirations with the often racist expectations of her patron and audience. For example, Mrs. Rufus Osgood Mason, was a generous benefactor; but "as perhaps with all patrons, . . . she expected some return on her money. In Hurston's case it was a report on the aboriginal sincerity of rural southern black folk . . . Her black guests were either primitive, or they were not being themselves" (Hemenway, p. 107).

Many of Hurston's critics viewed this external pressure as a handicap to her literary production. H. Nigel Thomas, for example, counts Hurston as one of a school of writers (including Charles Chesnutt and Paul Laurence Dunbar) who could not meet the challenge of simultaneously satisfying the demand for "minstrel-type buffoonery" and "ensuring that [s]he did not compromise the dignity of the black race."[6] Thomas mistakes Hurston's humor for buffoonery, and fails to recognize the dignity of her lowly characters. Furthermore, his dismissal of her work arises from the notion that a successful narrative seamlessly blends folklore with fiction. Thomas marks the 1930s as, in general, a time in which African American writers mastered the art of incorporating those elements of folklore that were necessary to their fiction, without pandering to the audience's "baser instincts" or hindering their art. From the 1930s on, black writers produced literature in which "rituals are not allowed to remain a thing apart or as caricatured quaint antics; instead they are integral aspects of the characters' struggle to survive" (p. 175). According to Thomas, Hurston is an exception to this rule, but he fails to acknowledge that her attempts to set apart and highlight some elements of the folklore (like the stories told by the townsfolk) may be deliberate. Rather than judging the obvious seams between the novel's third person, standard English narration and its first person, African American vernacular as a sign of Hurston's failure as a writer, it is possible to view it as an emotionally powerful juxtaposition of two very different kinds of language. Furthermore, like many other critics, Thomas does not recognize that she makes Ezili, a figure from Caribbean folklore and ritual, a central, yet nearly invisible, aspect in Janie's struggle for survival. Hurston achieves a double triumph over those in her audience who demanded primitive images. First, by setting apart the African American folklore within the central narrative, she makes a case for the recognition of the literary possibilities of folklore. Second, her use of Vodou achieves the harmonious blending of folklore and fiction that Thomas holds as a standard of successful, black creative expression.

During the 1920s and 1930s, the widespread desire for the primitive extended beyond a demand for minstrel stereotypes of "happy darkies" into the world of the exotic primitive. These demands dovetailed with Renaissance writers' struggles to define what was unique to African American culture. One way they did so was by attempting to articulate and define blacks' African heritage. But when imagining African culture's relevance to African American culture and identity, Hurston and her contemporaries often used stereotypical images of beating drums and the jungle, feeding American society's perceptions of Africa as a savage, primal and uncivilized place. Hemenway writes:

> Such tom-tom beats were almost a cliché in Harlem Renaissance writing, and both blacks and whites became enmeshed in the cult of exotic primitivism. For the whites it was the idea that Harlem was an uptown jungle, a safari for the price of cab fare, with cabarets decorated in jungle motifs. They went to Harlem to see the natural rhythm and uninhibited grace of America's link with the heart of darkness. For the black artists it was a much more serious concern, an attempt to establish a working relationship with what Locke called in *The New Negro* the "ancestral" past. (p. 75)

Harlem Renaissance writers' uses of African images frequently held a dual significance as expressions of a serious attempt to articulate the relevance of an African past to African Americans' present and futures, and as a base appeal to racist demands for exotic entertainment. Hurston's literary forays into blacks' ancestral past often made use of the clichés mentioned above. In *Jonah's Gourd Vine*, for instance, and in her 1928 essay, "How It Feels to Be Colored Me," she makes prodigious use of the metaphor of the drum to invoke an ancient African heritage as the foundation of African American identity.

One could view Hurston's turn to Vodou as another example of her exploitation of the primitive because, historically, representations of Vodou in the United States have been rife with clichés. For example, Eugene O'Neill's *The Emperor Jones* contains numerous stereotypes in its depiction of a voodoo cult of savages: Brutus Jones, the noble savage; the tom-toms beating incessantly in the background to foreshadow evil; and natives using black magic to depose their emperor. However, Hurston's weaving of Vodou imagery in *Their Eyes* completely evades such predictable stereotypes, delving instead into the complexities of the belief system, the culture from which it springs, and the ways in which those complexities address African American (and Afro-Caribbean) social and political concerns. The Vodou subtext represents a facet of the primitive that exceeds the scope of the plantation and jungle bunny stereotypes that dominated the Harlem Renaissance era. It links the southern folk with a Black Atlantic experience rooted in slavery, armed revolution, and African spirituality.

Vodou Imagery and Female Agency

The primary Vodou element in this novel is the implicit presence of the goddess Ezili. Hurston infuses Janie with the characteristics of two aspects of this spirit: Ezili Freda, the mulatta goddess of love, and Ezili Danto, the black goddess who is associated with maternal rage. These two spirits display attributes that are completely opposed. Freda is of an elite class; she is a mulatta, self-possessed and materialistic. Danto is working class, black, and associated with motherhood. These contradictory qualities reside in one spirit, and in the case of the novel, they also lie in one body—Janie's. The tensions that stem from these oppositions reflect the conditions and desires of African Americans; and while they cannot always be assimilated or resolved, they frequently result in cultural and individual expressiveness that is dynamic and powerful. Therefore, Hurston uses Vodou imagery, in particular the image of Ezili, in order to implicitly enter a discourse on the present and future of African American culture.

Just as all Vodou ceremonies begin with songs, dances, and prayers in honor of Legba, the novel starts with an implicit invocation of him. Janie calls forth the power of Legba, the keeper of the crossroads, which is the gateway between the spiritual and material worlds, as she searches "as much of the world as she could from the top of the front steps" (p. 11). And when she walks "down to the front gate"—the symbolic crossroads—"and [leans] over to gaze up and down the road" (p. 11), her air of expectation invokes the potential embodied by Legba. In *Tell My Horse*, Hurston calls Legba the "opener of gates"; he symbolizes opportunity (p. 115).[7] As Janie stands at the gate, "looking, waiting, breathing short with impatience. Waiting for the world to be made," she feels acutely this sense of opportunity (p. 11).

This invocation of Legba, a Black Atlantic god, takes place in a text marked by its multiple references to the Christian God, most notably in its title. During the storm that erupts near the end of the narrative, the folks stranded on the muck stare into the darkness, putting themselves at the mercy of a Christian God. But throughout the narrative, as they gaze upon Janie's body, they have also been looking to a New World goddess rooted in African spirituality. Rachel Blau DuPlessis notes that "there are a number of substitutions for God made in this book, usually in the form of big talkers—'Mouth Almighty' of the rural folk, and 'I God' for Joe Stark's comic blasphemous condensation of political and economic power."[8] The temporal powers of Jody and the gossiping Eatonville folk give scant competition to the all encompassing power of God to whom Janie, Tea Cake, and their friends silently appeal as they wait for the storm to arrive. But the novel refers in passing only to these false gods and to the ultimate authority, the God who controls the potentially devastating forces of nature. This God is Ezili's primary challenger in the competition for the characters' allegiance.

Janie resembles Ezili Freda physically. In *Voodoo in Haiti*, anthropologist Alfred Mètraux describes Freda, the goddess of love, as "a pretty Antillean half-caste. . . . a personification of feminine grace and beauty. She has all the characteristics of a pretty mulatto: she is coquettish, sensual, pleasure-loving and extravagant" (p. 110). Freda can make any man she chooses her husband, a characteristic that finds its parallel in Janie's search for a suitable mate. Janie dresses in blue (p. 2), Freda's favorite color.[9] The description of Janie's return to Eatonville echoes Mètraux's description of Ezili's entrance into a Vodou temple. Hurston writes:

> The men noticed her firm buttocks like she had grape fruits in her hip pockets; the great rope of black hair swinging to her waist and unraveling in the wind like a plume; then her pugnacious breasts trying to bore holes in her shirt. They, the men, were saving with the mind what they lost with the eye. (p. 2)

Mètraux writes:

> At last, in the full glory of her seductiveness, with hair unbound to make
> her look like a long-haired half-caste, Ezili makes her entrance to the peri-
> style. She walks slowly, swinging her hips, throwing saucy, ogling looks at
> the men or pausing for a kiss or a caress. (p. 111)

Janie's long hair and sensuality mark her as the object of sexual desire. Although, unlike Ezili Freda, Janie does not actively solicit male attention,
Freda's desire for sensuality and love blooms in Janie as she muses under
the pear tree in her grandmother's garden. And finally, the celebration of
love and sexuality symbolized by Freda culminates in Janie and Tea Cake's
playful, loving relationship.

The text celebrates female sexuality with its sensuous prose and its positioning of Janie's quest for love at its center. By linking Janie's sexuality
with Freda's, Hurston radicalizes it by associating it with the ritual of possession in which a god mounts an initiate. The goddess is said to "ride"
her horse. The implicit sexuality in this terminology is self-evident and
Ezili's desire for numerous "husbands" is well documented in the anthropological literature. The image of a woman, either human or spirit,
"mounting" a man proves significant because it implies the woman's control over her own sexuality and over the man's pleasure as well. For
Hurston, representing a woman's sexuality in full bloom is not just affirmative, it is revolutionary.

But Freda's presence also represents a desire for wealth and status,
which eventually leads to conflict for Janie. After joining in a loveless marriage with Logan Killicks, Janie tells her grandmother, "Ah wants things
sweet wid mah marriage lak when you sit under a pear tree and think, Ah
. . . ." (p. 23). Janie's desire for "things sweet" corresponds with the myth-
ology surrounding Ezili Freda, who also desires sweets.[10] Janie eventually
satisfies that desire when she marries a man with a sweet sounding name,
Tea Cake; but that only occurs when she shucks off her grandmother's belief that a secure, middle-class home should take precedence over romantic love. Nanny responds to Janie's rejection of the economically stable and
physically unattractive Logan Killicks in the following way:

> If you don't want him, you sho oughta. Heah you is wid de onliest organ in
> town, amongst colored folks, in yo' parlor. Got a house bought and paid for
> and sixty acres uh land right on de big road and . . . Lawd have mussy!
> Dat's de very prong all us black women gits hung on Dis love! (p. 22)

The similarities between Janie and Freda go only so far because, ultimately,
Janie rejects the aristocratic ideal that Freda embodies (represented by her

love of jewelry, brushes and combs, the valorization of her light skin and long hair and her preference for French over Creole, the language of the lower classes in Haiti). She laments to Pheoby the fact that "Jody classed me off"; and rejoices when she finds in Tea Cake not only romantic love but also the connection with the folk from which she has so often been discouraged. Janie finds no satisfaction in Logan Killicks's possessions, resents the fact that Jody sits her on the front porch like "a pretty doll-baby" (p. 28), and rejoices when Tea Cake asks her to work in the muck with all the "common" folk.

Although Janie resents being "classed off," most of the other characters crave and envy the status that comes with having material possessions and a light-skinned wife. They worship and desire the materialistic and elitist lifestyle represented by the mulatta Freda, which eventually proves their downfall. While most of the folk share these desires, Mrs. Turner, Janie's "visiting friend" in the muck, proves the most egregious example of this mindset because her worship of Janie's mixed-race features borders on self-hatred. Mrs. Turner "didn't cling to Janie Woods the woman. She paid homage to Janie's Caucasian characteristics as such" (p. 13):

> Once having set up her idols and built altars to them it was inevitable that she would worship there. It was inevitable that she should accept any inconsistency and cruelty from her deity as all good worshippers do from theirs. All gods who receive homage are cruel. All gods dispense suffering without reason. Otherwise they would not be worshipped. Through indiscriminate suffering men know fear and fear is the most divine emotion. It is the stones for altars and the beginning of wisdom. Half gods are worshipped in wine and flowers. Real gods require blood. (p. 138–139)

Mrs. Turner worships Janie's Caucasian features like an initiate worships the lwa—with blood sacrifices and an awareness that the gods can sometimes be arbitrary in their cruelty. This critique of Mrs. Turner's misplaced faith in whiteness is not a condemnation of Vodou, however. Rather, it is an honest assessment of the religion's tendency to respond to and reflect all of its worshippers' desires, including those that may be self-destructive. While the other characters are not as virulent in their internalized racism as Mrs. Turner, Nanny, Logan, Jody, the townsfolk, and even Tea Cake show signs of being color struck and materialistic. Thus, the text's condemnation of Mrs. Turner implicitly extends to a critique of other characters who share her views.

Despite the popular tendency to worship that which Ezili Freda represents, Janie eventually rejects the elitist trappings that characterize the lwa

and embraces the working-class folk identity of Ezili Danto. When she returns to Eatonville, the women remark on the changes in her appearance.
"What she doin' coming back here in dem overalls?—What dat ole forty
year ole 'oman doin' wid her hair swingin' down her back lak some young
gal?" (p. 2). While their vituperative comments reflect their envy of Janie's
appearance and wealth, the changes in her appearance reflect a profound
change in Janie's self-perception and a departure from the iconography of
Ezili Freda.[11] The references to Janie's "overalls" and age place her in the
province of Ezili Danto, the Petwo spirit, at the same time that her long
hair and sensuality continue to align her with Freda. This passage resonates
on multiple levels, positioning Janie as two kinds of woman: one who
benefits from and reaffirms gender, class, and color biases (signified by
Freda), and one who is noted for her willingness to work and for her maturity (signified by Danto).

McCarthy Brown describes Ezili Danto as an independent woman with
an unconventional sexuality. She has "dark black skin" and is "not too
proud to work" (p. 229). Although the fair-complexioned, relatively well-
off Janie must convince Tea Cake that she is not above working in the fields
with the other migrant laborers, she soon proves to be an enthusiastic
worker. Danto's black skin mirrors the blackness of the muck and that of
the people in whom Janie finds fulfillment. Unlike the light-skinned Mrs.
Turner who says she "can't stand black niggers" (p. 135), or the mulatta
Ezili Freda who detests those with black skin, Janie loves Tea Cake, his dark
skin and the affirmative connection with her community that blackness
represents.

But Danto also has the power to destroy, which earns her the reputation of being "red-eyed," or evil. Hurston calls her "the terrible Erzulie,
ge-rouge. . . . an older woman and terrible to look upon" (p. 123).[12]
That destructive force makes itself known during the hurricane, which
erupts in order to convey Danto's displeasure. This spirit, who represents
working-class values and an affirmative blackness, violently objects to the
African Americans' deference to white cultural, racial, and economic supremacy at the expense of their own autonomy. The danger of such attitudes becomes clear when the folk remain in the path of the storm, despite the warning signs they receive, because they are making "seven and
eight dollars a day picking beans." In contrast to the Native Americans
who know how to read the signs that nature gives them—"Sawgrass
bloom. Hurricane coming," they say as they flee the Everglades—the
African Americans ignore the warnings (p. 146). They stay where they are
because "De white folks ain't gone nowhere. Dey oughta know if it's dan-

gerous" (p. 148). This implicit trust in white people's authority proves their downfall and results in the deaths of scores of people. Tea Cake's "possession" by the rabid dog that bites him is the most graphic example of the consequences suffered by black folks who blindly worship whiteness.

Vodou stands in this novel as a reminder of black independence and expressiveness, and the Vodou goddesses demand payment when proper attention is not paid to these principles. Janie's deferral to Tea Cake, who insists that they follow the example of the white landowners, runs against her own instincts. Her acquiescence to his will mirrors the African American community's subordination to white authority and underscores the notion that their flaw is in the refusal to read the situation and interpret its meaning for themselves. When we first meet the young Janie, we learn that she can communicate with nature and understand its signs:

> . . . Janie had spent most of the day under a blossoming pear tree in the back-yard. She had been spending every minute that she could steal from her chores under that tree for the last three days. That was to say, ever since the first tiny bloom had opened. It had *called* her to come and gaze on a mystery. . . . She had been *summoned* to behold a revelation" (p. 11, emphasis added)

Janie's ability to "read" nature's signs mirrors that of the Native Americans who warn her and her friends to leave before the hurricane strikes. But her unwillingness to heed her own internal barometer results in a terrible price paid to nature's forces. Karla Holloway writes in *The Character of the Word*:

> Nature has bowed to human forces throughout the novel. Here she shows that she is a power that can control, as well as be controlled. Perhaps her fury is a lesson for Janie, who has been linked with natural imagery throughout the story and who needs to learn the potential strength of her own independence. (p. 65)

All of the folks living in the Everglades, and not just Janie, need to learn to honor their independence.

Ezili Danto makes her angry presence known at this point in the narrative. She is connected with water; a gentle rainfall signals her presence and a deluge signals her rage.[13] The hurricane is described as a terrifying and cosmic force that extracts the blood sacrifice that "real gods" demand: "Ten feet higher and as far as they could see the muttering wall advanced before the braced-up waters like a road crusher on a cosmic scale. The monstropolous beast had left his bed. The two hundred miles an hour

wind had loosed his chains" (p. 153). Danto's rage erupts as a violent reminder to the folk that their passive faith in Euro-Americans, or Christianity, to determine their fate is misguided. The events leading up to the
hurricane vividly illustrate the need for self-determination in the collective black consciousness. This lessons comes too late for Tea Cake to learn;
but his death is an example for other individuals. Likewise, Janie suffers for
her passivity, not only in losing Tea Cake but also in having to act as the
agent of his death.

Ezili Danto's brutal insistence that the folk maintain their independence defies Christian doctrine which traditionally advocated submission
to authority.[14] The passiveness of the folk as they wait for the onslaught to
begin underscores Christianity's traditional call for submissiveness: "They
sat in company with the others in other shanties, their eyes straining
against crude walls and their souls asking if He meant to measure their
puny might against His. They seemed to be staring at the dark, but their
eyes were watching God" (p. 151). In contrast to this situation which forces
the folk to assume a posture of defeat, Hurston saw Vodou as facilitating a
peasant self-expression that often subverted authority. Her account in *Tell
My Horse* of the events that take place when Gede, the peasant god of death,
mounts an individual, highlights the potential threat in the Vodou tradition to upend hierarchies and disrupt social order:

> On several occasions, it was observed that Guedé [sic] seemed to enjoy hum-
> bling his betters. On one occasion Guedé reviled a well-dressed couple in a
> car that passed. Their names were called and the comments were truly dev-
> astating to say the least. With such behavior one is forced to believe that
> some of the valuable commentators are "mounted" by the spirit and that
> others are feigning possession in order to express their resentment general
> and particular. That phrase "Parlay cheval ou" is in daily, hourly use in Haiti
> and no doubt it is used as a blind for self-expression. (p. 221)

When Gede speaks through the possessed, political, economic and social
injustices come under attack in ways that could never be possible in Haitian society under ordinary circumstances. If an individual pretends to be
possessed by the Iwa, in effect putting on a mask of Gede, that attack
becomes even more threatening than one from a possessed individual because it is a willful expression of anger, disgust, or defiance.

In Gede's burlesque antics we find the most striking, but not the only,
example of peasant self-expression that threatens the stability of a social
order. While possession by Gede results in the subversion of class hierarchies, the presence of Ezili Freda and Danto illustrates the ways in which

class identity and female agency are expressed in Haitian society (and, by extension, within Eatonville society as well). Vodou's implicit stress on self-expression echoes the novel's more explicit celebration of black expressiveness through the storytelling that takes place. Storytelling and, by extension, other forms of self-expression have the capacity to liberate Janie from the many constraints placed on her. Powerful truths about life and love exist in Janie's story, which she recounts to her friend Pheoby while they sit on the back porch of her house. Janie's story takes on a mythic dimension and her words transcend even the limitations of her own life. Mary Helen Washington aptly describes those limitations:

> One can hardly make . . . an unequivocal claim for Janie's heroic posture in *Their Eyes.* . . . Her friendship with Pheoby, occurring apart from the community, encapsulates Janie and Pheoby in a private dyad that insulates Janie from the jealousy of other women. Like the other women in the town, she is barred from participation in the culture's oral tradition. When the voice of the black oral tradition is summoned in *Their Eyes,* it is not used to represent the collective black community, but to invoke and valorize the voice of the black *male* community.[15]

While I concur that the novel primarily celebrates the black male oral tradition, I would reassert the significance of the frame story told by Janie to Pheoby. The frame story takes on the power and status of myth, which Leslie Desmangles describes as possessing "a paradoxical capacity to express complex truths in everyday language, to use common words and familiar objects to reveal what is most sacred in life" (p. 61). Janie's gender and race certainly circumscribe her experiences, but her story speaks to the potential she carries within. Desmangles notes that "myths are . . . powerful vehicles which can transcend the limitations of profane existence" (p. 61). While Janie may not fully realize her voice and agency in the time frame of the narrative, her mythic tale underscores the potential that exists within all black women. Janie entrusts Pheoby with the responsibility of passing on her story and "de understandin" that goes along with it: "You can tell 'em what Ah say if you wants to. Dat's just de same as me 'cause mah tongue is in mah friend's mouf" (p. 6). With this exhortation, the promise arises that a ritualized sharing of stories and experiences between women will develop. Pheoby will recount Janie's tale, but she will also revise it as she grows and experiences new things. She may inspire future listeners, just as Janie has inspired her. Janie's experience, her story, functions as myth for the folk, teaching them the value of self-expression and the necessity for self-determination.

Critical Schools: Tradition and Transformation

Hurston's incorporation into her novel of a religious tradition that she viewed as ancient and African does not preclude the text's relevance to the condition of modern African Americans. The Vodou intertext in *Their Eyes* actually enabled Hurston to grapple with issues that preoccupied black intellectuals in the 1920s and 1930s, such as class, gender, and inter- and intraracial conflicts. Critical responses to the text failed to perceive, however, its immediate relevance to current events and modern political thought. Because Hurston positioned herself as an authority on black culture in her lifetime, she practically instigated others to attack her representations of black people and black culture for their lack of authenticity or legitimacy. Alain Locke chastised Hurston in his annual literature review for *Opportunity* magazine (1 June 1938) for creating "those pseudo-primitives whom the reading public still loves to laugh with, weep over, and envy" (p. 18). More biting that Locke's review was the critique by the leading black novelist of the day. Richard Wright wrote that the novel, like minstrelsy, "carries no theme, no message, no thought," and functioned only to satisfy the tastes of a white audience for the simple and exotic primitive.[16] Locke and Wright registered their conviction that Hurston's characters are too cartoonish, simple, and docile to be real.

Locke and Wright expressed their squeamishness with Hurston's portrayal of local color during a time in which Northern black newspapers regularly instructed those in their readership who were newly arrived from the South on proper etiquette in public places. Their discomfort with her portrayal of folk characters echoed the sensitivity of many African American intellectuals to the public's perception of black culture. In his introduction to *New Essays on "Their Eyes Were Watching God,"* Michael Awkward notes:

> Sensitive to the need to improve white America's perception of Afro-Americans, some powerful black intellectuals, including Locke and W.E.B. Du Bois, believing that literature represented the most effective means by which to begin to dispel racist notions that black Americans were morally and cognitively subhuman, insisted that Afro-American writers were obligated to present Afro-Americans in the most favorable—and flattering—light possible. (p. 10)

Although Wright was subjected to similar criticisms upon the publication of *Native Son,* his review of *Their Eyes* reflects a touchiness regarding the proper strategy for depicting the African American lower classes. Although Locke and Wright couch their criticism in a rhetoric of authenticity, they seem to object more strenuously to Hurston's seemingly apolitical depiction of poor, uneducated blacks to a presumably racist white audience.

Hurston's reputation has benefited from a surge in scholarly interest since the publication in the early 1970s of Alice Walker's essay "Looking for Zora."[17] To this day, however, some critics retain a residual discomfort with her often flamboyant and controversial statements about black culture. For example, in *The Black Atlantic* Paul Gilroy asserts that Hurston's romanticization of "the folk" and idealization of rural, southern black culture prevent her from acknowledging African American cultural transformation.[18] Gilroy's critique of Hurston assumes that the desire to preserve a sense of tradition automatically marks one as antagonistic to change. Hurston's forays into Vodou symbolism illustrate her respect for a tradition and culture which she considered ancient and African. But more importantly, her appropriation of this African diasporic tradition allowed her to participate in an ongoing dialogue about social and cultural change within black communities in the United States, which preoccupied her contemporaries during and after the Harlem Renaissance. Hurston was absolutely interested in exploring the extent and effect of cultural transformation within African American communities; and Vodou was the primary avenue for accomplishing this exploration.

To illustrate his point, Gilroy teases out a compelling analysis of Hurston's contempt for the operatic performances of spirituals by the Fisk Jubilee Singers, focusing on her theories of authenticity and black culture:

> For Hurston, the success of the Fisk choir represented the triumph of musicians' tricks over the vital, untrained, angular spirit of the rural fok who "care nothing about pitch" and "are bound by no rules." . . . She attacked the choir's performances as inauthentic. (pp. 91–92).

Gilroy goes on to say:

> I would emphasize that as far as this chapter is concerned, whether Hurston was right or wrong about the Fisk Singers is not the primary question. The issue which interests me more than her correctness is her strongly felt need to draw a line around what is and isn't authentically, genuinely, and really black. . . . (p. 92)

The implied critique in Gilroy's observation is that by insisting on an authentic way of singing the spirituals, Hurston resists an inevitable and dynamic change that is an inherent part of the Black Atlantic experience. In order to make this point, he understates the desire for upward class mobility that motivated individuals and groups like the Fisk Singers to elevate a lowly folk art into "high" culture. I think it important, however, to focus on the reasons for her objections to what she considered the loss of integrity in a black cultural production. Hurston's criticism was directed primarily toward a group of formally educated African Americans who attempted to transform a rough, improvisational musical form born of illiterate blacks into an operatic, and therefore more "cultured," form of music.[19] Her refusal to see the operatic performances of spirituals as authentic stems from her resistance to an aesthetic which continued to view poor black culture as inferior, even as it attempted to rehabilitate and transform that culture for a wider audience.

While Hurston grappled with the significance and consequences of transformed cultural experiences, she was not willing to define a "New Negro" who was completely ignorant of, or free from, the influences of the past. Karla Holloway accurately notes that "Hurston's was an ancient spirit in an age that demanded modernism, that called the Negro 'new' and expected that Negro to be male" (p. 17). Hurston refused to submit to the demands of modernism and progress without question because she feared the loss or repression of African cultural fragments. Her objection to the choir's innovations was not so much that they diluted the music's blackness with their injection of class and educational privilege; rather, she objected to the compromise, or abandonment, of the principles on which the music was based.

In an essay titled "Spirituals and Neo-Spirituals," Hurston describes such unique characteristics of Negro singing as "jagged harmony," disharmony, shifting keys, "broken time," and improvisation (pp. 80–81). She was very much aware that most of these musical characteristics were African in origin. Eric Sundquist's comparison of black English and black music proves illuminating in understanding the rationale behind Hurston's supposed resistance to change. He asserts that the perceived strangeness of the language and the music (which we could also call African-ness) often led to anxiety in and ridicule from the dominant culture: "For whites' complaints about the ineffability of the black dialect, which led in turn to the grotesque caricatures of minstrelsy and some plantation romance, repeated comparable observations by musicologists . . . that the intonations of the black spiritual were difficult to transcribe."[20] The elements of the spirituals that seem wrong to the ear trained in Western music (like the polyrhythms and blue notes that Hurston called broken time and disharmony) are the very elements that Hurston sought to preserve. Her critique of the Fisk Jubilee Singers was directed as much at the westernization of the spirituals at the expense of their African elements as it was toward the elegant concert halls and bourgeois performers and audience members. Hurston expressed her rejection of white cultural supremacy through her insistence on an authentic mode of performance, which Gilroy reads as a rejection of modernity. While some might argue that westernization is an inevitable and not necessarily negative cultural transformation, to do so without reservation is problematic because it does not challenge the then widely held assumption that European values were superior to and more sophisticated than African ones.

Unlike Gilroy, Hazel Carby acknowledges Hurston's investment in deflating class-driven pretensions; but like Gilroy, she finds Hurston too quick to delineate who *the* folk might be, as if such a homogenous group identity ever existed. In "The Politics of Fiction, Anthropology, and the Folk: Zora Neale Hurston," Carby notes that Hurston avoids any mention of the newly emergent northern, urban black and chooses to focus on an almost mythical South:

> Hurston was concerned to establish authenticity in the representation of popular forms of folk culture and to expose the disregard for the aesthetics of that culture through inappropriate forms of representation. She had no problem in using the term "the people" to register that she knew just who they were. But critics are incorrect to think that Hurston reconciled "high" and "low" forms of cultural production. Hurston's criticisms were not reserved for the elitist manner in which she thought the authentic culture of the people was reproduced. The people she wanted to represent she defined as a rural folk, and she measured them and their cultural forms against an urban, mass culture. (p. 75)

Carby concludes that Hurston displaces the migration of blacks to the urban North with a nostalgic discourse about the rural South, resisting the cultural transformation that resulted from that migration. Carby stresses the need to recognize the transformation of black culture and warns against the impulse to romanticize a homogenous experience. Her critique, like Gilroy's, is facilitated by Hurston's many assertions of the genuine and authentic in black culture.[21] But Hurston's polemics do not preclude an active engagement in her literature with African American social and cultural change.

While Carby astutely observes that, in *Their Eyes,* Janie reverses the direction of most black migrants, moving deeper South rather than North, she does not investigate the reasons for and implications of this movement.[22]

She notes that Hurston situates "the southern, rural folk and patterns of migration in relation to the Caribbean rather than the northern states," viewing that migration ever southward as yet another displacement (p. 82). Hurston's evocation of the Caribbean through Vodou, however, allows her to grapple with many of the issues being debated in cosmopolitan, intellectual circles during the Harlem Renaissance.[23]

In *Their Eyes,* Hurston comments on issues of class, gender, sexuality, and cultural identity primarily through her use of Vodou imagery. The novel takes up many of the same issues being debated by her contemporaries during the 1920s and 1930s. For example, Harlem was frequently celebrated as unique because it was a gathering place for diverse people of the African Diaspora. Alain Locke writes in *The New Negro:*

> Here in Manhattan is not merely the largest Negro community in the world, but the first concentration in history of so many diverse elements of Negro life. It has attracted the African, the West Indian, the Negro American; has brought together the Negro of the north and the Negro of the south; the man from the city and the man from the town and village; the peasant, the student, the business man, the professional man, artist, poet, musician, adventurer and worker, preacher and criminal, exploiter and social outcast. Each group has come with its own separate motives and for its own special ends, but their greatest experience has been the finding of one another.[24]

In asserting that "their greatest experience has been the finding of one another," Locke minimizes any social or cultural tensions that may have existed between the different groups gathered in Harlem and celebrates Harlem as a center of African diasporic culture. This emerging and changing culture, noted for its diversity, is but one of the social transformations Carby believes Hurston should have recognized.

Locke's optimism actually was shared by Hurston, however, and is implicitly echoed in an easily overlooked passage in the novel. In it she describes how the Bahamians and Black Americans working in the Everglades overcome their initial trepidation over each other's foreignness by dancing together. The Bahamians "quit hiding out to hold their dances when they found that their American friends didn't laugh at them as they feared. Many of the Americans learned to jump and liked it as much as the 'Saws.' So they began to hold dances night after night in the quarters, usually behind Tea Cake's house" (p. 146). The relative ease with which these groups overcome their differences suggests that national and ethnic identification can be blurred with a greater awareness and cultivation of cultural similarities, and a greater tolerance of and interest in cultural difference. So, in the midst of their dances, we cannot distinguish between American and Bahamian as they make "living, sculptural, grotesques in the dance" (p. 147). This reference to "sculptural grotesques," African sculptures brought to life, evokes the dancers' shared ancestry.

This allusion to Africa and the passage's naïve suggestion that cultural, political, and economic differences can be easily eradicated by social inter-action reveal that Hurston ascribed to the notion of a unified and idyllic African past. Carby and Gilroy have accurately identified Hurston's ten-dency to romanticize the past in this novel, yet I argue that the allusions to Vodou reveal a more complex vision of Black Atlantic cultures. Her im-mersion in tradition, specifically Haitian Vodou tradition, opens the novel up to politicized readings of contemporary African American racial, gen-der, and class politics.

Just as Locke saw the social and political potential of Harlem because it was a site of "group expression and self-determination," Hurston saw that same potential in Haitian Vodou. The elements of the text that Carby iden-tifies as displacements to the South and to the Caribbean actually allow Hurston to explore through metaphor and symbolism the social and po-litical concerns of African Americans in the North, South, and throughout the Caribbean. Hurston was not solely interested in elevating African American folk culture; she was also invested in collecting and recreating through fiction what black people had to say about themselves. Haitian Vodou provided Hurston with the ideal vehicle to voice African diasporic peoples' (especially women's) views on their social status and unique expe-riences, demonstrating that ancient tradition can effectively shape our comprehension of modern cultures that are constantly evolving.

Notes

1. In *The Faces of the Gods: Vodou and Roman Catholicism in Haiti* (Chapel Hill: Univer-sity of North Carolina Press, 1992), Leslie Desmangles writes, "Thanks to Hollywood and the film industry, what average persons conjure up in their minds when they think of *Voodoo* is a picture of witches and sorcerers who, filled with hatred, attempt to inflict diseases or even death on other persons by making wax or wooden repre-sentations of them, and perforating them with pins. Another popular image of *Voodoo* or *Hoodoo* is that of a conglomeration of exotic spells celebrated clandestinely by blacks inebriated with blood . . ." (pp. 1–2). Given that the terms "voodoo" and "hoodoo" are saddled with misleading and defamatory meaning, I have chosen to use in this paper the Creole spelling of Vodou and other terminology related to it,

except when citing sources that may spell them differently. The Creole spelling also approximates the etymological root, the Dahomean term *"vodu"* or *"vodun,"* which means "spirit."

2. Roseann P. Bell et al., *Sturdy Black Bridges: Visions of Black Women in Literature* (New York: Anchor Books, 1979).

3. Karen McCarthy Brown, *Mama Lola* (Berkeley: University of California Press, 1991).

4. Trudier Harris claims that Hurston "excessively packs in folk expressions and beliefs to the extent that the excessively metaphorical folk language becomes an added character, plugging up the cracks between theme and plot, not a smoothly woven, integral part of the whole; language and story seem to have mutually exclusive functions" (p. 6). Although the American folklore functions separately from, and sometimes competes with, the narrative, the Haitian folklore blends in with and extends the narrative's themes *(Fiction and Folklore: The Novels of Toni Morrison* [Knoxville, University of Tennessee Press, 1991]).

5. Robert E. Hemenway, *Zora Neale Hurston: A Literary Biography* (Chicago: University of Illinois Press, 1977), 154.

6. H. Nigel Thomas, *From Folklore to Fiction: A Study of Folk Heroes in the Black American Novel* (New York: Greenwood Press, 1988), 175.

7. Hurston's characterization of Legba as the master of potentiality *(Tell My Horse: Voodoo and Life in Haiti and Jamaica* [New York: Harper & Row, 1938]) is supported by other sources. For example, Robert Farris Thompson writes that "God granted Eshu [the Yoruba manifestation of Legba] the force to make all things happen and multiply *(ashé)*. . . . He is . . . the ultimate master of potentiality *(Flash of the Spirit: African and Afro-American Art and Philosophy* [New York: Random House, 1983], 18–19).

8. References to God and godlike figures abound. Rachel Blau DePlessis notes that "the absolute beginning of the book begins playing with title materials and meanings by opening issues about words and the Word in relation to gender and racial power. The third paragraph starts with a revisionary articulation of Biblical rhetoric, 'So the beginning of this was a woman', taking the world-creating place of Word or God" (p. 109) ("Power, Judgment, and Narrative in a Work of Zora Neale Hurston: Feminist Cultural Studies," in Michael Awkward, ed., *New Essays on "Their Eyes Were Watching God"* [New York: Cambridge University Press, 1990], 95–123).

Lorraine Bethel writes, "Hurston's first description of Nanny in *Their Eyes* establishes her as a representative of the religious experience that stands at the center of Afro-American folk tradition. She is described in terms suggestive of a Christ figure. Janie makes Nanny a wreath of 'palma christi leaves,' and the words 'bore' and 'pierce' used in this passage invoke images of the crucifixion" (pp. 13–14) "'The Infinity of Conscious Pain': Zora Neale Hurston and the Black Female Literary Tradition," in Harold Bloom, ed., *Zora Neale Hurston* [New York: Chelsea House Publishers, 1986] 9–17).

Barbara Johnson and Henry Louis Gates, Jr., note that "Joe Starks . . . fondly and unconsciously refers to himself as 'I-God.' During the lamp-lighting ceremony . . . Joe is represented as the creator (or at least the purchaser) of light" (p. 73) ("A Black Idiomatic Free Indirect Discourse," in Harold Bloom, ed., *Zora Neale Hurston* [New York: Chelsea House Publishers, 1986] 73–85).

9. "Each *loa* has its representative colour—red for Ogu, white for Damballah, blue for Ezili etc. . . ." (p. 167) (Alfred Métraux, *Voodoo in Haiti* [New York: Schocken Books, 1959].

10. "Ezili being a white *loa* and a 'woman of the world' has a fondness for pale and sugary drinks" (Métraux, p. 176).

11. Janie's donning of the overalls can be read as a moment of symbolic transvestitism that disrupts and challenges Eatonville's social order. In *Vested Interests: Cross-Dressing and Cultural Anxiety*, Marjorie Garber argues that "transvestitism was located at the juncture of class and gender, and increasingly through its agency gender and class were revealed to be commutable, if not equivalent. To transgress against one set of boundaries was to call into question the inviolability of both, and the set of social codes—already demonstrably under attack—by which such categories were policed and maintained" (p. 32). The townsfolk react to Janie's transgression of class and gender boundaries, seeing the overalls as a violation of their social codes (New York: Routledge, 1992).

12. While some anthropologists mistakenly represent the Rada and Petwo spirits as symbolizing good and evil (Hurston included), the actual significance of these two Vodou pantheons is more complicated than suggested by this binarism. Mc-Carthy Brown writes: "The Rada spirits are sweet-tempered and dependable; their power resides in their wisdom. . . . They are intimate, familial spirits who are given family titles such as Papa and Kouzen [cousin]. . . . The Petwo spirits, in contrast, are hot-tempered and volatile. They must be handled with care and precision. Debts must be paid and promises kept, or they will badger and harass those who serve them. The power of the Petwo spirits resides in their effectivity, their ability to make things happen" (pp. 100–101) (Karen McCarthy Brown, *Mama Lola* [Berkeley: University of California Press, 1991]).

13. "Danto's anger can exceed what is required for strict discipline. At times, it explodes from her with an irrational, violent force. Ezili Danto, like Lasyrenn, has connections with water. A gentle rainfall during the festivities at Saut d'Eau, a mountain pilgrimage site for Ezili Danto (Our Lady of Mount Carmel), is readily interpreted as a sign of her presence; but so is a sudden deluge resulting in mud slides, traffic accident, and even deaths. . . . Thus Danto's rage can emerge with the elemental force of a torrential rain, which sweeps away just and unjust alike.

This aspect of Ezili Danto might be described as an infant's-eye view of the omnipotent mother" (McCarthy Brown, p. 231).

14. Donald A. Petesch notes that during the period of enslavement, in sermons and catechisms, "grand moralizing gave way to immediate practical ends: the language of religion became the language of social control" (p. 60) (*A Spy in the Enemy's Country: The Emergence of Modern Black Literature* [Iowa City: University of Iowa Press, 1989]).

15. Mary Helen Washington, "'I Love the Way Janie Crawford Left Her Husbands': Zora Neale Hurston's Emergent Female Hero," in Henry Louis Gates, Jr. and K. A. Appiah, eds., *Zora Neale Hurston: Critical Perspectives Past and Present* (New York: Amistad, 1993), 99.

16. Richard Wright, "Review of *Their Eyes Were Watching God*," in *New Masses*, 5 October 1937," in Henry Louis Gates, Jr. and K. A. Appiah, eds. ibid., 17.

17. Alice Walker, "Looking for Zora," in *I Love Myself When I Am Laughing . . . And Then Again When I Am Looking Mean and Impressive* (New York: The Feminist Press, 1979).

18. Paul Gilroy, *The Black Atlantic: Modernity and Double Consciousness* (Cambridge, Mass.: Harvard University, Press, 1993).

19. Arnold Rampersad's assessment of the contributors to *The New Negro*, some of the most influential black intellectuals of the day, supports my suggestion that the desire to elevate the spirituals to a "higher" art form betrays a belief in the cultural inferiority of African Americans. Rampersad writes, "It is fair to say that, in the face of racial 'science,' most of the contributors to the volume accepted the notion of black racial and cultural inferiority compared to the standards of European civilization. Most also believed, however, that the African race was on the move forward, that politically, economically, and culturally, peoples of African descent around the world were engaged in the first stages of a transformation that would eventually lead to independence from Europe" (p. xvi). Ironically, most believed that independence from Europe could only be achieved by successfully replicating, with minor adaptations, its cultural, social, and political paradigms (Introduction, Alain Locke, ed., *The New Negro* [New York: Anthenaeum, 1992] ix–xxiii).

20. Eric Sundqust, *The Hammers of Creation: Folk Culture in Modern African-American Fiction* (Athens: The University of Georgia Press, 1992), 60.

21. For example, in "Spirituals and Neo-Spirituals" (*The Sanctified Church* [Berkeley: Turtle Island] 79–84) Hurston asserts, "There never has been a presentation of genuine Negro spirituals to any audience anywhere. What is being sung by the concert artists and glee clubs are the works of Negro composers or adaptors [sic] *based* on the spirituals" (p. 80).

22. Carby is far from alone in perceiving the novel as being removed from history and reality ("The Politics of Fiction, Anthropology, and the Folk: Zora Neale

Hurston," in Michael Awkward, ed., *New Essays on "Their Eyes Were Watching God"* [New York: Cambridge Univ. Press, 1990] 71–93). Robert Stepto writes, "The narrative takes place in a seemingly ahistorical world: the spanking-new all-black town is meticulously bereft of former slave cabins; there are no railroad trains, above or underground, with or without Jim Crow cars; Matt's mule is a bond with and catalyst for distinct tribal memories and rituals, but these do not include the hollow slogan 'forty acres and a mule'; Janie seeks freedom, selfhood, voice, and 'living' but is hardly guided—or haunted—by Sojourner Truth or Harriet Tubman, let alone Frederick Douglass" (p. 6). What Stepto calls an "ahistorical world" Carby names a displacement. Carby remarks upon the text's avoidance of the present, while Stepto focuses on its avoidance of the past. But just as Hurston implicitly signifies on then-contemporary debates and experiences, so does she signify on African American history. One can read the fact that Logan Killicks owns not just forty but sixty acres and a mule not as a historicism but as an ironic commentary on the nation's unwillingness to realize its promise to the newly emancipated slaves ("Ascent, Immersion, Narration," in Harold Bloom, ed., *Zora Neale Hurston* [New York: Chelsea House Publishers, 1986] 5–17).

23. Deborah E. McDowell ("Lines of Descent/Dissenting Lines," in Henry Louis Gates, Jr., and K. A. Appiah, eds., *Zora Neale Hurston: Critical Perspectives Past and Present* [Amistad, 1993] 230–240) makes a similar point about Hurston's willingness to engage in political dialogue in an essay on *Moses, Man of the Mountain*. McDowell discusses the ways in which the text's symbolism critiques the United States' rhetoric of liberation and reveals its hypocrisy by implicitly juxtaposing the United States' oppression of African Americans with the ideology of racial purity that fueled Germany's entry into a world war in 1939. McDowell concludes, "All too often Hurston's readers have consigned her to Eatonville and left her there on the porch. . . . Even when readers stretch her province to New Orleans and the Caribbean, the sites of her fieldwork, they often read these migrations as extensions of Eatonville, seen as the repository of black folk culture on which all Hurston's work is dependent. But reducing Eatonville and its symbolic geographic coordinates to the repositories of black 'folk' expression that Hurston mined so well regionalizes her work and ensures her removal from a more global context of cultural production and exchange" (p. 240).

24. Alain Locke, *The New Negro* (New York: Athenaeum, 1992), 6.

Suggested Reading

Awkward, Michael. *Inspiriting Influences: Tradition, Revision and Afro-American Women's Novels*. New York: Columbia University Press, 1989.

———, ed. *New Essays on "Their Eyes Were Watching God."* New York: Cambridge University Press, 1990.

Baker, Houston. *Blues, Ideology and Afro-American Literature*. Chicago: University of Chicago Press, 1984.

———. *Workings of the Spirit: The Poetics of Afro-American Women's Writing*. Chicago: University of Chicago Press, 1991.

Callahan, John. *In the African-American Grain: The Pursuit of Voice in Twentieth-Century Black Fiction*. Urbana: University of Illinois Press, 1988.

Carby, Hazel. *Reconstructing Womanhood: The Emergence of the Afro-American Woman Novelist*. New York: Oxford University Press, 1987.

Christian, Barbara. *Black Women Novelists*. Westport, CT: Greenwood Press, 1980.

Davie, Sharon. "Free Mules, Talking Buzzards and Cracked Plates: The Politics of Dislocation in *Their Eyes Were Watching God.*" *PMLA* 108 (1993): 446–459.

DuCille, Ann. *The Coupling Convention: Sex, Text, and Tradition in Black Women's Fiction*. New York: Oxford University Press, 1993.

DuPlessis, Rachel. *Writing Beyond the Ending: Narrative Strategies of Twentieth-Century Women Writers*. Bloomington: Indiana University Press, 1985.

Gates, Henry Louis, Jr. *The Signifying Monkey: A Theory of Afro-American Literary Criticism.* New York: Oxford University Press, 1989.

————, and Anthony Appiah, eds. *Zora Neale Hurston: Critical Perspectives Past and Present.* New York: Amistad Press, 1993.

Glassman, Steve and Kathryn Lee Seidel. *Zora in Florida.* Orlando: University of Central Florida Press, 1991.

Hemenway, Robert. *Zora Neale Hurston: A Literary Biography.* Urbana: University of Illinois Press, 1977.

Hill, Lynda. *Social Rituals and the Verbal Art of Zora Neale Hurston.* Washington, DC: Howard University Press, 1996.

Holloway, Karla F.C. *The Character of the Word: The Texts of Zora Neale Hurston.* Westport, CT: Greenwood Press, 1987.

Howard, Lillie. *Zora Neale Hurston.* Boston: G. K. Hall, 1980.

Johnson, Barbara. *A World of Difference.* Baltimore: Johns Hopkins University Press, 1987.

Jones, Gayl. *Liberating Voices: Oral Tradition in African American Literature.* Cambridge: Harvard University Press, 1991.

Jordan, Jennifer. "Feminist Fantasies: Zora Neale Hurston's *Their Eyes Were Watching God.*" *Tulsa Studies in Women's Literature* 7, 1(Spring 1988): 105–117.

Jordan, June. "On Richard Wright and Zora Neale Hurston: Notes Toward a Balancing of Love and Hatred." 1974. Reprinted in *Civil Wars.* Boston: Beacon Press, 1981.

Kaplan, Carla. *The Erotics of Talk: Women's Writing and Feminist Paradigms.* New York: Oxford University Press, 1996.

Kubitschek, Missy Dehn. *Claiming the Heritage: African-American Women Novelists and History.* Jackson: University Press of Mississippi, 1991.

Lowe, John. *"Jump at the Sun": Zora Neale Hurston's Cosmic Comedy.* Urbana: University of Illinois Press, 1994.

Meese, Elizabeth. *Crossing the Double Cross: The Practice of Feminist Criticism.* Chapel Hill: University of North Carolina Press, 1986.

Nathiri, N.Y. *Zora! Zora Neale Hurston: A Woman and Her Community.* Orlando: Sentinel Communications, 1991.

Plant, Deborah. *Every Tub Must Sit on Its Own Bottom: The Philosophy and Politics of Zora Neale Hurston.* Urbana: University of Illinois Press, 1995.

Stepto, Robert. *From Behind the Veil: A Study of Afro-American Narrative.* Urbana: University of Illinois Press, 1979.

Walker, Alice. *Anything We Love Can Be Saved: A Writer's Activism.* New York: Random House, 1997.

————. *In Search of Our Mothers' Gardens.* New York: Harcourt Brace Jovanovich, 1983.

————, ed. *I Love Myself When I Am Laughing . . . A Zora Neale Hurston Reader.* New York: The Feminist Press, 1979.

Wall, Cheryl A. *Women of the Harlem Renaissance.* Bloomington: Indiana University Press, 1995.

————, ed. *Zora Neale Hurston: Folklore, Memoirs and Other Writings.* New York: The Library of America, 1995.

————, ed. *Zora Neale Hurston: Novels and Stories.* New York: The Library of America, 1995.

Wallace, Michelle. *Invisibility Blues: From Pop to Theory.* London: Verso, 1990.

Washington, Mary Helen. *Invented Lives: Narratives of Black Women.* New York: Anchor Books, 1987.

Willis, Susan. *Specifying: Black Women Writing the American Experience.* Madison: University of Wisconsin Press, 1987.